CONTENTS

Helion & Company Limited
Unit 8 Amherst Business Centre, Budbrooke Road, Warwick CV34 5WE, England
Tel. 01926 499 619
Fax 0121 711 4075
Email: info@helion.co.uk   Website: www.helion.co.uk   Twitter: @helionbooks   Visit our blog http://blog.helion.co.uk/

Published by Helion & Company 2019
Designed and typeset by Farr out Publications, Wokingham, Berkshire
Cover designed by Paul Hewitt, Battlefield Design (www.battlefield-design.co.uk)
Printed by Henry Ling Ltd, Dorchester, Dorset

Text © Tom Cooper & Abdallah Emran 2019
Photographs © as individually credited
Colour profiles © Tom Cooper 2019
Maps © Tom Cooper 2019

Every reasonable effort has been made to trace copyright holders and to obtain their permission for the use of copyright material. The author and publisher apologize for any errors or omissions in this work, and would be grateful if notified of any corrections that should be incorporated in future reprints or editions of this book.

Cover Photograph: The two primary means of defence of Egyptian air bases during the October 1973 War: left, active defence in the form of a 20D missile of the S-75M Volkhov (SA-2 Guideline) SAM-system in combat position on its SM-63 launcher; and passive defence provided by hardened aircraft shelters. (Tom Cooper Collection & Photo by Tom Cooper)

Cover Artwork: A reconstruction of an F-4E Phantom from the Tel Nov-based No. 119 Squadron, as equipped for a nuclear strike mission, in around 1973. In addition to an ALQ-101 ECM-pod and AIM-9D Sidewinder missiles for self-defence purposes, the aircraft would have carried the nuclear device (or 'cradle') on a special pylon installed under its centreline. It is widely assumed that the design of early Israeli nuclear weapons was strongly influenced by the second generation of French-made tactical nuclear weapons – especially the AN-52 nuclear bomb (first tested on 28 August 1972), roughly equivalent to such US-made tactical nuclear weapons as the Mark 7, Mark 8, Mark 11 and Mark 12. (Artwork by Tom Cooper)

ISBN 978-1-911628-71-2

British Library Cataloguing-in-Publication Data.
A catalogue record for this book is available from the British Library.

For details of other military history titles published by Helion & Company Limited contact the above address, or visit our website: http://www.helion.co.uk. We always welcome receiving book proposals from prospective authors.

ABBREVIATIONS

AAA	anti-aircraft artillery
AAM	air-to-air missile
AB	air base
AMAN	Military Intelligence Agency (Israel)
ASCC	Air Standardisation Coordinating Committee
BAI	battlefield air interdiction
CAP	combat air patrol
CAS	close air support
CBU	cluster bomb unit
CEP	circular error probability
CIA	Central Intelligence Agency (USA)
CO	commanding officer
COMINT	communications intelligence
DIA	Defence Intelligence Agency (USA)
EAF	Egyptian Air Force (official designation from 1952 until 1958)
ECM	electronic countermeasures
ECCM	electronic counter-countermeasures
ELINT	electronic intelligence
EMOD	Egyptian Ministry of Defence
FTD	Foreign Technologies Division (USAF)
GCI	ground-controlled intercept
IAEC	Israeli Atomic Energy Commission
IDF	Israeli Defense Forces
IDF/AF	Israeli Defense Forces/Air Force
IFF	identification friend or foe
IR	infrared
IP	initial point (typically a visual reference on the ground used as an aid to begin attack run)
IRBM	intermediate-range ballistic missile
KAMAG	Nuclear Research Centre in Dimona (Israel)
KIA	killed in action
Km	kilometre
MBT	main battle tank
Mi	Mil (the design bureau led by Mikhail Mil)
MiG	Mikoyan i Gurevich (the design bureau led by Artyom Ivanovich Mikoyan and Mikhail Iosifovich Gurevich, also known as OKB-155 or MMZ' 'Zenit')
NATO	North Atlantic Treaty Organisation
Nm	nautical mile
NPT	non-proliferation treaty
NUMEC	Nuclear Materials and Equipment Corporation (USA)
PoW	prisoner of war
QRA	quick reaction alert
RHAWS	radar homing and warning system
RIO	radar intercept officer
RWR	radar warning receiver
SAM	surface-to-air missile
Su	Sukhoi (the design bureau led by Pavel Ossipowich Sukhoi, also known as OKB-51)
TEL	transporter/erector/launcher
UAR	United Arab Republic (Union of Egypt, Syria and Yemen, 1958–1961)
UARAF	United Arab Republic Air Force, designation of the Egyptian and Syrian air forces between 1958 and 1962, and of the Egyptian Air Force until 1969
UAV	unmanned aerial vehicle
USAF	United States Air Force
USN	United States Navy (includes US Naval Aviation)
V-PVO	Voyska Protivo-Vozdushnoy Oborony, the Soviet Air Defence Forces
RAFAEL	Weapons Development Authority (Israel)
WIA	wounded in action

INTRODUCTION & ACKNOWLEDGEMENTS: WHY 'THE FIRST NUCLEAR WAR'?

The topic of this book is as complex as it can get. The original idea was to cross-examine a number of myths about aerial warfare during the October 1973 Arab-Israeli War. The usual histories of this conflict stress that air power did not play an important role and the war was almost exclusively decided on the ground. Such conclusions are quite surprising considering that the research and cross-examination of details provided by all involved parties clearly indicated something entirely different. In particular, there were strong indications that the Israeli Defence Force/Air Force (IDF/AF) ran an intensive, week-long campaign against unknown targets in the Port Said area, provoking numerous clashes and dozens of claims. Seemingly at least, this campaign culminated in an 'Air Battle of el-Mansourah', on 14 October 1973: according to the Egyptian sources, this was the biggest clash between the two air forces in this war and it ended with such a success, that ever since the Egyptian Air Force (EAF) has celebrated that date as its official day; according to the Israeli sources, all such claims are either outright lies, or the operation in question is barely worth mentioning. At most, the air battles on – amongst others – 14 October were a result of the Israeli Air Force/Defence Force (IDF/AF) attempts to achieve an entirely different objective than the one usually assessed by the Egyptians or, indeed, anybody else. The related research came forward with quite satisfactory results until an – apparently – 'entirely unrelated' question surfaced: this was the delivery of 9K72 Elbrus (ASCC/NATO-codename 'SS-1c Scud-B') surface-to-surface missiles (SSMs, also 'ballistic missiles') made in the Union of Soviet Socialist Republics (USSR, also 'Soviet Union'), and their possible deployment by Egyptian armed forces, though in association with Soviet-made nuclear warheads. The 'appearance' of Scuds in Egypt in turn prompted us to take a closer look at similar armament in service with the IDF/AF: considering both the importance and sensitiveness of such an affair – no matter where – this imposed the question of how much did the availability of both of these influence military thinking on either side, and that at a strategic-, an operational-, and a tactical level? After all, nuclear warfare is widely perceived as the ultimate military discipline, one overarching all other priorities and aims, and heavily influencing all military thinking of so-called 'nuclear powers'. If this was influencing the decades-long confrontation between the North Atlantic Treaty Organisation (NATO) and the Warsaw Pact, and embroiled them into constant manoeuvring for position favourable for deployment of nuclear weapons – resulting 'just' in the so-called 'Cold War' – then the logical question is: how much did the availability – true or perceived – of nuclear weapons and suitable means of their deployment influence the thinking, strategic-, operational-, and tactical planning of the Egyptian and Israeli militaries during a 'shooting war' like the one in October 1973?

Our related findings have eventually resulted in the title of this volume: 'The First Nuclear War' is the story of the first ever 'hot' war in which at least one of the parties involved not only contemplated the deployment of nuclear weapons, but went on nuclear alert, too. That said, this is the only conclusion drawn and provided by the authors in this book: we are leaving the rest to the reader to decide. The reason for this is rather ironic: while finding plenty of participants ready to share their recollections, and at least as many secondary sources, crucial documentation about the related decision-making processes at strategic and operational levels is unlikely to be released any time soon. Official Egyptian military archives remain not only 'locked', but 'well hidden' from the public; some parts of those in Israel are meanwhile open for public access, but certain of their segments remain secret, too. Thus, finding the ultimate answers to questions about reasons for specific Israeli-, and a few of Egyptian operations remains outside of what is currently possible.

Most of the research for this project is based on our earlier work, and became possible only through the help of many individuals. Many are likely to find our methods of research at least 'unusual', if not futile: while heavily supported by secondary sources of Israeli and Western origin, most of the following narrative is based on recollections of Arab participants. However, one should keep in mind that not only the majority of Israeli military historians, but nearly all Western military historians, analysts and students of Arab-Israeli Wars are following a subjective approach to nearly everything reported by Israel: the country and its politics are supported regardless of the reason and circumstances, official explanations for backgrounds of its military operations and diverse claims are never questioned, and even less so subjected to a critical review. In comparison, the other side is next to never explained. Indeed, reporting by Arab sources is much too often explained away with the Israeli legend according to which 'Arabs always lie'. Unsurprisingly, the result is that the Israeli points of view about the October 1973 Arab-Israeli War are widely published, considered as 'well-known' and 'a given': Egyptian – and indeed 'Arab' positions – not the least so. Our standpoint is that wars take two to fight: correspondingly, we intentionally sought to offer and emphasise the Egyptian points of view, and Egyptian experiences, because these remain largely unknown, and because our standpoint is that these are at least as valid as those of the Israelis.

The personal stories retold in this volume are intriguing and throw an especially interesting light on specific events. The list of those to whom we owe our gratitude is long, and as usual begins with the officers, pilots, non-commissioned officers and other ranks of various air forces, particularly (in alphabetical order) those in Egypt, Iraq, and Israel. They include the Major-General Qadri Abd el-Hamid (EAF, ret.), the late Major-General Mohammad Abdel-Moneim Zaki Okasha (EAF), Major-General Nabil el-Shuwakri (EAF, ret.), Major-General Mamdouh Taliba (EAF, ret.), Major-General Ahmed Abbas Faraj (EAF, ret.), Major-General Ayman (ADC, ret.), Major-General Zia el-Hefnawi (EAF, ret.), the late Major-General Farid Hafroush (EAF, ret.), Major-General Mamdouh Heshmat (EAF, ret.), Major-General Reda el-Iraqi (EAF, ret.), Major-General Hussein el-Kfass (EAF, ret.), Major-General Ahmed Kilany (EAF, ret.), Major-General Samir Aziz Mikhail (EAF, ret.), Major-General Nassr Moussa (EAF, ret.), Major-General Reza Saqr (EAF, ret.), Major-General Siad Shalash (EAF, ret.), Major-General Ahmed Yusuf el-Wakeel (EAF, ret.), Major-General Magdy el-Wakeel (EAF, ret.), Major-General Medhat Zaki (EAF, ret.), Brigadier-General Iftach Spector (IDF/AF, ret.), Brigadier-General Ahmad Sadik (IrAF, ret.), the late Air Commodore Gabr Ali Gabr (EAF, ret.), Colonel Dawoud Makarem (EAF, ret.), and others. In this place, we would like to take the opportunity to stress that

following a gentlemen's agreement with Brigadier-General Spector, out of respect for his person and the knowledge that he is privileged to, we have never addressed specific issues to him publicly known to be 'sensitive' in Israel, and he has never divulged anything related to such matters.

Special thanks are due to a number of other researchers for their kind help, comparable with near-authorship of this book: in particular, Nour Bardai from Egypt. His support enabled the acquisition of many of crucial details that helped us prepare and provide a much more detailed narrative.

We would like to express our special gratitude to Sherif Sharmi, Franz Vajda, Jeroen Nijmeijer, Menno van der Wall, Frank Olynyk, Robert Szombati, Peter Weinert, Thomas Nachtrab, Alexander Hunger and Ferenc 'Franz' Vajda, for their kind permission to use some of their research and photographs, and to Ali Tobchi from Iraq, and Hicham Honeini from Lebanon for their patience and kind help with the translations of various publications and documentation from Arabic.

Last but by no means least, we would like to thank a number of friends who have helped with additional information, commentary, translations or encouragement over a prolonged period of time, foremost Tom Long. All of them, as well as our families, have consistently supported our work with the greatest enthusiasm and patience, and our special thanks are due to each one of them.

1

BEN-GURION'S TEXTILE FACTORY

As far as is known, Egypt never developed, and never operated nuclear weapons. Although Cairo did launch a nuclear programme in 1954 and constructed a number of reactors since, it ratified the Non-Proliferation Treaty (NPT).

While not officially recognized as a 'nuclear weapons state', Israel never ratified the NPT. Instead, the country has maintained the policy of 'deliberate nuclear ambiguity': for more than 50 years, the official standpoint of the Israeli government seems to be that the country would 'not be the one to introduce nuclear weapons to the Middle East', leaving ambiguity as to whether it means it will not create, will not disclose, will not make first use – or any other interpretation of that statement. In fact, and despite insistence of successive US governments that they have no knowledge about such projects, over time more than enough evidence has surfaced that Israel is not only running a very big and successful project for the development of nuclear bombs, but has meanwhile heavily armed itself with such weapons.

The documentation and photographs released in 1986 by Mordechai Vanunu especially, a technician at the Negev Nuclear Research Centre, have provided clear evidence not only about the extents of the Israeli nuclear programme, but also that the country is in possession of dozens of nuclear weapons.

AN ACCIDENTAL DISCOVERY

Late in the afternoon of another of the oppressively hot and dusty days of October 1965, a pair of metallic MiG-17Fs wearing the insignia of the United Arab Republic Air Force (UARAF) on their wings, and the red 'Winged Bat' insignia of No. 18 Squadron on their noses, entered the Israeli airspace low over the western Negev Desert. Leading the pair was Lieutenant Salah Mansour, an experienced pilot serving his second tour of duty in the Sinai.

Classic 'mushroom cloud' caused by the plutonium-type device dropped by the US Air Force (USAF) over Nagasaki, on 9 August 1945. (US National Archives and Records Administration)

During one of these flights, late Salah Mansour reached Dimona. There he saw some very strange construction and thought it looked like a nuclear reactor. He immediately informed me and so I decided to fly with him to confirm what he had seen. This time there was no doubt about it: a nuclear reactor was under construction.[1]

On their own, such airspace violations between Egypt and Israel were really 'nothing new' of the period 1958-1965: radar coverage over both countries was still rudimentary. Unsurprisingly, the reconnaissance aircraft of the IDF/AF were penetrating the Egyptian airspace over the Sinai Peninsula at least once a week. On its part, the UARAF had ceased flying reconnaissance sorties over Israel in September 1961: at the time, its only aircraft equipped for reconnaissance purposes were old and slow Ilyushin Il-28R bombers. Although these managed to avoid Israeli air defences on a number of occasions in the period 1958-1961, the mere service entry of the Dassault Mirage IIICJ radar-equipped supersonic interceptors in 1962 convinced the Egyptians that their Il-28Rs would be too slow and too vulnerable. Never keen to provoke another war with Israel, Cairo thus issued a general moratorium on any kind of flights into Israeli airspace. Mansour's, and then Zaki's overflight of Dimona in 1965 was thus not only an exception, but also the first time any Egyptian had ever seen what was going on in that part of Israel. The story of exactly what Mansour and then Zaki saw in Dimona is a longer one though.

He guided his wingman in an eastern direction low over the sandy dunes until reaching a few farms in the Tlalim area. Continuing due east, the two jets then jinked above the peaks of several low hills to reach Jerocham, before turning north-east. Following a dusty road, Mansour and his wingman next saw a massive, tall concrete tower in front of them: startled by what they saw, both Egyptians banked hard left and flew straight back to their home-base in el-Arish. Their commander, Tahsin Zaki, recalled:

In 1965, I commanded the 2nd Air Group with MiG-17s, plus an additional attached squadron of MiG-17s permanently stationed at el-Arish, the Egyptian air base closest to the cease-fire line between Egypt and Israel. Our orders were not to fly closer than 35 kilometres to Israel, but the Israelis often penetrated our airspace, even flew very low across el-Arish air base. This made my pilots feel bad, as our High Command ordered us not to cross into the Israeli airspace. So, to boost my pilots' morale, I sometimes allowed them to penetrate Israel at low level as far as Beersheba.

FRANCO-ISRAELI COOPERATION

While it is certain that Zaki – although risking court-martial for violating the standing order not to fly over Israel – had filed a comprehensive report to his superiors on what he, Mansour, and their wingmen had seen in Dimona, it remains unknown how officials in Cairo reacted. Indeed, although the government of the Egyptian President Gamal Abdel Nasser had already pledged a 'preventive war' to stop Israel from developing nuclear weapons in 1960, nothing happened for years afterwards, and even the Israelis did not take such threats seriously. This might not be surprising considering the fact that the principal objective of all the Egyptian intelligence services in the period 1954-1967 was the prevention of a coup against Nasser's government: in other words, that Egyptian intelligence almost certainly failed to obtain additional information. However, it should be surprising considering not only the strategic importance of the Israeli project, but especially its duration and intensity.[2]

The story of the coming into being of Israeli nuclear weapons is almost as old as the State of Israel. For most of the last 1,500 years, Western Europe received innovations in different sciences – but especially mathematics and physics – from the Middle East. One of the combined effects of Fascist terror and the Zionist underground in the 1930s and 1940s was to return the latest scientific knowledge back to the area – almost exclusively to newly-created Israel. Amongst the refugees and settlers that streamed into Palestine as this was converted into Israel during these times were many eminent physical scientists from universities in Berlin, Bucharest, Prague and Warsaw. Unsurprisingly, the Israeli Atomic Energy Commission was already established under the auspices of the Israeli Ministry of Defence in 1949, only a year after the establishment of the State of Israel. However, while funding from the diaspora in the USA and Europe enabled the start of this program, development of the necessary industrial infrastructure became possible only through cooperation with France, which resulted in a relationship that would mutually benefit both countries through the following decades.[3]

In early 1957, Israel and France signed a secret agreement for the construction of a 26MW reactor and an underground plutonium separation plant at Dimona. During the following years, Israeli scientists were granted unrestricted access to data from experiments with early French nuclear weapons – run at the testing grounds in Raggane and Ekker, in Algeria – developed because Paris was enraged over the US-British 'special relations' in this field.[4]

From the official standpoint of the US government, nothing of this was known before 1960, when the Central Intelligence Agency (CIA) got the first wind of the actual nature of the facility in Dimona. Indeed, when the administration of US president Dwight D Eisenhower officially inquired into the nature of the same, Israeli Prime Minister David Ben-Gurion responded with solemn assurances that it was a 'textile factory'.[5]

Privately, of course, the US intelligence community did not miss links between the French and the Israeli cooperation with regards to the development of nuclear weapons, or about related protests from Cairo. For example, after the French announced their third nuclear test at Reganne, on 27 December 1960, the CIA did pay attention to Radio Cairo 'coupling French tests with reports France [is] aiding Israel in nuclear weapon production', and the Arab League's spokesman threatening, 'possible severance [of] political and economic relations with France'.[6]

Almost desperate to force Israelis into confession, the State Department (the foreign ministry of the USA) then publicly disclosed its intelligence, eventually prompting the Israeli government to admit that there was a nuclear reactor under

Developed 'for peaceful purposes only', the first nuclear reactor in Dimona became the centrepiece of the Israeli program for development of nuclear weapons. This post-card from the 1960s shows the 'tall concrete construction' as sighted by Mansour and Zaki in 1965 – the 'dome' over the original reactor before this was expanded to a capacity of about 150MW. (Tom Cooper Collection)

construction in Dimona.[7]

Not only this disclosure, but certainly the knowledge about the actual Israeli intention then prompted the French President Charles de Gaulle to cancel nuclear cooperation with Israel – unless the facility in Dimona would be opened to international inspections, declared peaceful, and no plutonium produced there would be reprocessed. This resulted in two years of often emotional negotiations in the course of which Ben-Gurion went as far as to promise to stop development of nuclear weapons in Israel. Although deeply distrusting the Israeli prime-minister, de Gaulle agreed to fulfil the Dimona contract – minus the planned plutonium separation plant.[8]

In 1964, US intelligence seems to have run a 'comprehensive inspection' of the Dimona facility, with the conclusion that there was, 'no indication that the Israelis have started the chemical separation plant that would be needed to produce the fissionable material for a nuclear explosion', and – also because the Israelis had meanwhile signed the nuclear test ban treaty – become, 'less inclined than in May 1963 to believe that Israel will attempt to produce a weapon sometime in the next several years'.[9]

Later the same year – and at the same time that the Israeli government officially declared itself 'unable' to support US efforts to publicly declare the Dimona reactor as 'peaceful' – Israel's Deputy Minister of Defence (and Ben-Gurion's *protégé*) Shimon Peres reached a new agreement with the French Foreign Minister Maurice Couve de Murville. Accordingly, French companies would continue fulfilling their contract obligations – albeit without providing uranium fuel, deliveries of which were stopped in 1963 – while Israel would declare the project as 'peaceful'. Ultimately, Israel never issued a corresponding declaration but obtained uranium for the Dimona reactor nevertheless – indeed, from a French company based in Gabon – in 1964. More importantly, up to 206 pounds of 'strategic nuclear materials' – including weapons-grade enriched uranium – were acquired via companies like the Nuclear Materials and Equipment Corporation (NUMEC) and ISORAD in the USA, both of which were involved in production of highly enriched uranium fuel assemblies for the US Navy. This acquisition was what enabled the Israelis to start the final work

March 19, 1964

Dear Mr. Prime Minister:

I am distressed to learn from Ambassador Barbour that you feel unable to approve of our reassuring President Nasser about the peaceful character of the Dimona reactor. We are far from confident that apprehension as to Israel's atomic potential will, as you suggest, help deter Nasser from attacking Israel. Quite the contrary, we believe that Nasser's fear of a developing Israeli nuclear power may drive him to a choice between accelerating the UAR military buildup or a desperate pre-emptive attack. Either of these choices would have the gravest effects on the security of Israel. We think it plain that any possible deterrent value that might come from keeping Nasser in the dark is trivial compared to these risks.

It is also hard to see how Nasser could adversely exploit reassurance that Israel's nuclear activities are for peaceful purposes. We certainly do not intend to provide him with details. Nor did he misuse our reassurances when, with the agreement of your government, we last informed him along these lines. Indeed our doing so served to ease Arab-Israeli tensions.

Therefore I hope you will reconsider your decision on this matter, on which I am sure you will agree that our ultimate interest--enhancement of Israel's security--is the same as yours.

With warm regards,

Sincerely, Lyndon B. Johnson.

A scan of a letter from US President Johnson to the Israeli Prime Minister Levi Eshkol, in which the former expressed serious doubt that Israel's possession of nuclear weapons might deter Egypt from attacking Israel. (Lyndon B. Johnson Library)

on actually constructing nuclear bombs. Immediately afterwards, the two hubs of related activities – the Negev Nuclear Research Centre in Dimona (KAMAG) and the Weapons Development Authority (RAFAEL) – were merged under the management of the administration of the Israeli Atomic Energy Commission (IAEC), presided over by the prime minister. Concerned about a possible Egyptian reaction – especially so in the aftermath of the overflight by UARAF's MiG-17s – in November 1965, the Chief of the General Staff IDF, Yitzhak Rabin, ordered the Military Intelligence (AMAN) to develop a 'special intelligence collection system', codenamed 'Senator', to provide the IDF with an early warning about possible hostile intentions regarding Dimona.[10]

MAY 1967

At least as unsurprising was the Israeli reaction to the next occasion at which the Egyptians overflew the nuclear complex in Dimona. Although the IDF/AF continued flying its weekly reconnaissance missions over Egypt, no new reconnaissance missions by UARAF aircraft over Israel had ever been planned, authorized, or undertaken by the UARAF since 1960. From the Israeli point of view, this changed only on 17 May 1967 – a day after President Nasser had mobilised the Egyptian armed forces in response to fake Soviet reports about an 'imminent Israeli invasion of Syria' – when a pair of Egyptian aircraft launched from Meliz AB in central Sinai, passed south of the port Eilat in southern Israel at an altitude of more than 18,000 metres (59,050ft) before reaching Jordan. After flying north for a while, the jets then turned west and made a pass not only over Israel, but directly over the Dimona complex, this time reaching an altitude of 21,340 metres (70,000ft). The battery of US-made Hughes MIM-23A HAWK surface-to-air missiles (SAMs) deployed to protect the strategically important installation opened fire but failed to shoot the intruders down: the unknown aircraft flew above its engagement envelope.[11]

To say that this overflight caused 'consternation' within the Israeli government and top ranks of its armed forces would be an understatement: combined with reports (which turned out to be bogus) about the deployment of the Egyptian Il-28 bombers to bases

in the Sinai, it resulted in the IDF/AF being put on full alert and its Mirage-pilots given the authorisation to cross the border in pursuit of overflying 'MiGs' if necessary.[12]

The sources differ over the date of the next Egyptian overflight of Dimona: according to one version, this took place around midday on 26 May, and included four aircraft: while two returned early, the other two overflew Dimona. According to the other version, it took place only on 3 June. What is certain is that with his military informing him about the Egyptians 'possibly preparing a coordinated attack on Dimona including up to 40 aircraft', the Israeli Prime Minister Levi Eshkol then authorized the IDF/AF to promptly hit back against all of the Egyptian air bases (ABs) in the Sinai should anything of that kind happen. Although some of the Israeli and Western sources stress that this intelligence was substantiated, and that even the later Egyptian Chief-of-Staff Muhammad Fawzy alluded that Egypt was actually planning to open an aerial offensive on Israel on the morning of 27 May – but that this was cancelled by Nasser at the very last moment – the authors have never found any kind of evidence for such plans: if they ever existed, they must have remained one of best-protected secrets of Egypt, ever.[13]

Moreover, while all sorts of UARAF plans for sporadic and disorganized air strikes on Israel were captured – and widely published – by Israel during and after the June 1967 Arab-Israeli War, not one is known to have aimed at Dimona. More likely, such rumours were based on failed Soviet attempts to de-escalate the crisis originally caused by Moscow.[14]

FISHBEDS OVER DIMONA

Some of the shock-waves caused by the Egyptian overflights of Dimona from May 1967 can be felt to the present day. In recent years scholarly publications concerning this and the following series of overflights of southern Israel have suggested that the aircraft involved was a Soviet-owned and flown MiG-25R reconnaissance fighter, and that these overflights were undertaken with the aim of preparing some sort of a Soviet attack on Israel, at least a military

A youngster who was joy-riding MiG-21F-13s high over the Israeli nuclear complex in Dimona as of May-June 1967, Qadri Abd el-Hamid went on to pursue a distinguished career with the EAF. Amongst others, he claimed at least one Israeli Mirage during the War of Attrition and then a Phantom during the October 1973 War. This photograph was taken when he was flight-testing BAe HAWK training jets in the UK in the mid-1970s. (Qadri Abd el-Hamid Collection)

intervention on the Arab side – set up by Moscow because they were gravely concerned about Israeli nuclear weapons.

While there is little doubt that the Soviets had known about the Israeli project to develop nuclear bombs at least since the early 1960s – and while there is no doubt that it was a fake Soviet report about an 'imminent Israeli invasion of Syria' that sparked the crisis that eventually culminated in the June 1967 War and the catastrophic defeat of Arab militaries – there is also little doubt that Moscow was doing its best to maintain the status quo in the Middle East, to prevent any kind of armed conflicts, and to keep itself non-involved. Foremost, there is no trace of evidence about any deployment of Soviet MiG-25Rs in Egypt at that time: if for no other reason, than because as of May 1967 the type was available in prototype form only (designated Ye-266), and still years away from entering operational service. Indeed, the development of the reconnaissance variant of the MiG-25 began only in 1969, the resulting MiG-25R first flew in 1970, and was still very much undergoing testing when actually deployed in Egypt for the first time in 1971. Unsurprisingly, some sort of a 'definitive confirmation' that such aircraft had been deployed in Egypt, and then at an air base as exposed and as relatively primitive as Meliz AB – in the middle of the Sinai desert, only 50 kilometres from the border to Israel – as of May 1967 is less than 'unlikely' to ever become available.[15] …even more so considering the aircraft in question were

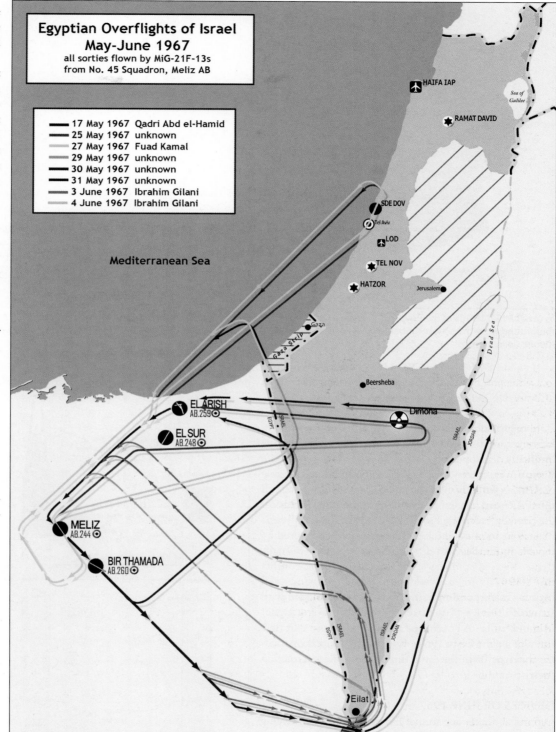

A map illustrating known Egyptian penetrations of Israeli airspace during the second half of May and early June 1967. While causing grave concern within the Israeli government and the top ranks of the IDF, as is obvious not only from the routes taken by UARAF MiG-21s, but also from descriptions from the pilots involved, these operations were undertaken by joyriding pilots and resulted in no collection of any kind of useful intelligence. (Map by Mark Lepko, based on Shalom, 'Like a Bolt out of the Blue')[18]

MiG-21F-13 from No. 45 Squadron, UARAF and that their pilots were Egyptians – which is a matter of fact that failed to attract the attention of researchers daydreaming about MiG-25s overflying in Dimona as of May 1967 foremost because the same never attempted to directly research the Egyptian air force. Indeed, one of the two pilots involved in the overflight of 17 May was Qadri Abd el-Hamid:

I was with No. 45 Squadron at Meliz AB in the central Sinai… None of us thought we would really have to fight with Israel, but we felt we were very good… [and thus felt like] …flying above Israel at a flight level above 18km [11 miles]. They shot at us with their HAWK missiles, but because of our height they didn't hit us. We were flying over Israeli territory but stayed over it just a short time, so the (Dassault) Mirage (IIICJ interceptors) couldn't reach us. On 29 May 1967, we had seen Eshkol [on TV] with President

A row of MiG-21F-13s of the Egyptian air force as seen in 1962 – in livery and markings as worn during the June 1967 Arab-Israeli War. The aircraft in the foreground wore the serial number 5006. As of May-June 1967, not one Egyptian MiG-21 was capable of flying photo-reconnaissance missions. (David Nicolle Collection)

[Lyndon B] Johnson in the USA. He was begging for US support because the Egyptians were flying over them every day, and they could not stop us.[16]

It might sound unusual for MiG-21s to fly so high. However, one should keep in mind that this type was originally developed on the basis of experiences from the Korean War, where Soviet-made MiG-15 proved capable of flying *higher* than all types in US- and allied service and thus remained a major problem throughout three years of the conflict. From the standpoint of top military decision-makers in Moscow the logical conclusion – bolstered by reports about the USA developing several types of high-flying strategic bombers – was that in any future conflict the Soviet air force would need a fighter flying even higher. Correspondingly, the MiG-21 was designed with flying at altitudes of up to 18,000m (59,055ft) and higher in mind, and – as confirmed not only by those that flew the type in the early 1960s, but also by tactical manuals for this type from the same time – their pilots trained in such operations.[17]

DEVICES OF JUNE 1967

Of course, the Israeli military knew that the high-flying MIG-21s were no direct threat to Dimona. Nevertheless, top commanders of the IDF took nothing for granted. By 28 May 1967, a combined civilian and military team of the KAMAG/RAFAEL/IAEC had assembled the first two or three – improvised – nuclear bombs, and drawn a preliminary contingency plan codenamed 'Shimshon' (Samson). This envisaged a demonstrative deployment of a nuclear device by two Aerospatiale SA.321 Super Frelon helicopters in a desolate part of the eastern Sinai, as the 'last trump card' for the (very unlikely) case that Israel found itself in peril.[19]

While the crisis that eventually led to the June 1967 Arab-Israeli War thus marked the moment in which Israel crossed the nuclear threshold, the available information

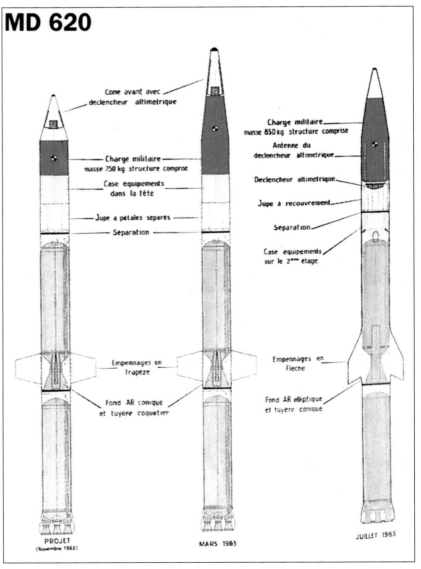

Official drawing of the MD.620 as developed by Dassault and delivered to Israel by January 1969. (Dassault, via Albert Grandolini)

indicates that these early nuclear weapons assembled as of 28 May were clumsy, spider-like, improvised constructions unsuitable for deployment by classic platforms such as combat aircraft or ballistic missiles. Moreover, their possible deployment was quickly overtaken by developments. On the morning of 5 June 1967, the IDF/AF launched an all-out attack on 14 major air bases in Egypt, followed by two in Jordan and six in Syria. In five successive waves the Israelis launched 470-474 combat sorties to *claim* the destruction of 374 Egyptian, Jordanian, Syrian, and Iraqi aircraft, while losing just 19 of their own. Although the claims in question were significantly exaggerated, this hammer blow stunned the chain of command of the entire Egyptian military to a degree where this remained paralyzed for most of the following 24 hours, and then quickly lost control. Egypt, the power-house of the Arab world, was not only defeated, but lost most of its Army and nearly all of the Sinai Peninsula. In turn, the IDF was thus free to maul the Jordanian armed forces, and then prompt the Syrians into a hasty retreat. By 10 June 1967, Israel was in control of all of the Golan Heights in the north, the entire West Bank and Gaza – the only two remnants of the original Palestine as designed by the United Nations in 1947 – and the Sinai Peninsula in the south.

An MD.620 undergoing final phase of assembly before a test-launch in France. (Dassault via Albert Grandolini)

Two MD.620s undergoing assembly at Dassault's facility in Martignas. (Dassault via Albert Grandolini)

JERICHO

Having established itself in a position of military hegemony over the entire Middle East – precisely as planned by the Israeli leaders since 1947 – the IAEC and the IDF returned to the project of completing the weaponisation of the country's nuclear potential.[20]

While it is possible that Israel did initiate the work related to a project for a 'carrier' of its future nuclear weapons as early as of 1946-1952 – when its representatives hired the leading US rocket engineer and rocket propulsion researcher, John Whiteside 'Jack' Parsons – the first confirmed effort in this direction was launched around the same time that Israel placed the order for the Dimona reactor. Correspondingly, the Israeli Ministry of Defence contracted

Test-launch of an MD.620 in France. (Dassault, via Albert Grandolini)

the French company Dassault for the development of a surface-to-surface missile capable of carrying nuclear weapons. For the next few years, related work was run by the state-owned SEPR consortium, until de Gaulle's reservations resulted in the transfer of this project back to privately-owned Dassault – found 'more suitable' to continue the work in a clandestine fashion. The first related official contract with the Israeli Ministry of Defence was signed on 7 September 1962, while the definitive contract – signed on 26 April 1963 – stipulated production of 25 test rounds in France, and Dassault subsequently helping the Israelis to launch licence production at home.[21]

Originally based on the unmanned variant of the Mirage IV supersonic bomber, the resulting MD.620 missile had a length of 13.4m (43.96ft) and diameter of 0.80m (41.50in). It weighted 6.7

tonnes (14,771lbs), could be launched from fixed or mobile sites within two hours of corresponding orders, and carry a 750kg (1,653lbs) warhead over a range of 500 kilometres (270nm). It had an ascending speed of Mach 6 up to an altitude of 150km before re-entering the atmosphere at around Mach 8. While the Israelis were originally satisfied with a circular error probability (CEP) of as much as 1,000m (1093yds), the French managed to make the missile quite precise: trials proved that the MD.620 had a CEP of only 300m (328yds). The first series of missiles was assembled at the newly-constructed facility in Martignas, which employed around 100 French technicians, starting from 15 May 1964. The first test firing of a single-stage structure took place on 1 February 1965, but failed due to a malfunction in the inertial navigation system (INS). It was followed by the first firing of a complete, two-stage missile in December 1965, and the first successful test of the full system, on 16 March 1966, after which the missile hit a target 450km (243nm) away. Following the fifth test-launch, on 13 December 1966, the French arrived at the decision to transfer production of further missiles to Israel. Nevertheless, testing in France was continued until 30 September 1968, by which time 16 MD.620s were fired: ten tests were considered successful, three semi-successful, and three ended with a failure.[22]

The US intelligence community followed the related developments with growing concern. In 1965, the air attaché at the US Embassy in Tel Aviv reported that a senior IDF source was boasting about early testing of the MD.620 on the Isle de Levant, off the southern coast of France, and that once the missile was ready, it would have 'the right kind of warhead'.[23]

DAVID'S ARROWS …

By January 1969, when France imposed its second and 'total' embargo on arms exports on Israel, ten missiles manufactured in France had been delivered. The IDF then ran the seven final qualification-firings and the weapon entered service with the Sdot Micha-based No. 150 Squadron IDF/AF under the designation YA-1 Jericho (later 'Jericho 1' to distinguish it from subsequent developments). According to US intelligence reports, Israel received 12 missiles from France, and – since 1968 – was in the process of setting up a production line with the intention of having a total force of 24-30 within two years – 'ten of which were programmed for nuclear warheads'. Moreover, the Americans were aware of the likelihood of Israel to equip its McDonnell Douglas F-4E Phantom II for deployment of nuclear weapons, once these were delivered, starting in 1969.[24]

Although the Israeli government officially agreed with Washington that the French-designed missiles would not be used as 'strategic missiles' (with nuclear warheads) – 'until at least 1972' – the Jerichos were mated with nuclear warheads about a year after their delivery. Reportedly, the production of the latter began in 1968 and reached an annual output rate of three 'devices' per year by 1973. During the same year, Israel officially patented the laser enrichment process that further accelerated their production rate. For all the official friendship between the two nations, the American efforts to monitor related developments then reached a point where, when a military attaché at the US Embassy in Tel Aviv 'got close to' the Jericho, he was declared *persona non grata* by the Israeli government. Nevertheless, before being forced to leave the country, he obtained enough intelligence for the Jericho to be featured in the so-called 'Gray Book': a constantly updated catalogue of nuclear weapons in active service around the World maintained by a nuclear proliferation sub-group of the US Intelligence Board.[25]

A formation of F-4E Phantom IIs from No. 119 Squadron, IDF/AF – the unit explicitly described by US intelligence as including 10 aircraft modified to carry nuclear weapons as of October 1973. (Albert Grandolini Collection)

According to estimates of the US intelligence community, by October 1973, Israel was in possession of 14 20kt warheads (weighing 450kg/992lbs) and six 50kt warheads (each weighing 700kg/1,543lbs), with six further devices undergoing assembly. Most of the 20kt warheads were planned for deployment with the help of Jerichos, between 10 and 13 of which were in service with No. 150 Squadron under the reported code-name 'David's Arrow'.[26]

... AND DAVID'S SHIELDS

Soon after acquiring the first of 44 F-4E Phantom II fighter-bombers – the release of which the US president Johnson conditioned with Israel signing the NPT, expressing its support for the US commitments in Vietnam, and 'maintaining a flexible position in the ongoing UN-sponsored Middle East peace negotiations' – the IDF/AF launched the work on making these compatible with nuclear weapons. Johnson was to get none of the Israeli concessions. Indeed, even the next US president that attempted to condition the delivery of F-4Es to Israel on at least indirect peace negotiations with Egypt – Richard Nixon – was to receive nothing in return: on the contrary, the provision of advanced technologies to Israel only increased once the Rockwell Corporation became involved in the country, in the 1968-1969 period. Rockwell not only helped establish the Israeli Aircraft Industries (IAI): the corporation also arranged a clandestine deal for the delivery of 50 Mirage 5s officially 'embargoed' by France, in 1970 (where these were assembled under the official designation 'IAI Nesher'), and then provided the personnel and technical expertise to launch a project for the installation of US-made General Electric J-79 engines into the same – which eventually resulted in the IAI Kfir fighter-bomber. With or without help from experts from Rockwell and similar US companies, by October 1973, the IDF/AF had '10 F-4Es based at Tel Nov AB', equipped to carry nuclear weapons. Reportedly code-named 'David's Shield', the Phantoms in question could be armed with both of the available devices – those with the yield of 20kt and those with the yield of 50kt.[27]

PURPOSE

The usual explanation for Israel developing nuclear weapons is that it is a small country surrounded by hostile neighbours, 'all of whom have sworn to destroy it', indeed to, 'sweep the Israelis into the sea'. While there is no doubt that no Arab statesman could ever dare be known as anything less than a 'bitter enemy of Israel', and while there is even less doubt that diverse Arab media outlets have repeatedly run outrageous anti-Israeli propaganda campaigns stipulating nothing less than its complete destruction, the reality is that Israel has never faced such a threat. Ever since 1947 (i.e. before the State of Israel officially came into being), all the known professional military assessments of the balance of forces between Jewish armed forces in Palestine, and then the Israeli military, and the armed forces of Israel's neighbours, have repeated the same conclusion – according to which the Jewish forces, and then the Israeli armed forces were always in a position of military superiority to one or the other degree, and this to all of their neighbours combined.[28]

For example, during negotiations between Ben-Gurion and de Gaulle in 1960, the President of France – a former military officer and acting Commander-in-Chief of the French armed forces – proved impossible to fool with such Israeli arguments as that the newly-delivered Egyptian MiG-19s would be capable of, 'attacking and destroying Tel Aviv and Haifa', plus 'our four aerodromes', in a matter of 'one hour', 'killing most of IDF/AF's cadre', 'Jews born in the country and those who came from Europe and the United State and who form the core of our nation'. Thus, after explaining that, '... the other Jew immigrants coming from backward and undereducated countries are less relevant...', Ben-Gurion attempted the explanation that Israel, 'needs a credible deterrence'. Still unimpressed, de Gaulle replied that the Egyptian air force could not destroy the Israeli cities, and that Israel was in a perfect position to defend itself with available, conventional military forces.[29]

Considering that the IDF certainly knew better than Ben-Gurion, it is on hand that the Israeli decision to develop nuclear weapons must have been quite different than usually accepted. Indeed, in the early 1970s a notable Israeli expert of his country's nuclear weapons program explained that '... *acquiring a superior weapons system would mean the possibility of using it for compelling purposes – that is, forcing the other side to accept Israeli political demands...*'[30]

Of course, like every professional military service, the Israeli Defence Force went to quite some lengths to – soon after acquiring nuclear weapons and Jerichos – develop a suitable doctrine for their deployment. Apparently based on the original planning for Shimshon, the related work resulted in the emergence of plans with code-names like 'Situation Intensity', 'Samson Ended', 'Last Genius', 'Forced Resolution', and 'Bitter Freedom'. Precise details remain unknown but one such plan may have called for Israel to warn the Arab governments via the UN in advance of deploying such weapons; another for Israel issuing a direct warning to Cairo and Damascus; one called for deployment of a single nuclear weapon against the Egyptian military on the Sinai without any previous warnings; and another for the destruction of Cairo and Damascus with nuclear weapons and that without any warning. Finally, the 'ultimate' of these plans envisaged the continued deployment of all available Israeli nuclear bombs against a combination of Arab capitals and field armies until the war was ended – 'one way or another'. The source concluded:

> Our assessment was that the Israelis were ready to make use of their nuclear weapons, and we had little doubt that they would use them, even if only as a last resort – for example *if Egyptian troops would break through in the Sinai, or Syrians reach the Jordan River*' (emphasis added by authors).[31]

2
TOOLS OF THE TRADE

While diverse forms of warfare – aerial, ground, naval, and even the nuclear – are usually considered in total isolation, each is actually a part of a much larger pattern, and each must be seen within context: as a part of the military service and the conflict in question. Nuclear and aerial warfare in particular are both extremely complex – and very technical too. For easier understanding of the subsequent narrative, this chapter will provide an overview of Egyptian and Israeli military branches, their doctrine, strategy, tactics, equipment, training, and the crucial units involved in the story in question. Moreover, it is going to provide coverage of the specific weapons systems cited – by one or the other side – as influential to their decisions, and the resulting combat operations described in subsequent chapters of this book.

LIMITED WAR

Considering it is at least 'likely' that Cairo was aware that Israel was in possession of nuclear weapons as of the early 1970s, the question arises: how Sadat and his military commanders came to the decision to plan and then 'attack' what was a 'nuclear power' while knowing they had no similar armament at their disposal?

In Western military thinking, a total military victory – one including the conquest or even a total annihilation of the defeated party – is often considered the principal objective of every war. Indeed, there is much obsession with the so-called 'Cannae scenario': one in which the enemy military is encircled and completely annihilated. However, modern warfare has shown that this solution is not always necessary, and often not even desired. Indeed, many modern wars are fought for other purposes – because one of their lessons is that the desired result can be achieved alone by eroding the ability and the will of the opponent to continue waging a war. Moreover, while there are plenty of other reasons and objectives for fighting wars, two things are common to all of them:

a) in the words of the legendary Prussian general and military theoretician Carl Philipp Gottfried von Clausewitz, they are,

'the continuation of politics by other means', and

b) 'wars usually erupt when politicians cease communicating with each other and resort to violence'.[1]

During the war of June 1967, Israel defeated the Egyptian military and conquered the Sinai Peninsula. With the IDF/AF not only in a position of vast superiority over the Egyptian air force, but also actively exercising control of the airspace well to the west of the Suez Canal, with Israel unilaterally annexing Jerusalem, and General Ariel Sharon boasting that every national force in Europe was weaker than that of Israel, and that the IDF could conquer the area from Khartoum to Baghdad and Algeria in one week, Cairo saw no point in any kind of negotiations. In attempt to at least regain control over its own sky – necessary to enable its military to reach positions along the western side of the Canal required as a springboard for a possible counteroffensive – Nasser then initiated what he called the 'War of Bloodletting', that is generally known as the 'War of Attrition', in 1968. As far as is known, even at that point, the Egyptian president remained unimpressed with the Israeli nuclear weapons. When one of his generals observed that Israel was on the way to getting an atomic bomb and that this posed a need for Egypt to build its own, Nasser replied 'You must not worry about that. If Israel gets the bomb, Egypt will immediately get it too.'[2] Obviously, Egypt had a promise of nuclear assistance from a friendly country if Israel ever became a nuclear power.

Indeed, Israel remained insistent on preventing the Egyptian military from establishing itself in positions along the Suez Canal and then, in autumn 1969, began flying air strikes ever deeper into Egypt. By February 1970 the situation reached a point where the Soviet Union launched a military intervention with the nominal intention of lessening the IDF/AF's pressure upon the Egyptian military, and buying time necessary for this to bolster its air defences on the western side of the Suez Canal. The fighting ended with a US-negotiated cease-fire in August 1970. A month later, Nasser suddenly died and was replaced by Anwar el-Sadat as president of Egypt. Sadat faced two options: one was to continue pursuing the plan for an all-out counteroffensive into the Sinai, and the other to negotiate with Israel. An attempt to do the latter under US-supervision failed in 1971, and Cairo was thus left without options other than to fight another war.[3]

For the purpose of planning that war, Sadat appointed Major-General Sa'ad Mohammed el-Husseiny el-Shazly as the Chief-of-Staff of the Egyptian Armed Forces in May of the same year. Soon after assuming command, Shazly concluded that the Egyptian military lacked the arms and supplies for another large-scale war: it could not hope to 'win' and 'defeat' Israel. He advised Sadat correspondingly and the president repeatedly requested the supply of both from Moscow, but the Soviets proved partially unwilling, partially unable, and certainly slow, to deliver. Short on options, Sadat and Shazly then sought for alternatives. One was to fight a war that Egypt could afford with means on hand, make a good start and achieve a limited yet maintainable success that would produce political conditions favourable for further negotiations with Israel. In cooperation with Major-General Ahmad Ismail Ali, appointed the Minister of Defence in October 1972, Shazly and Sadat thus developed the idea of a 'limited war': one in which the Egyptian military would cross the Suez Canal, and then entrench itself to beat back any expected Israeli counterattacks, until politicians could negotiate – and thus without directly threatening the security of Israel.[4]

In other words: contrary to what is usually expressed in diverse English-language publications, Egypt was not seeking the

Sadat (centre), with top generals, including Ismail (on Sadat's right), Gamasy (on Sadat's left) and Mubarak. Notable is the absence of Shazly, who fell out of favour with the Egyptian president during the October 1973 War. (Albert Grandolini Collection)

'destruction' of Israel during the resulting October 1973 Arab-Israeli War, nor even to destroy the IDF: indeed, Israel was neither under a direct threat, nor ever in need of being 'saved', but the Egyptians fought a war with an actually minimalistic objective of breaking the deadlock in negotiations. While this message was expressed in public several times before, during and after that conflict – and especially so in relation to the series of Israeli air strikes against civilian and military targets in the Cairo area of late 1969 and early 1970 – it seems to have been accepted only by parts of the Israeli government. As we are to see, especially Minister of Defence Moshe Dayan was to think quite differently during the October 1973 War.[5]

Until Cairo ever releases the related documentation, the conclusion to hand is that, whatever intelligence Sadat, Ismail, and Shazly might have had about the status of the Israeli nuclear weapons, and the circumstances under which these might be deployed, they were hoping that their enemy's government would understand there was no need to deploy these.[6]

WEAKNESSES OF THE EGYPTIAN AIR POWER

The next issue Shazly had to solve was that of lacking arms to actually fight Israel: certainly enough, the Egyptian Army was reasonably well-supplied with tanks, artillery, and infantry weapons. However, while ground forces have the paramount role in any conflict – because only foot soldiers can hold territory – the majority of modern wars are won by the side capable of providing better air support to its ground forces. This factor was dramatically demonstrated during the June 1967 Arab-Israeli War, when the IDF/AF first knocked out the Egyptian air force, and then played the decisive role in supporting the advance of the Israeli ground troops. During the subsequent War of Attrition, 1969-1970, the Egyptians were forced into the realisation that although completely rebuilt and

better trained than ever before, their air force was in no condition to seriously challenge the technological superiority of the IDF/AF created by deliveries of the latest combat aircraft from the USA. Not only the availability of growing numbers of McDonnell Douglas F-4E Phantom II, AIM-9D Sidewinder and AIM-7E Sparrow air-to-air missiles, but also an entire IADS – including advanced COMINT/SIGINT/ELINT- and ECM/ECCM-systems – made the Israelis capable of exercising aerial dominance deep inside the Egyptian airspace west of the Suez Canal. At least as severe was the lack of armament necessary to hit back at the very essence of Israeli air power: the IDF/AF's bases in central Israel.[7]

SILVER BULLETS

The Egyptian and Israeli conclusions about the inability of the Egyptian military to threaten IDF/AF air bases were well-substantiated. Egypt had no nuclear weapons and possessed next to no capacity to hit Israel. Indeed, at the time Shazly assumed his position of the Chief-of-Staff, Cairo actually had no ability to do so at all: no fighter-bombers with sufficient range and payload to reach Israel and no ballistic missiles. Certainly enough, and just as in June 1967, one could argue that the Egyptian Air Force (EAF) was equipped with light bombers and medium-bombers that, without doubt, did possess the range and payload-carrying capability to reach Israel. However, as mentioned above, it was due to the appearance of the Mirage IIICJ interceptors that the Egyptians concluded that their old and slow Il-28s to be far too vulnerable to penetrate Israeli-controlled airspace. The few attempts to operate them in combat in June 1967, and then during the War of Attrition, all resulted in heavy losses and thus confirmed such conclusions beyond any doubt. Unsurprisingly, the surviving aircraft of this type were concentrated into only one unit – the 77th Independent Tactical

An Egyptian Tu-16K-11-16 bomber armed with two KSR-11 anti-radar missiles, as seen during a military parade in October 1974. (Ahmed el-Keraidy Collection)

A formation of four out of 16 Su-17 fighter-bombers delivered to Egypt in 1971 (inset is shown the centre section of an example used for testing the Egyptian-made runway-cratering bomb). All drawn from the '0-series' (pre-production), they proved a maintenance nightmare and were quickly withdrawn from service, to be replaced by Su-20s in early 1973. (Albert Grandolini Collection)

(ASCC/NATO-codename 'AS-5 Kelt') guided air-to-surface missiles. However, the service entry of these with No. 36 Squadron EAF changed nothing in Israeli assessments: the matter of fact was that not only were Tu-16s vulnerable to IDF/AF interceptors but the same was valid for their big and slow AS-5s.[8]

The capability of the EAF to hit any Israeli air bases remained limited even after the delivery of 16 Sukhoi Su-17 fighter-bombers, which arrived around the same time as the Tu-16K-11-16s: although entering service with No. 55 Squadron, all belonged to the pre-production series, which was poorly manufactured and marred by diverse technical problems. All 16 had to be grounded and withdrawn from service within six months of delivery to Egypt. It was only in summer 1973 that the Soviets replaced them with 16 much more mature Su-20 fighter-bombers.[9]

SADAT'S KICK-OUT ORDER

The situation did experience a *slight* change late in 1971, when the EAF became involved in the Libyan project to acquire 110 Dassault Mirage 5 fighter-interceptors, fighter-bombers and reconnaissance

Bomber Squadron – relegated to secondary duties, and as far as is known, they did not fly a single combat sortie in October 1973.

Potentially, the Egyptian medium bomber fleet of mid-1971 – consisting of 14 Tupolev Tu-16 bombers organized into two squadrons of the 403rd Bomber Brigade – packed much more punch: each of them could carry up to 9,000kg of bombs over ranges sufficient to reach Israel. However, not only the experiences with Egyptian Il-28s, but also those with Iraqi Tu-16s during the June 1967 War, had shown that the type was much too vulnerable when operating within enemy-controlled airspace without protection. With the EAF having no fighter-interceptors with sufficient endurance to escort them to Israel, simply sending them in that direction promised to result in unacceptable losses for no gain in return. In autumn 1971, Moscow finally granted permission for the delivery of ten slightly improved Tu-16K-11-16, equipped with KSR-2 and KSR-11

fighters, ordered two years earlier. The first group of 'Libyan' pilots sent to Dijon AB in France for conversion courses for this type largely consisted of Egyptian pilots with Libyan passports. After working up on the type through 1972, they were organized into No. 69 (Independent) Squadron. Commanded by Colonel Ali Zien al-Abideen Abdul-Jawwad, this unit included 20 pilots, 19 Mirage 5D fighter-bombers and two Mirage 5DR reconnaissance fighters (all still owned by Libya, but lent to the EAF), and it re-deployed to Tanta AB in Egypt in April 1973.[10]

Even then, and even if combined, the 10 AS-5-armed Tu-16s, 16 Su-20s, and 19 Mirage 5Ds were far too few to enable the EAF to directly challenge the far superior IDF/AF. Resenting not only the slow deliveries of additional equipment demanded by him, but also angered by Soviet lack of will to support Egypt, and Moscow's 'private' dealings with the USA, on 16 July 1972 president Sadat ordered the majority of 970 Soviet military advisors and around 7,000 other military personnel to leave his country by the end of the month. Already resenting the Egyptian 'ingratitude for past services' and alarmed by the post-Nasser 'trend towards the right in Egyptian political and economic life', the Soviet government accepted this 'kick-out' order.[11]

This decision had far-reaching consequences – in so far that it convinced the Israelis that Sadat was not preparing for another war: on the contrary, the Israeli intelligence community expected that the entire Egyptian military would collapse without Soviet support. Actually, Sadat's order was carefully timed, and resulted in no outright end of relations with the USSR: several groups of Soviet technical experts continued serving in Egypt.

Egyptian (and a few Libyan) pilots, together with their French instructors during conversion training for Mirage 5s in France, in 1971. (Albert Grandolini Collection)

BALLISTIC MISSILES

While not pursuing the development of nuclear weapons, Cairo did request the delivery of ballistic missiles from the USSR as early as of 1957. However, Moscow flatly refused to supply any, leaving the Egyptians with no option but to launch an attempt to develop ballistic missiles at home. With no rocket science being available in Egypt, Nasser's government followed the Israeli example and launched an effort to import the necessary know-how and technology: Hassan Sayed Kamil, an Egyptian-Swiss arms dealer was contracted to find and recruit scientists from West Germany and Switzerland. A dummy company was set up in Munich, run by Heinz Krug, that began providing materials and tools necessary to

The first Mirage 5D manufactured for Libya wore the serial number 401. This photograph was taken shortly before its delivery and shows it in a test-configuration with – amongst others – JL.100 combined rocket launchers and drop tanks on inboard underwing pylons. (Dassault via Albert Grandolini)

The first two-seat conversion trainer made for Libya wore the serial number 201. This photograph shows it shortly after delivery in 1972. The aircraft was used extensively for converting the first few groups, with about 30 Egyptian pilots, to this type. (Albert Grandolini Collection)

A prototype of the al-Qaher-1 rocket, as seen during a test-launch on 20 July 1962. No less than 20 were shown on a parade that marked the 10th anniversary of Nasser's ascent to power, a day later. (Albert Grandolini Collection)

and the Egyptian program had come to a standstill.[12]

This effort left behind three semi-finished designs for ballistic missiles: the smaller al-Qahir and az-Zafir, and the bigger one, ar-Raid. No less than 12m (39ft) long and weighing 2,500kg (5,511lbs) when fully loaded, al-Qahir was originally designed as a road-mobile missile, with a range of about 160km (100nm). The az-Zafir was slightly smaller: like al-Qaher, it consisted of a cylindrical body, conical pointed nose, flared skirts, fixed fins and single, fixed-thrust chamber. The biggest of the three was ar-Raid: claimed to be able to carry a 1,000kg (2,205lbs) 'scientific payload', it was only ever shown as a mock-up, indicating two stages. Due to the early cancellation of all three projects they lacked guidance: al-Qahir and az-Zafir could only be aimed with the help of tilting and aligning the launching ramp. Unsurprisingly, both proved woefully short-ranged and inaccurate. During a series of test-firings run on Shazly's order in September 1971, al-Qahir reached less than eight kilometres (five miles). Az-Zafir proved to be even shorter-

set up Factory 333 at Helwan. The project progressed at a reasonably good pace, although marred by a major issue: none of the involved scientists was capable of developing an operational guidance system. Moreover, when it was revealed in public, during a parade in Cairo of July 1962, it prompted Israel into launching Operation *Damocles*, a covert campaign of state-sponsored terrorism targeting the scientists and technicians involved: after letter bombs failed to produce any effects, Krug was kidnapped and murdered in Germany, while two other scientists narrowly avoided assassination attempts. Although causing a major scandal and severely straining relations between West Germany and Israel, Operation *Damocles* was highly successful: all 70–80 scientists involved were out of Egypt by the end of 1963,

ranged, but possessing marginally better accuracy. Despite all the shortcomings, Shazly decided to deploy the handful of available missiles under the designation at-Tin and az-Zaytoon, respectively.[13]

When Israel launched its deep penetration raids against military and economic targets in the Cairo area, in 1969-1970, the Egyptians approached Moscow with another request for ballistic missiles – and this time the Soviets agreed to deliver 24 9K52 Luna-M systems (ASCC/NATO-codename 'FROG-7') – including ZIL-135 transporter/erector/launchers (TELs) and a similar number of 9M21 rockets. These entered service with the 64th Missile Brigade of the Egyptian Army, which by 1973 acquired 80 additional rockets from the USSR. Staffed by officers of the Army's Artillery Corps that underwent preparatory training in the USSR between late 1966 and July 1967, and officially established in October 1970 after ten additional months of intensive training in Egypt, this brigade was organized into three battalions.[14]

With FROG-7s having a maximum range of only 70km (38nm) and a CEP of no less than 500-700 metres (546-765 yards), and with the 64th Missile Brigade becoming operational only in October-November 1970, it was not only hopelessly incapable of deterring Israeli air raids striking targets in central Egypt, flown in late 1969 and through early 1970, but also entered service much too late for participation in the War of Attrition. Unsurprisingly, Cairo remained persistent. Related negotiations went on and in October 1972 Moscow finally agreed to deliver enough missiles and support equipment of the system known under the codename 'Scud' by the ASCC/NATO, for Cairo to equip two units with 12 launchers each. Following training of Egyptian personnel in the USSR, two groups of Soviet specialists arrived in Egypt to receive the equipment and help

The younger brother in flight: az-Zafir was 50% smaller than the 39-foot al-Qaher. Lacking a guidance system, both could be aimed only by tilting their launchers, and were extremely short ranged. (Albert Grandolini Collection)

The most ambitious part of the Egyptian missile project of the late 1950s and early 1960s was the ar-Raid. This mock-up of a two-stage missile was revealed in public during a military parade in Cairo, on 21 July 1962 – an act that proved counterproductive: it prompted the Israelis to launch Operation *Damocles* and force all of the associated German scientists to leave Egypt. (Albert Grandolini Collection)

working up the Egyptian units, in late July 1973. The first 10 TELs and 18 missiles arrived by ship in Alexandria a few days later, and on 1 August 1973 the Soviets initiated the training of the first Egyptian unit slated to operate Scuds: the 65th Missile Brigade. Ironically, while the official Egyptian documentation indicates that the unit promptly became involved in the planning for the coming war, and was operational as of 6 October, the Israelis assessed that the Scuds would have gained operational status only in early 1974, and – generally – their political and military leadership did not consider them a high-level threat. With one exception: that of the Minister of Defence, Moshe Dayan.[15]

Moreover, there is still quite a dose of uncertainty regarding the quantity and the exact variant of the R-17 system Moscow had provided before the October 1973 War. One recently published

Israeli source cites the delivery of 10 old 8A61 launchers and R-11 or R-11M (ASCC/NATO-codename 'SS-1a Scud-A' and 'SS-1b Scud-A', respectively) missiles 'during the summer of 1973'. Along the same lines, the Soviets would have been very reluctant to provide their 'newest weapons' to Egypt. Earlier US intelligence reports and publications cite the delivery of 9 MAZ-543 TELs and 18 R-17E missiles 'shortly before the outbreak of the October War'. While a delivery of 8A61 TELs cannot be excluded – simply because the Soviets were delivering 'unusual' pieces of equipment to diverse Arab clients time and again, and there are still plenty of unknowns about Arab militaries in general – there is no evidence that any vehicles associated with the Scud-A system have ever been operated by Egypt. On the contrary, all the available documentary films and photographs from before, during and immediately after

A still from a documentary film showing a ZIL-135 transporter/erector/launcher (TEL) of the 64th Missile Brigade of the Egyptian Army in 1973. (Albert Grandolini Collection)

This still from a documentary film released by the MOD in Cairo leaves no doubts about the type of TELs and missiles delivered to Egypt in 1973: it shows a MAZ-543 with an R-17E missile atop of it. (Egyptian MOD)

defence equipment to Cairo. Correspondingly, the ADC received unlimited funding in the period 1971-1973 and, drawing upon Soviet military theories, its commander – Major-General Ali Fahmy – set up a highly-centralised, integrated air defence system (IADS), the purpose of which was to integrate the information from all the sensors and observation posts, and to coordinate the work of all the weapons deployed along the length of the Suez Canal, and also to prevent Israeli aircraft from reaching the airspace over Cairo and Aswan. In other words, the purpose of the ADC's IADS was to enable the accomplishment of the air defence mission through providing one authority with all the command, control, and communication ('C3') functions.

The backbone of the ADC's IADS was a total of 180 radar sites (including 3 equipped with P-14 long-range/early warning radars, ASCC/NATO-codename 'Tall King'), with a maximum range of 400km (215nm) and 174 SAM-sites acquired from the USSR in the period 1956-1973. The obvious purpose of the ADC was to prevent Israeli air power from carrying out its task, but also in thwarting their attempts to spoil strikes by the EAF. Overall, its role was preventive by nature and had an essential function.[18]

the October 1973 War show the personnel of the 65th Missile Brigade with MAZ-543 TELs – which are usually associated with the R-17E (ASCC/NATO-codename 'SS-1c Scud-B') system. That said, the War Diary of the 65th Missile Brigade explicitly cites the deployment of 'Scud-A' missiles: whether this means that the Egyptians actually received a unique system consisting of R-11 or R-11M missiles from the Scud-A and MAZ-543 TELs from the Scud-B system, or something else, is currently still unclear.[16]

AIR DEFENCE COMMAND

Due to Cairo's inability to significantly bolster its offensive capabilities, and the combination of the Soviet refusal and inability to sell fighter-interceptors that could at least match the Israeli air superiority, Shazly soon concluded that the only way to provide at least 'adequate' air defence for the Egyptian ground forces was to significantly bolster their ground based air defences. This conclusion was confirmed by experiences from the final phase of the War of Attrition, when the Air Defence Command of Egypt (ADC) – an independent branch of the Egyptian military established in 1967 – proved successful in neutralizing the Israeli air campaign, even if not successful in neutralizing the Israeli aerial superiority.[17]

Another advantage of this approach was that Moscow proved ready to continue supplying 'unlimited' quantities of air

SA-2 GUIDELINE

For the reasons described above, contrary to what might be expected – and to some disagreement amongst Egyptian veteran fighter-pilots interviewed – the primary weapon of the ADC in October 1973 were not manned interceptors, but the Soviet-made SAM-systems. The oldest of these was code-named 'SA-2 Guideline' by the ASCC and NATO: originally designated the 'Dvina' by the Soviets, it was developed for strategic defence of major urban areas and military facilities against high-flying aircraft. First put to service in 1956, it was subjected to a series of upgrades and further development, which eventually resulted in the emergence of variants like Volkhov, Desna and Dvina. Very bulky (all of components of just one SAM-site together weigh well over 100 tonnes), the system was made mobile (even if at a relatively slow rate), and gradually adapted as a general-purpose air defence weapon, capable of engaging even tactical aircraft down to altitudes of around 300 metres (990ft). The centrepiece of each SA-2 SAM system – or a battalion – was the fire control radar designated 'Fan Song' by the ASCC/NATO. Supported by three other radars, and controlled from the command post, this served the purpose of engaging one target at a time with up to three (though usually two) SAMs. Egypt had acquired its first

Volga SAM system (widely known as 'SA-1' within the ADC and the EAF) – in 1962. By 1973, this was reinforced through the acquisition of 106 additional Volgas, Volkhovs, Desnas and Dvinas. Consisting of the equipment listed in Table 1, the latter was also the most numerous in service with the ADC.

One typical unit equipped with the SA-2 was the 418th Air Defence Battalion: officially established on 4 December 1964 from personnel trained by Soviet advisors in Egypt, as of early October 1973 this was deployed at el-Qanka, south-west of Inchas AB, where it was assigned to the 92nd Air Defence Brigade – a unit responsible for the defence of el-Mansourah AB – and protecting the nearby Cairo International Airport (IAP). Staffed by seasoned

The RSNA-75M (Fan Song) fire-control radar was the core of every SA-2 site. It used electro-mechanical scanning to emit a pair of beams from its two perpendicular antennae, which formed a cruciform pattern to determine the height and azimuth of the target. The round antenna on the side was used for missile guidance. (JH)

veterans of the War of Attrition, 418th Air Defence Battalion was commanded by Colonel Ayman Hob el-Din. Another of the SA-2-equipped units to become involved in the drama described in this book was the 425th Air Defence battalion: this unit was deployed in the Port Fuad area, in the north-western corner of the Sinai – the only part of the peninsula that remained under the Egyptian control through the time between 1967 and 1973.[19]

Table 1: Equipment of a typical SA-75MK Dvina (SA-2 Guideline) SAM-site of the ADC, October 1973

Equipment and Remarks	Number of Systems per SAM-Site/ Battalion
UV fire-control station (command post)	1
P-10 (ASCC-code 'Knife Rest') VHF-band early warning radar (range 75km/47nm)	1
P-12 (ASCC/NATO-codename 'Spoon Rest') early warning and P-15 ('Flat Face') C-band acquisition radar (range 250-300km/155-186nm)	2
PRV-10 (ASCC/NATO-codename 'Rock Cake') or PRV-11 ('Side Net') E-band height-finding radar (range 200km/124nm or 240km/149nm respectively)	1
RSNA-75M (ASCC/NATO-codename 'Fan Song') E/F/G-band fire-control radar (detection range 140km/87nm; acquisition range 100km/62nm); capable of simultaneously tracking up to six targets, but engaging only one at a time	1
SM-63-I launcher	6
PR-11 transporter-loaders (each with one spare missile)	3

SA-3 GOA

Originally developed as the medium-altitude partner to the SA-2, the Neva SAM system and its further development, the Pechora (both

received the ASCC/NATO-codename 'SA-3 Goa'), emerged in the early 1960s, and – essentially – functioned on the same principle as the SA-2: after being supplied with necessary targeting information, its command post used the sole fire-control radar to engage one target at a time with up to three missiles. However, contrary to the older system, the Neva/Pechora family was equipped with either double or quadruple launchers, which meant that even though still capable of engaging just one target at a time, they could engage the same target with a higher number of missiles, or a higher number of different targets in quick succession before having to reload.

The ADC began acquiring a total of 67 SA-3 SAM-systems in 1970 and deployed them for three purposes: for the defence of installations of strategic importance, for the defence of major air bases, and – in combination with SA-2s – for the protection of ground units deployed along the Suez Canal.[20]

Table 2: Equipment of a typical S-125 Neva (SA-3 Goa) SAM-site of the ADC, October 1973

Equipment and Remarks	Number of Systems per SAM-Site/ Battalion
UNK fire-control station	1
P-12 VHF-band early warning radar	1
P-15 C-band acquisition radar	1
PRV-11 E-band height-finding radar	1
SNR-125 (ASCC/NATO-codename 'Low Blow') fire-control radar	1
SP71 launcher for 2 V-601P missiles	4
PR-14 transporter-loaders with two spare missiles each	8
spare missiles	32-45

INTEGRATED AIR DEFENCE SYSTEM[21]

As the number of SA-2 and SA-3 SAM-systems operated by the ADC continued to grow, the issue of exercising control over them reached such proportions that by 1970 the Egyptians began acquiring so-called 'automated tactical management systems' (ATMS): cable-and computer-supported systems serving the purpose of connecting

A 5P71 launcher with two V-601P missiles, part of an ADC SA-3 site as of 1970s. Visible in the background (between the two missiles) is the SNR-125 (Low Blow fire-control radar, which was actually a pedestal for a complex that included one OUV-10 transmitter/receiver antenna, two OUV-11 antennae inclined at 45 degrees and the large OUV-12 main antenna for missile guidance. (Tom Cooper Collection)

The P-37 early-warning radar had a range of 300-370km (186-230nm) and an integral D-band IFF-system. Originally developed to support the SA-5 strategic SAM, in Egypt of the early 1970s it was a primary tool of the ADC's control over EAF fighter-interceptor operations. (Albert Grandolini Collection)

and coordinating the work of multiple radar stations and SAM-systems at the regimental-, brigade- and divisional level (for types and number of ATMS acquired by Egypt by 1973, see Table 2). The information collected by ATMS like Sneg, but also all of the available radar systems, ground observers, all available stations for communications-intelligence- (COMINT), electronic-intelligence- (ELINT), and signals-intelligence (SIGINT) gathering, stations for electronic countermeasures (ECM) and electronic counter-countermeasures (ECCM) assigned to each of the four ADC divisions – was fed into the *AZURK-1ME* ATMS: this was a fully automated, computer-supported system capable of automated coordination of the work of SAM-sites *and* manned interceptors. Essentially, it made the commander of the ADC capable of running the entire air battle with all of the forces assigned to him via 'remote control' from the Air Defence Operations Centre (ADOC), constructed in the form of an underground bunker in the desert east of Cairo.

Obviously, some of the SAM-sites were destroyed, and many SAMs were fired in the fighting during the 1967-1970 period, while a few were held in reserve and others were undergoing periodic maintenance. Thus as of 6 October 1973, the ADC operated a total of 138 SA-2 and SA-3 SAM-sites with a total of 700 launch rails, as follows:

•	74 batteries of SA-2s (6 launchers each)
•	64 batteries of SA-3s (4 launchers each).

As of October 1973, the units under the ADC's control were organized into three air defence divisions and two (nominally) 'independent' air defence brigades (as listed in Table 5): the most powerful of these was the 149th Air Defence Division, deployed along the Suez Canal, which exercised control over 30 SA-2 and 14 SA-3 SAM-sites, and 10 anti-aircraft artillery batteries. North of it was the 10th Air Defence Division; further west was the 139th Air Defence Division; while southern Egypt – and the gigantic Aswan Dam in particular – was protected by units of an unknown 'Southern' Air Defence Brigade.

By 1973, Egypt also received 10 SAM-sites equipped with a total of 40 SA-6

Taken from significant distance, this photograph shows a typical early warning radar station of the ADC deployed along the Mediterranean Sea. Visible are antennae of a P-18 ('Spoon Rest') early warning radar installed on two Ural-4320 trucks. (Photo by Alexander Hunger)

Another photograph of the same site, showing two PRV-11 (ASCC/NATO-code 'Side Net') height finding radars. Their purpose was to determine the altitude of tracked targets. (Photo by Alexander Hunger)

launchers. However, these units were assigned to the Egyptian Army – together with most of about 100 ZSU-23-4 self-propelled 23mm anti-aircraft artillery pieces – and operated independently from the ADC. Furthermore, Egypt acquired 366 launchers for 9K32 Strela-2 and 9K32M Strela-2M (ASCC/NATO-codenames 'SA-7A Grail' and 'SA-7B Grail') man-portable air defence systems (MANPADS), and 1,500 other anti-aircraft artillery pieces of calibres ranging from 23mm to 100mm. Contrary to what might be expected, the Egyptian Army's SA-6s were not to play any role in the drama that is the topic of this book: they were deployed for protection of the units fighting on the frontlines along the Suez Canal. Indeed, even most of the ADC's SAMs were to play only an indirect role, regardless how often described as the 'technologically the most advanced ever used' by even well-informed Western observers.[22]

Another difference between the two branches was that the ADC made extensive use of equipment for electronic identification friend or foe (IFF), while the Army did not: combined with the lack of a centralized command and control over the army's air defence weapons, this was to cause plentiful problems to the Egyptian fighter-interceptors. In essence, these could only pass over the army's positions along carefully selected corridors at carefully determined points in time, and never remained in that area for any extended periods of time. Nevertheless, the army units still tended to open fire at EAF aircraft, especially when these were returning from attacks on Israeli targets. Therefore, the majority of commanders of the Egyptian fighter-bomber units preferred to fly around, instead of over, areas protected by Army air defences.[23]

Table 3: ATMS delivered to Egypt, 1970-1973[24]

Designation	Number
Polye (also 'Polyot')	4
Sneg	45
AKKORD 75/125A	2
AZURK-1ME	4

PEOPLE'S SUPERSONIC SPORTS AIRCRAFT

While the ADC exercised not only the operational but also administrative control over the radar network and majority of air defence systems protecting Egypt, contrary to its Soviet equivalent – the Air Defence Forces (*Voyska Protivovozdushnoy Oborny*, PVO) – it included no units equipped with manned interceptors: the administrative control over these was exercised by the EAF.

The primary weapon system of all the manned interceptor units of the EAF as of October 1973 was the Mikoyan i Gurevich MiG-21 (ASCC/NATO-codename 'Fishbed'). Developed in reaction to the experiences of the Korean War, the original concept of the MiG-21 was that of a simple, lightweight, high-altitude fighter-interceptor for day and fair weather conditions only. Striving to extract as much performances as possible while keeping the aircraft simple enough to be operated under austere conditions and flown by inexperienced pilots, the designers sacrificed nearly everything – especially the firepower and endurance. While the 40 aircraft of the pre-production version MiG-21F (Izdeliye-72) were armed with two 30mm cannons, the MiG-21F-13 – the first version manufactured in large numbers, and the first to include a slightly increased fuel capacity – was armed with only one 30mm cannon with 60 rounds, and a pair of R-3S short-range, infra-red homing air-to-air missiles (ASCC/NATO-codename 'AA-2 Atoll'). Unsurprisingly, while highly popular with pilots, the nimble and very fast, but rather short-ranged and poorly armed jet became known as the 'People's Supersonic Sports Aircraft' in the Indian Air Force (IAF).[27]

Egypt acquired more than 70 MiG-21F-13s between 1962 and 1967, but less than half of these had survived the June 1967 War. Units equipped with this version were subsequently reinforced by deliveries of second-hand MiG-21F-13s from Algeria and Czechoslovakia. As of October 1973, the resulting mix of about 50 airframes formed the backbone of two squadrons of the Inchas-based 102nd Fighter Brigade (for an overview of manned interceptor units of the EAF as of October 1973, see Table 6). While their pilots were considered the elite of the Egyptian Air Force, operationally, this unit was subjected to the ADC.

The next major variant, the MiG-21PF (Izdeliye-76) was envisaged as an interceptor capable of nocturnal operations. The cannon armament was completely abandoned in exchange for a larger inlet centre body housing the TsD-30T R1L radar (ASCC/NATO-codename 'Spin Scan'), and additional fuel capacity. Egypt originally acquired about 30 examples of two slightly improved sub-variants with a larger fin – the MiG-21FL (Izdeliye-77) and the MiG-21PFM (Izdeliye-94), in 1965-1967. The latter was the first to have a new, two-piece canopy, blown SPS flaps and a more powerful engine. Most Egyptian MiG-21FLs and MiG-21PFMs were written-off in 1967: agreeing to replace losses from a war it has caused, Moscow promptly delivered 65 second-hand MiG-21PFS – essentially MiG-21PFs upgraded to a standard similar to that of the MiG-21PFM. Since 1969, some of these were made compatible with the 200kg GP-9 gun-pod for a 23mm twin-cannon with 200 rounds of ammunition. However, this was next to never used: the majority of combat operations over Egypt were flown at high speeds

Table 4: Deliveries of SA-2 and SA-3 to Egypt, 1962-1973[25]

System Type	Number	Number of Missiles
SA-2 (Volga, Volhov)	9	348 V-755/V-759
SA-2 (Desna/Dvina)	98	3402 V-750/V-750BMB
SA-3 (Neva, Pechora)	67	1808 V-601, 82 training rounds
total	174	5558

Table 5: ADC Divisions, 6 October 1973[26]

Unit	Headquarters	Notes
10th Air Defence Division	Port Said	operational zone Port Said; 4 SA-2 and SA-3 SAM-sites
149th Air Defence Division	Inchas AB	operational zone Suez Canal; 8 regiments, each with 5-8 SA-2 and SA-3 SAM-sites
139th Air Defence Division	el-Mansourah AB	operational zone Nile Delta
'Southern' Air Defence Brigade	Aswan	exact numeric designation unknown; operational zone Aswan and upper Egypt

Table 6: EAF Fighter-Interceptor Units operationally subordinated to the ADC, October 1973

Brigade	Squadron	Base	Equipment	Commanding Officers (COs)
102nd Air Brigade		Inchas AB		Colonel Nabil Shuwakry (deputy: Hassan Khadr)
	No. 25 Squadron	Wadi Qena	MiG-21F-13	Lieutenant-Colonel Ala'a Shakir
	No. 26 Squadron	Inchas, Jiyanklis, Gardeka, Abu Hammad	MiG-21F-13	Lieutenant-Colonel Ahmad Abd el-Aziz Ahmad Nur
	No. 27 Squadron	Inchas, Shubrakhat	MiG-21M/MF	Lieutenant-Colonel Mohammad Kamal as-Sawy
104th Air Brigade		el-Mansourah AB		Colonel Jamal Abd ar-Rahman Nassr
	No. 42 Squadron	Gardeka, Luxor, Saiyah el-Sharif	MiG-21M/MF	Lieutenant-Colonel Essam Muhammad Muqadam Sadiq
	No. 44 Squadron	el-Mansourah, Shubrakhat	MiG-21PFS/PFM	Lieutenant-Colonel Amir Ahmad Riyadh
	No. 46 Squadron	el-Mansourah	MiG-21M/MF	Lieutenant-Colonel Magdy Kamal Mahmoud Sadiq
111th Air Brigade				Colonel Ahmad Adil Nassr
	No. 45 Squadron	Kom Awshim	MiG-21PFS	Lieutenant-Colonel Ahmad Muhammad Shafiq
	No. 47 Squadron	Qutamiyah	MiG-21PFM	Lieutenant-Colonel Hisham Sayd Abduh
	No. 49 Squadron	Beni Suweif	MiG-21MF	Lieutenant-Colonel Tamim Fahmy Abd Allah

Commanders of the 102nd Air Brigade EAF, and its squadrons, as of October 1973. From left to right: Colonel Nabil Shuwakry (CO 102nd Air Brigade), Lieutenant-Colonel Ala'a Shakir (CO No. 25 Squadron), Lieutenant-Colonel Ahmad Abd el-Aziz Ahmad Nur (CO No. 26 Squadron). (Abdallah Emran Collection)

and low altitudes, where the short endurance and high fuel consumption of all MiG-21 variants were a distinct disadvantage. Due to a mix of inability and the lack of will of Moscow to deliver aircraft with better performance, and despite losses suffered in combat and training during the War of Attrition, together with few remaining MiG-21FLs and MiG-21PFMs, as of October 1973 the MiG-21PFS still formed the backbone of the 111th Fighter Brigade and one squadron of the 104th Fighter Brigade: the latter was the second and last unit of EAF manned interceptors operationally assigned to the ADC.

Ironically, while most of accounts of the October 1973 War emphasise the appearance of the advanced MiG-21MF variant (*Izdeliye-96F*), the matter of fact is that this version – probably the best MiG-21 fighter-interceptor ever – entered production only in 1972, and thus relatively few were delivered to Egypt by 1973. On the contrary, most of MFs encountered in combat by the Israelis during the October 1973 War were actually the slightly less-powerful MiG-21Ms (*Izdeliye-96*), deliveries of which began in 1970. This was an export variant of the MiG-21SM (*Izdeliye-95*), equipped with internally installed GSh-23 cannon, SPS-flaps, a slightly more powerful engine, and also four underwing pylons for R-3S missiles. Even then, because the EAF was critically short on fighter-bombers, the majority of MiG-21M/MFs delivered by October 1973 were serving in the 203rd Fighter-Bomber Brigade: only about 40 were assigned to the interceptor-units of the 104th Fighter Brigade.[28]

Overall, the EAF could thus provide the ADC with a maximum of about 120 MiG-21F-13s, MiG-21FL/PFM/PFS and MiG-21M/MFs – provided all of these were operational, manned, and available for instant action at the same time. Due to the tasks assigned to diverse units – foremost the necessity to fly CAPs over different parts of the huge Egyptian airspace – on average only about 60% of this force was available for combat operations at any time.

ISRAELI DOCTRINE: THE CONCEPT

It is notable that the Israelis had drawn precisely the same conclusions about the Egyptian capability to hit their air bases as Shazly had. Indeed, the

One of the few MiG-21FLs (serial number 6128) that survived the June 1967 War seen while undergoing overhaul at one of several works at Helwan tasked with providing such services. Notable is that this aircraft received the Nile Valley camouflage pattern by the time this photograph was taken (see Colour Section for details). (David Nicolle Collection)

Commanders of the 104th Air Brigade EAF, and its squadrons as of October 1973. From left to right: Colonel Jamal Abd ar-Rahman Nassr (CO 104th Air Brigade), Lieutenant-Colonel Essam Muhammad Muqadam Sadiq (CO No. 42 Squadron), Lieutenant-Colonel Amir Ahmad Riyadh (CO No. 44 Squadron), and Lieutenant-Colonel Magdy Kamal Mahmoud Sadiq (CO No. 46 Squadron). (Abdallah Emran Collection)

Contrary to many reports, MiG-21M/MFs were still relatively rare in EAF service as of 1973. Furthermore, lack of fighter-bombers forced the Egyptians to use many of them for ground attack. These two examples (serials 8611 and 8652) even wore a small stylized 'bomb', applied in black on their forward fuselage as their unit insignia. (Albert Grandolini Collection)

weakness of the Arab air power resulted in the emergence of what is known as 'The Concept' in Israel: following this thesis – developed by the Israeli intelligence community in the 1971-1972 period – the IDF/AF was so clearly superior to the Arab air forces that the chance of the Arabs attempting to attack Israel was next to non-existent for up to the following ten years. Egypt would not do so without obtaining the ability to at least partially neutralise the Israeli air bases and attack objectives in Israel, while Syria would never attack Israel without Egypt. Correspondingly, no war was to be expected until Egypt could achieve strategic balance and would have a serious chance of inflicting a military defeat upon Israel. Emphasis – indeed: insistence and overreliance – on 'The Concept' in turn became the major reason why Egypt (in cooperation with Syria) achieved a strategic surprise when 'attacking Israel' on 6 October 1973.[29]

Moreover, disdainful of Arab fighting abilities, the Israelis convinced themselves that their intelligence system would provide timely warning of any possible attack, and that the attacking enemy could be sufficiently slowed down, if not stopped, by the defence lines composed of isolated strongpoints anchored to an obstacle system along the Suez Canal, the so-called 'Bar Lev Line'. The regular Israeli military could then be mobilized and – supported by superior air power – quickly destroy any enemy build-ups.[30]

While the Egyptian doctrine for fighting the October 1973 War thus relied on denial of the airspace over the battlefield to the enemy, the essence of the Israeli doctrine – and, indeed, the centrepiece of the IDF's war plan – was based on seizure of the initiative and taking the battle into enemy airspace and territory at the earliest opportunity. Although not everybody in the IDF/AF felt that way, the force generally considered itself victorious during the War of Attrition, and thus expected to start any new war by destroying enemy air defences through the deployment of superior technology and firepower, then establishing air superiority by attacking enemy air bases, and then resorting to the role of 'flying artillery' for the tank-reliant ground forces.

MCDONNELL DOUGLAS F-4E PHANTOM II

The centrepiece of the IDF/AF as of October 1973 was four squadrons equipped with the F-4E Phantom II. Originally designed as an attack aircraft with four cannons, then re-designed into a supersonic, gunless, all-weather interceptor for the US Navy and then the US Air Force, the Phantom gradually emerged as the greatest fighter that entered service between 1955 and 1970. The F-4E was a dramatically improved variant with increased engine thrust, an internal gun, and an AN/APQ-120 radar with nine major working modes and about two dozen sub-modes, with a search range of out to 321km (200nm).

Israel placed its first order for 44 F-4Es in 1968, and Washington subsequently granted permission for the release of four additional batches of Phantoms: indeed, the deliveries of the aircraft from that first order were still incomplete (they were to last until January 1971), by the time the IDF/AF was granted six additional aircraft as replacements for losses suffered during the War of Attrition. By October 1973, Israel received a total of 122 F-4Es (and 6 RF-4E reconnaissance fighters). While the published Israeli sources usually stress that 13 of these had been written off by 6 October 1973, US reports point out that only 99 F-4Es (and all six RF-4Es) were still available to four squadrons of the IDF/AF operating the type by that date. Another important detail with regards to the Israeli F-4E fleet is that in 1972 the USAF introduced to service the F-4E TO.556 sub-variant, equipped with – amongst others – leading edge slats (LES) for improved manoeuvrability. Deliveries of such Phantoms to Israel – and conversion of older examples to the same standard –

An F-4E Phantom II of the IDF/AF as put on display before the October 1973 War. In the foreground are some of the weapons carried by the type, including (from left to right), LAU-3 launchers for unguided 68mm rockets, a trio of M117 bombs (on a triple ejector rack), six Mk.82 bombs (on a multiple ejector rack), and M118 – at 3,000lbs (1,400kg) the biggest conventional bomb carried by the type. (US Air Force Photo)

Table 7: IDF/AF Units with Strategic Reach, October 1973

Base or Wing	Squadron	Base	Equipment	Commanding Officers (COs)
1st Air Wing		Ramat David AB		Colonel Arlozor Lev
	No. 69 Squadron		F-4E	Lieutenant-Colonel Yoram Agmon
4th Air Wing		Hatzor AB		Colonel Amos Lapidot
	No. 201 Squadron		F-4E	Lieutenant-Colonel Yiftah Zemer (WIA, 13 October; replaced by Major Eitan Ben-Eliyahu)
2nd Air Wing		Sdot Micha AB		
	No. 150 Squadron		MD.620 Jericho	
6th Air Base		Hatserim AB		Brigadier-General Amihai Shmueli
	No. 107 Squadron		F-4E	Lieutenant-Colonel Iftach Spector
8th Air Base		Tel Nov AB		Colonel Ran Ronen
	No. 103 Squadron		Noratlas	Lieutenant-Colonel Eli Mor
	No. 118 Squadron		S-65C/CH-53A	Lieutenant-Colonel Yuval Efrat
	No. 119 Squadron		F-4E, RF-4E	Lieutenant-Colonel Eliezer Prigat
27th Air Base		Lod IAP		
	No. 120 Squadron		C-97 & EC-130H	Lieutenant-Colonel Yehushua Shani
30th Air Base		Palmachim AB		
	No. 200 Squadron		Model 124I	Lieutenant-Colonel Shlomo Nir

began later the same year, with the first modified aircraft entering operational service with the IDF/AF in May 1973. Exactly how many Israeli Phantoms were upgraded to the TO.556 standard by 6 October 1973 remains unclear.[31]

Approximately 90 of Israel's F-4Es were operational at any given time, but the IDF/AF lacked enough crews to man all of them at once. Moreover, and as described above, up to 10 Phantoms assigned to the Tel Nov AB-based No. 119 Squadron were held back as carriers of nuclear weapons. As far as can be assessed, Phantoms were *de-facto* the only Israeli-operated fighter-bombers to play a role in affairs covered in this volume.[32]

SUPPORT ASSETS

According to the pre-war planning of the IDF/AF, combat-support aircraft – and helicopters – were to play an important role in any future conflict. These included some of 11 Boeing KC-97 Stratotanker transport-, tanker- and aircraft for electronic support measures (ESM), several Nord N.2501 Noratlas transports equipped to act as airborne command posts and radio-relays, two Lockheed EC-130H electronic warfare aircraft, and several Sikorsky S-65/CH-53A Stallion helicopters equipped to carry ECM-systems of US-origin, known only by their Israeli designation, *Katef*. The shock caused by the surprising simultaneous attack by Egypt and Syria on two frontlines virtually blew all such plans out of the

Two of the big and powerful S-65A/CH-53A Stallion transport helicopters were equipped with Katef ECM-systems of US origin, and were supposed to act as stand-off jammers during the IDF/AF's air strikes. According to Egyptian and Soviet reports, their presence was felt only later during the October 1973 War. (Albert Grandolini Collection)

window, and the IDF/AF's combat-support platforms were to play a role only later during the war. [33]

3

LIMITED WARFARE VS. SWIFT AND EASY VICTORY

Because flying is a four-dimension activity (if time is included), it is often misunderstood as one 'unlimited' in regards of manoeuvre and reach. In another extreme, it is often misunderstood as a knightly tournament between specific types of aircraft, resulting in these wheeling around each other in a clear blue sky until achieving a favourable position to open fire. Actually, aerial warfare and so also air combats are incredibly complex. The following chapter provides an overview of the basic principles of aerial warfare, while paying special attention to peculiarities of the situation between Egypt and Israel as of October 1973.

FACTOR 'ARAB PILOTS'

While details on the organisation of the ADF and EAF, and performances of their equipment are relatively easy to obtain, assessing the ability of their Egyptian crews to operate them is not only much harder to acquire, but a matter of much controversy, too. To this day, the Israeli pilots are generally accepted as the 'best in the World'. On the contrary, one of the most common, most widespread prejudices about 'Arab' air forces spread in the mass of related Western publications over the last 70 years is that their pilots were – and remain – not only poorly trained, but outright incompetent, indeed 'stupid' – especially in comparison to, supposedly, 'super competent' Israelis. While obviously having no clear picture about the amount and nature of contemporary tactical training of the EAF's interceptor pilots, even US intelligence reports emphasised the, 'Israel's excellent aircrew selection and training programs' in comparison.[1]

The reasons for such assessments were countless, though predominantly coloured by the fact that Israeli propaganda was highly successful in presenting the Arab-Israeli conflict through the prism of the Cold War. Correspondingly, 'Arabs' were understood as 'Soviet clients', if not 'Soviet marionettes', and the training of their air forces explained as 'based to a large extent on Soviet techniques': the latter being only 'basic', providing the pilot with only the most rudimentary ideas about tactics and weapons deployment. Along the same lines, all the crucial decisions would be made by ground controllers – exactly in the way this was expected to be done by the Soviets. Furthermore, immediately after the June 1967 War, Israeli propaganda created the myth about IDF/AF pilots regularly flying 7-8 combat sorties a day, while – supposedly – all the Arab air forces were suffering from a chronic lack of qualified native personnel and heavily dependable not only on foreign advice, but indeed: on foreigners flying for them.[2]

It is next to impossible to explain the results of the related campaign. Certainly enough, many Arab air forces were created out of literally nothing in the 1940s-1970s, but those really short on pilots were those such as the air forces of Kuwait or Oman, not to mention the United Arab Emirates, Bahrain or Qatar. On the contrary, the air forces of Egypt, Iraq and Syria actually never lacked in numbers: rather in qualifications, training and experience. For example, already prior to and during the Suez War of 1956, and contrary to the IDF/AF, the Egyptian Air Force had more than enough pilots and flying crews to operate all of its aircraft,

Samir Aziz Mikhail, a Coptic Christian who joined the Egyptian air force in 1960. Aziz first flew MiG-17F and MiG-17PFs before converting to MiG-21F-13s in 1963-1964. After scoring at least one confirmed kill against an Israeli Mirage IIICJ, during the War of Attrition, he served as deputy commander of No. 46 Squadron during the October 1973 War. (David Nicolle Collection)

but relatively few of these were converted to Soviet-made aircraft in time to face the tripartite aggression. Despite repeated requests by Nasser, and contrary to endless related reporting in the West, the Soviets never deployed their pilots to fly combat sorties for any Arab air force before they did so in what was then the Republic of (North) Yemen, in late 1967.[3]

Certainly enough, the Soviets then did deploy two MiG-21 equipped regiments to Egypt, in 1970, but these became involved in exactly two clashes with the IDF/AF: no Soviet pilots were ever assigned to any EAF/UARAF units, nor did they fly combat sorties *for* the Egyptian air force. Moreover, while there can be no doubt about the heavy Soviet influence upon the doctrine of the Egyptian Army and the ADC, the EAF in particular was always operating entirely according its own tactics: whenever Soviet 'advisors' assigned to it during the War of Attrition attempted to intervene, it either suffered heavy losses, or outright refused to follow their advice. Unsurprisingly, the Egyptian pilots of October 1973 were operating entirely in accordance with their own tactics that reflected – and emphasised – not only their very own experiences, but also put great emphasis on planning and execution: higher ranks only assigned them the target or the aim of the mission. The MiG-21s of the units assigned to the ADC were also flying in genuine formations – roughly similar to what became known as 'lose deuce' in the US Navy – unique for Egypt of the time, and fighting in a different fashion than one could expect Soviet or other Eastern European pilots to do at the time.[4]

Ironically, while several dozen books have been published praising the special quality of the IDF/AF's system of training its pilots, and its excellent results, Egyptian experiences in this

Nassr Moussa joined the Egyptian air force in 1968, and continued serving – and flying fast jets – for more than 25 years, before retiring with the rank of Major-General. (Nassr Moussa via Abdallah Emran)

regard particularly – and then especially those from the 1967-1973 period – remain next to unknown. This is why it remains largely unknown that the Egyptian and Israeli pilot training programs as of 1967-1973 were at least equal. Both the Egyptian and the Israeli air forces had had high washout rates in primary and basic training – at 50% for the Egyptians and 75% for the Israelis. Regardless of how famed the IDF/AF was (and remains), differences between the Israeli advanced training and continuation training and those of the Egyptians, were minimal – and mostly related to the complexity of their equipment: US-made aircraft operated by the Israelis were much more complex than Soviet aircraft operated by the Egyptians, thus more demanding and taking longer to master. On the other side, the Egyptians greatly expanded and intensified their training curriculum: originally aiming to produce 800 new aviators between 1968 and 1973, this was further enhanced through extremely tough and thorough tactical exercises. The result was the emergence of an entirely new generation of Egyptian pilots.[5]

Typical amongst these was Nassr Moussa, a youngster evacuated from Suez City when this was mercilessly shelled and bombed by the Israelis in 1968, and then convinced to join the air force by nobody less than Hosni Mubarak – the then Commander of the Air Force Academy at Bilbeis. Following elementary military- and flight-training, Moussa underwent a jet training course in Egypt, followed by a MiG-21-conversion course in the USSR. Back to Egypt in 1970, he was assigned to one of the el-Mansourah AB-based squadrons of the 104th Air Brigade, equipped with brand-new MiG-21Ms:

On return to Egypt, I was assigned to No. 46 Squadron at el-Mansourah AB, commanded by Samir Aziz Mikhail. He had a fierce reputation as disciplinarian, and I was told he sometimes has beaten his pilots. I almost broke in tears when learning about my assignment... Mikhail turned out to be a strict disciplinarian, but also a great mentor and teacher that was devoting every minute of his time to training his pilots. I learned a lot from him within shortest period of time, including all the details of the famous 'zero speed manoeuvre'. We further studied the theory of air combat, different manoeuvres, details about our and enemy aircraft and weapons. We ran intensive air combat exercises, with our tasks getting harder every time. The peak of our training

were two-versus-four mock combats, which were specially demanding. Within the first two years of serving with No. 46 Squadron I clocked *nearly 500 hours of flying time*, and in July 1973 was promoted to the rank of a Captain...'[6]

MIRAGES FOR EVERYBODY

In addition to a much intensified training syllabus, one of the reasons for major improvement in the EAF's advanced training was the acquisition of Mirage 5 fighters-bombers by Libya: this was exactly the same type of aircraft clandestinely delivered to Israel in 1970, where they were declared as 'IAI Nesher'. Ignored by the French, and entirely unknown to the outside world, was the fact that nearly all of the early 'Libyan' pilots that underwent not only conversion to-, but also advanced operational courses on Mirage 5s at Dijon AB in France during the same year, were actually Egyptian fighter-pilots provided with Libyan passports. Amongst them were veterans like Farouk el-Ghazzawy – former MiG-17F-pilot that shot down the future Commander IDF/AF, David Ivry, in the course of a dogfight over the Sinai, in November 1959 – but also relative novices, like Magddin Rifaat:

I graduated from the Air Force Academy on 15 May 1967, then underwent an advanced jet training course at Marsa Matruh, and a conversion course to MiG-21 before being assigned to an operational squadron in June 1968...We trained very intensively:

Magddin Rifaat with one of the 'genuine' Egyptian Mirage 5SDEs, obtained in 1974 with support from Saudi Arabia. Due to an extremely intensive training syllabus and plentiful combat experience from the War of Attrition, even relative 'novices' within the fraternity of Egyptian fighter-pilots were seasoned veterans by October 1973. (Magddin Rifaat Collection, via Nour Bardai)

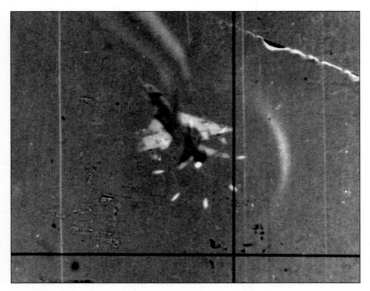

A still from a gun-camera film taken during one of the nearly endless air combat training exercises run by the EAF in the 1971-1973 period, and showing a MiG-21MF 'hit' by another MiG-21. (David Nicolle Collection)

Ghazzawy, Ahmed Shafiq, Samir Aziz Mikhail and our other instructors taught us to fly MiG-21F-13s to the limit. There was plenty of competition between us young students and at least four were killed in accidents during this period…. In 1970, we moved to el-Mansourah AB, and our units were re-designated as Nos. 42 and 44 Squadrons of the 104th Air Brigade…. In September 1971, I was sent to Libya for conversion to Mirages. While waiting for delivery of these, I converted to US-made [Lockheed] T-33A two-seat jet trainer and [Northrop] F-5A… then the training on Mirages began, supported by a group of French, Pakistani, and Egyptian instructors. We trained a lot, used all types of weapons, and by April 1973 I had 450 hours on the new type.[7]

In Libya, the Egyptians received a total of 39 Mirage 5DD fighter-bombers, Mirage 5DE radar-equipped interceptors and Mirage 5DR reconnaissance-fighters. In April 1973, they formed No. 69 (Independent, Mirage) Squadron and transferred 19 of its Mirage 5DDs and 2 Mirage 5DRs to Tanta AB.[8]

Another of the early Egyptian Mirage-pilots of the time was Dawoud Makarem, who recalled:

A Mirage 5D manufactured for Libya, as seen during pre-delivery testing in France. (Dassault via Fana de l'Aviation)

After months of long and hard training, by October 1973 we had reached the maximum levels of combat readiness. We had high confidence in our capabilities, good knowledge of the enemy's combat capabilities, and were filled with enthusiasm and ready to fly any kind of operations. Still, the exercises went on. On 4 October 1973, we were ordered to fly a training sortie against Tahrir airfield. I did not fly the mission, but observed it from a helicopter and recorded the results for subsequent review. Six Mirages came in and deployed French-made, parachute-retarded 250 and 400 kilogram bombs (500 and 900lbs, respectively). The results were excellent – with one exception: the parachute of one bomb failed to deploy and it narrowly missed our helicopter. Following exhausting de-brief, our commander ordered six of us to prepare for a similar mission on 6 October 1973, this time

A MiG-21M (serial number 8238) returning to el-Mansourah AB following an air combat training sortie. Notable is the R-3U acquisition round used for training purposes under its left outboard underwing pylon. While they trained as intensively as humanly possible in the period 1967-1973, hopeless obsolescence of Soviet air-to-air weaponry and massive amounts of related Israeli propaganda were main factors in the poor reputation of 'Arab' fighter-pilots. (David Nicolle Collection)

against a target near Marsa Matruh. That formation was to be led by Lieutenant-Colonel Mohammed Okasha, with four in front and two in the rear. I was to fly as Number 6.[9]

With hindsight, and irrespectively of what happened before or after, there is no reason to conclude that the advanced – and continuation training of 1967-1973 of Israeli pilots was any more thorough or more demanding than comparable Egyptian programs, as usually insisted upon by all Israeli and Western sources. Even if the Israelis might have possessed superior intelligence on the characteristics of enemy aircraft – due to their extensive efforts to acquire detailed information, and even intact MiG-17Fs and MiG-21s – already as of 1972 the EAF was gaining an advantage in this regard. On the contrary: considering they began running intensive air combat manoeuvring exercises already as of 1967, that by 1973 all of the EAF's interceptor units ran extensive DACM training exercises against Libyan Mirages, and that this type of aircraft was not only considered as superior to the F-4E and the MiG-21 in air combat, but proved as such in reality too, it is to hand that as of 1972-1973, Egyptian interceptor pilots possessed more and better-quality training in regards of air combat than not only their counterparts from the IDF/AF, but also any other air force around the world.[10]

DARN 'TECHNICAL DETAILS'

While the EAF thus improved the tactical training of its fighter pilots by several magnitudes in the period 1967-1973, as described in Chapter 2, it remained unable to effect similar changes with regards to available technology and thus its equipment. Indeed, irrespective of the influx of new MiG-21 variants, its primary air-to-air weapon – the combination of MiG-21 and the R-3S air-to-air missile – remained very much the same it was as of June 1967. Regardless of their variant, all the MiG-21s were suffering from exactly the same issues. Medhat Zaki, a veteran MiG-21F-13-pilot, explained:

The MiG-21F-13 was very manoeuvrable – really an excellent dogfighter – but suffered from a very short range. We ran out of fuel after nearly every exercise. After every air combat with the Israelis there were always a few pilots forced to land somewhere short of their home base because of the lack of fuel.[11]

Reda el-Iraqi, as of 1973 a seasoned veteran of the War of Attrition during which he was credited with three aerial victories, summarised the MiG-21F-13 as follows:

The MiG-21F-13 was an excellent aircraft, very special…But, it was also a very limited aircraft, carrying only 60 rounds of 30mm calibre…in an attack, these 60 rounds were spent within two seconds. This meant that in order to hit the enemy aircraft, the pilot had to be an excellent marksman…The other problem was that the Soviet Union refused to supply any two-seat MiG-21s to Egypt [before 1968; authors' note]: under terrible pressure, we were forced to convert a large number of pilots to the type with help of nothing but theory and subsonic MiG-15UTIs.[12]

Even the introduction of such advanced variants as the MiG-21M and MiG-21MF failed to improve the situation. Reza Saqr, a veteran MiG-21 pilot that was involved in the downing of the Mirage IIICJ flown by Giora Rom on 11 September 1969, recalled about his introduction to the MiG-21MF of the No. 42 Squadron, EAF, as follows:

When the first MiG-21MFs arrived, in 1973, I served at Luxor. I travelled to el-Mansourah AB to see it: it was the first ever version based on our earlier combat experiences. Still, to have the necessary range it had to carry three drop tanks, which in turn limited its armament to two R-3S missiles and the internal 23mm cannon.[13]

In comparison, the primary armament of the MiG-21 was still just a pair of Soviet-made R-3S air-to-air missiles: a poor, first-generation weapon rushed into production in the early 1960s, which could only be fired from an aircraft pulling no more than 2gs, and which could only track targets pulling no more than 2.5gs. The Israelis had captured at least 38 R-3S at the Meliz AB in June 1967, subjected them to throughout testing and even some operational service on their Mirage IIICJs a year later: thus, their pilots knew that whenever targeted by one, they 'only' needed flying a turn at 3gs or more in order to evade. On the contrary, although often praising North Vietnamese pilots for their 'excellent' deployment of R-3S in combat against the Americans – and using this 'argument' to counter Egyptian complains about the poor quality of Soviet-made missiles – the Soviets not only failed to study combat experiences with their missiles seriously enough, but also have never released any statistics detailing how many of the R-3S that were fired had actually hit their targets. There seems to be a good reason why: it is unlikely that on average even 4-5 out of 100 such weapons fired in anger has actually scored a hit, even less so a kill. Moreover, numerous examples are known of Israeli fighters making safe landings even after receiving a direct hit from an R-3S.

The disadvantages of the R-3S were to become particularly obvious in 1969, by when the IDF/AF began operating the advanced, US-made AIM-9D Sidewinder, and the indigenous Sharfir Mk 2 (developed with French assistance) – both of which had much more sensitive, cooled seeker heads with a far higher tracking capability and an expanded engagement envelope, more effective warheads, and the capability to be deployed from aircraft at much higher acceleration. Indeed, contrary to the R-3S, the AIM-9D – followed by AIM-9G, a number of which were delivered to Israel starting from 10 October 1973 – were to prove highly reliable, capable of very flexible deployment and murderously effective, easily outmatching the Soviet-made missile by a wide margin.

Similarly, Soviet-made 23mm guns (on MiG-21M/MF) and 30mm (on MiG-21F-13) fired heavy shells but at a slow rate of fire, which in air combat between fast jets meant that their shells were less likely to hit their target. Moreover, their shells were not causing enough damage: lessons from air combats during the Suez War of 1956 should have already taught not only the Egyptians but the Soviets too, that they were repeatedly failing to bring down their targets. However, no related studies are known to have been undertaken, and no useful lessons were drawn.[14]

The MiG-21 was very 'heavy' on the controls, especially during air combat manoeuvring: most pilots reported pains in their hands after only one, or at least the second 4-6g turn. Finally, the big delta wing acted as a sort of a giant brake in every turn, while the engine was accelerating very slowly. All of this meant that a MiG-21 pilot had a major problem tracking a target in front and below him (as often necessary in an air combat), that a turning combat was rapidly tiring the pilot, but also that the type tended to bleed off speed very fast and took time to accelerate even with the help of the afterburner. Combined with the fact that the F-4E also had a better climb rate and acceleration that the MiG-21, the conclusion is that the Soviet type was a clear underdog: while certainly relatively vice-free, safe,

Reda el-Iraqi, veteran of at least a dozen of air combats from the War of Attrition and one of the top Egyptian MiG-21-pilots of the period 1967-1973. During the October 1973 War he served with the MiG-21F-13-equipped No. 26 Squadron. (Reda el-Iraqi, via Abdallah Emran)

Reza Saqr, another veteran of the War of Attrition, served with MiG-21MF-equipped No. 42 Squadron during the October 1973 War. (Reza Saqr, via Abdallah Emran)

even fun to fly, much beloved by its pilots, and excelling in peace-time exercises, it was actually no match for the F-4E Phantom.

One of the primary reasons why the F-4E Phantom was such a superior – indeed: outstanding – aircraft for its time was its brute power. The two General Electric J-79 engines were producing so much thrust that while carrying a load of 3,000kg (6.613lbs) of bombs and underway at an altitude of less than 100 metres (328ft) the F-4E could still accelerate to speeds of up to 600 knots. This meant it could approach undetected by enemy radars to at least 45-50 kilometres from the target, then actually reach the target, bomb, and escape from the combat zone within less than two minutes – thus leaving most of the contemporary air defences too little time to react. In comparison, originally designed for operations at high altitudes, all the MiG-21 variants up to the MiG-21PFM were limited to a speed of 540kts at an altitude of less than 1,000 metres (3,280ft): operations at higher speeds were certain to subject the

aircraft to such vibrations and thus structural stress, that it was likely to disintegrate. Only the structure of the MiG-21M/MF was rugged enough to enable speeds of about 600kts at altitudes below 3,280ft: even then, even these could not turn as hard as the F-4E could.[15]

The speed advantage of the F-4E was even more dramatic if the aircraft was in clean configuration: while when underway at an altitude of 5,000ft even the more powerful MiG-21MF would cover a distance of 36nm (66.7km) within three minutes at most, the F-4E would cover a distance of 44nm (81.4km). In other words, the Phantom was certain to outrun all of its primary opponents in the skies over the Middle East.[16]

The Phantom was not only fast and powerful, but could carry huge amounts of ordnance. While all the MiG-21 variants were only armed with two, at most four R-3S missiles and one cannon with a very limited supply of ammunition, the F-4E had one General Electric M61 six-barrel gun with 640 20mm rounds installed internally: when configured for air combat it could carry up to four AIM-7E Sparrow and four AIM-9D Sidewinder air-to-air missiles. When armed as a fighter-bomber, a single F-4E could carry up to three CBU-30/As, CBU-52/Bs or CBU-58/Bs and six Mk.82 general-purpose bombs (weighting about 3,000kg/6,614lbs in total), or up to eight M117 general purpose bombs (about 1,500kg/3,000lbs in total), and still carry two AIM-9 Sidewinders, three AIM-7 Sparrows and one ECM-pod for self-defence. Alone such capabilities made it clearly superior to any other fighter aircraft in the Middle East of the early 1970s: a single F-4E could deploy more bombs in one sortie than six MiG-17s, and still had three or four air-to-air missiles and its internal gun for self-defence.[17]

If this was not enough, the F-4Es in Israeli service were further bolstered through the deliveries of AN/ALQ-71, AN/ALQ-87 and AN/ALQ-101 pods for electronic countermeasures (ECM) – also known as 'jammer pods'. Available from the start of the October 1973 War, these three had proven effective against Egyptian-operated SA-2s, and 'moderately effective' against SA-3s. The fourth, much more advanced pod – the AN/ALQ-119(V)-7 – was provided by the USA during the last days of war and promptly proved effective against the ZSU-23-4. However, neither the Americans nor the Israelis found

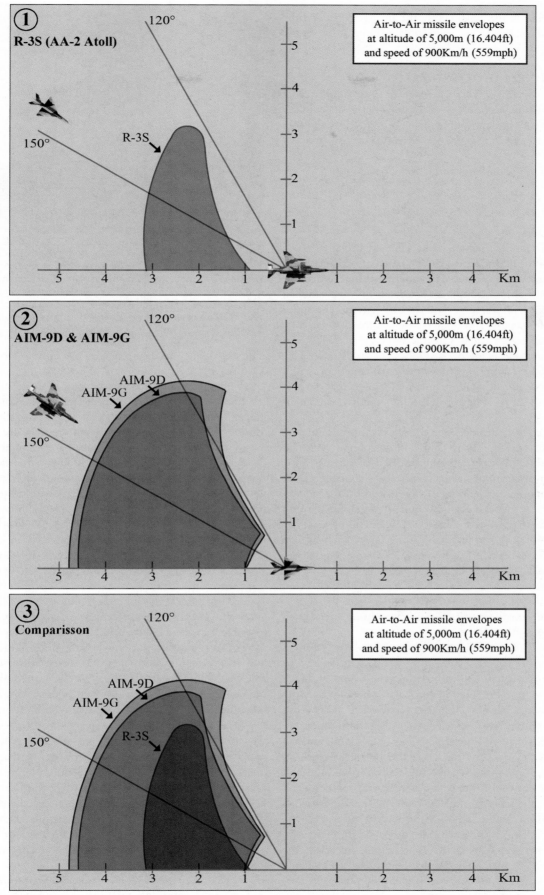

Three diagrams based on a Soviet tactical manual, describing engagement envelopes of three primary air-to-air missiles in service with the EAF and the IDF/AF as of October 1973. On the left is the engagement envelope of the R-3S, the only air-to-air missile in the Egyptian arsenal during that conflict; in the centre are engagement envelopes of the AIM-9D and AIM-9G; and the diagram on the right side has these superimposed for direct comparison. (Diagram by Tom Cooper)

an effective solution to the SA-6 before the final ceasefire. As the story below will show, this factor played only an indirect role in the operations in question.[18]

PHASES OF AIR COMBAT: DETECTION

For better understanding of how air warfare was conducted at the time, the available technology and personnel applied in air combat, and for better understanding of an entire myriad of factors influencing everything, every aerial operation can be broken down into five phases:

- detection (and its corollary: avoidance of detection)
- closing
- attack
- manoeuvre
- disengagement

Factors essential for the function of detection are brutally simple. The Earth is a giant ball, the hard part of surface of which consists of uneven terrain. Because light and most electronic emissions cannot penetrate the terrain, objects are detectable only if positioned above the Earth's curvature; atop or above the terrain. The speed of jet-powered interceptors and fighter-bombers makes their early detection vital: otherwise, their threat cannot be met on time. Therefore, the detection is the decisive phase of air warfare. This is even more valid for air combat: the principal experience from over 100 years since this discipline came into being is that the side that detects the other first is nearly always the one that wins an air combat.

At the strategic level, already since the late 1940s, the ultimate Israeli method of detection was taping of telephone cables in neighbouring countries. Early on, systems used to tap telephone cables were relatively primitive: they consisted of containers with the necessary equipment, which had to be placed on the cable – usually by the IDF's General Staff Reconnaissance Unit (Sayeret Matkal), in cooperation with Unit 848 (IDF Intelligence Corps' Central Collection Unit), and preferably buried in order to remain concealed. These containers were equipped with equipment capable of recording relatively limited amount of traffic and had to be retrieved by their users in order for the intelligence collected to be sorted out. As far as is known, by the mid-1960s the Israelis had also acquired containers capable of transmitting intercepted telecommunications in real time.[19]

In the course of dozens of clandestine operations, the IDF then taped all the major telephone cables in Egypt, Jordan, and Syria, and later also in Iraq. These taps turned into the 'secret of Israeli success' during the June 1967 War in particular, when not only top Arab political leaders, but also military commanders at all levels were making extensive use of telephones for communication. While details on subsequent Israeli operations of this kind remain a closely guarded secret, there is little doubt that they continued at a later date: indeed, a cross-examination of details obtained through interviews with major commanders of different Arab militaries and Israeli reactions to the same during the October 1973 War leaves no doubts that the Israelis continued using this kind of intelligence.

While the intelligence obtained through listening to telecommunications was helping the Israelis find out about the intentions of their enemies, they did not help them track enemy aerial movements. Instead, the most common method of modern-day early detection of aircraft is radar: since the early 1960s, the entire airspace over countries like Egypt and Israel was constantly monitored by an overlapping chain of ground radar stations. The resulting 'radar network' was essential for nearly everything each

Since the late 1960s, the P-12 early warning radar (ASCC/NATO-codename 'Spoon Rest') belonged to the family of most widely used systems of this kind in Egyptian service. With their maximum detection range of about 250 kilometres (135nm) and primary function of supporting such IADS as the one operated by the ADC, they were heavily dependent on the Kremniy IFF-system to recognize friendly from enemy aircraft. (Albert Grandolini Collection)

side was doing – in the air, but on the ground too, whether before October 1973, during that war, or ever since.

Preferably, ground-based radar stations are positioned atop higher elevations, so as to be able to peer far over the normal horizon and detect aircraft from further afar. The capture of the Sinai Peninsula during the June 1967 War had put the IDF in an advantageous position: it could position its radars atop mountain peaks in the western Sinai, and thus see over 250 kilometres deep into Egyptian airspace. On the contrary, with most of their radars positioned low in the Nile Delta or in the deserts east of it, the Egyptian view into the airspace over the Sinai was greatly limited. This situation became plainly obvious following the Israeli acquisition of the F-4E Phantom IIs in 1969, when this type enabled the IDF/AF to run low-level raids even against targets deep in Egypt at such a speed, that they were detected only when there was no time for the Egyptians to react.

Radar stations tend to be large facilities, vulnerable to diverse types of attacks. Because of the necessity to deploy them as far forward as possible, but also because of their sensitive electronics, during the War of Attrition they not only became prime targets for air strikes, but also for commando raids, and for electronic countermeasures (ECM). The October 1973 War was to be no exception to this rule.[20]

Running a very close second to early detection is positive identification. Traditionally, positive identification was dependent on the ability to visually acquire an aircraft and identify either its type or national markings. Not only the appearance of fast jet fighters, but especially the widespread deployment of radars and then SAMs made more complex methods of identification urgently necessary: after all, while the situation in the air tended to be 'clear' before any battle – simply because friendlies were 'over here' and the enemy 'over there' – as soon as the battle was joined, and up to dozens of different aircraft began moving at high speeds within the same portion of airspace, the situation tended to slip out of everybody's control.

Thus, during the 1950s it became common for the identification to be done electronically, foremost with help of so-called 'Friend or Foe' (IFF) systems. The IFF-systems of the early 1970s generally consisted of IFF-transponders installed into aircraft, and of IFF-interrogators installed into ground-based radars. The latter would

A reconstruction of one of 24 ZIL-135 TELs for the 9K52 Luna-M systems operated by the 64th Missile Brigade of the Egyptian Army as of October 1973. This example is shown as painted in beige (BS381C/388) overall: some seem to have received disruptive camouflage patterns consisting of wide, wavy strips of an unknown colour atop of it. Most Luna-Ms were painted overall; some in light grey as shown here, and seem to have worn only a bare minimum of handling and maintenance stencils. The 64th Missile Brigade fired a total of 80 Luna-Ms during the conflict: the majority against various Israeli HQs and forward airfields; 6 in support of the 21st Armoured Division's retreat after a failed offensive on 14 October; and 20 against the Deversoir Gap, in the period 18-20 October. (Artworks by David Bocquelet and Tom Cooper)

A reconstruction of one of the MAZ-543 TELs and R-17E/SS-1c Scud-B missiles as operated by the 65th Missile Brigade of the Egyptian Army as of October 1973, and shown during a military parade in Cairo a year later. By that time, the unit would have received 9 or 10 TELs in September and another 6 TELs during October 1973, together with a complement of up to 45 missiles. As far as is known, all of its MAZ-543s were painted in beige (BS381C/388) overall, while the missiles were either in white or light grey overall. The missile shown in this colour profile is an R-17E/SS-1c Scud-B: note that the War Diary of the 65th Missile Brigade explicitly cites the deployment of 'Scud-A' in the only combat firing of these on 22 October 1973.

As of October 1973, many of the MiG-21F-13s of No. 25 and No. 26 'Black Raven' Squadron (102th Air Brigade), EAF wore the camouflage pattern shown here, consisting of beige (BS381C/388) and olive drab (BS381C/398) on top surfaces and sides, and light admiralty grey (BS381C/697) on undersurfaces. Notable are the unusually large roundels applied on the rear fuselage and the upper surfaces of the wing. This aircraft, serial number 5843, was something like the personal mount of Reda el-Iraqi: it not only received the famous 'Black Raven' insignia of No. 26 Squadron applied on the front fuselage, but also wore three 'Stars of David' applied in white under the right side of the canopy, commemorating three kills with which el-Iraqi was credited during the War of Attrition. (Artwork by Tom Cooper)

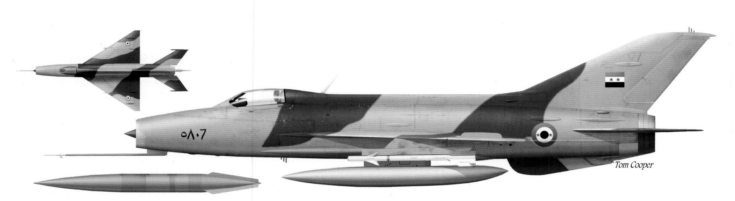

A sizeable number of MiG-21F-13s operated by No. 25 and No. 26 Squadron belonged to a batch of 30 acquired from Czechoslovakia in 1969-1970. The aircraft in question (known are examples with serial numbers 5528, and 5706) all wore the same camouflage pattern applied in Czechoslovak colours known as khaki (S2013/5450) and green (S2013/5300) on upper surfaces and sides, and blue (S2013/4265) on undersurfaces. Notable is the carriage of the Egyptian-designed (and manufactured) 800-litre (211-US gal) drop tank under the centreline: its design was subsequently adopted by the Soviets and saw widespread service around the world. (Artwork by Tom Cooper)

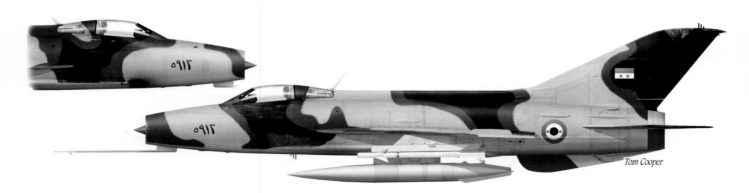

Most of the Egyptian MiG-21F-13s that underwent overhauls at Helwan in the period 1971-1973 received the so-called 'Nile Valley' camouflage pattern in beige (BS381C/388), grey-green (BS381C/283) or olive green (BS381C/437), and black-green (BS381C/298) on upper surfaces and sides, and light admiralty grey on undersurfaces. Always applied in black on the front fuselage only (sometimes on the drop tank too), their serials consisted of four digits: older aircraft and those donated by Algeria in June 1967 wore serials in the range 5001 up to 5999. Available during the October 1973 War were MiG-21F-13s with serials 5110, 5258, 5358, 5396, 5435, 5502, 5528, 5540, 5584, 5590, 5808, 5811, 5813, 5818, 5820, 5824, 5826, 5834, 5872, 5901, 5903, 5907, 5908, 5909, 5911 (shot down on 7 October 1973), 5912, 5913, 5914, 5916, 5917, 5918, 5919, and 5940. (Artwork by Tom Cooper)

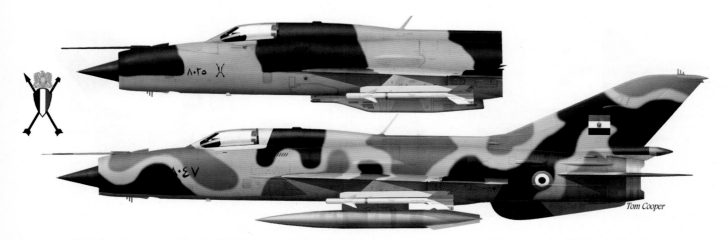

During mid-June 1967, the USSR delivered a total of 65 MiG-21PFS to replace Egyptian losses from the June 1967 War with Israel. This variant bore the brunt of operational training and combat operations during the War of Attrition. By October 1973, surviving examples were concentrated within No. 44 Squadron of the 104th Air Brigade. Most wore a relatively simple camouflage pattern, similar to that of many MiG-21F-13s, but in yellow sand and olive drab (BS381C/398) on top surfaces and sides, and light admiralty grey (BS381C/697) on undersurfaces. Some, like serial number 8025, even received the insignia of their unit, shown inset left. However, quite a number received the Nile Valley camouflage pattern in beige, grey-green (BS381C/283) and black-green (BS381C/298) on upper surfaces and sides, and medium grey (BS381C/627) on undersurfaces, as shown on 8047 on the main drawing. (Artwork by Tom Cooper)

As obvious from its ventral fin painted in light blue, this MiG-21PFM – serial number 8081 – was assigned to No. 47 Squadron (111th Air Brigade), a unit that also saw action during clashes over Port Said and the Nile Delta. Most were camouflaged in the 'Nile Valley' camouflage pattern, consisting of beige (BS381C/388), either green (BS381C/283) or olive drab (BS381C/437), and black green (BS381C/298) on top surfaces and sides, and light admiralty grey (BS381C/697) on undersurfaces. Although this variant was compatible with the GP-9 gun-pod, the same was next to never used in Egypt because fuel was at a premium: instead, the centreline hardpoint was used to carry the 400-litre drop tank. (Artwork by Tom Cooper)

A reconstruction of the MiG-21M serial number 8320 assigned to No. 46 Squadron and flown by Nassr Moussa in several combat sorties during the October 1973 War. The aircraft was painted in a camouflage pattern standardised by one of the factories in Helwan responsible for overhauls, and subsequently applied on numerous MiG-21Ms and MiG-21PFMs of the EAF, and a few MiG-21MFs of the Iraqi Air Force. The pattern consisted of beige (BS381C/388) and olive drab (BS381C/398) on top surfaces and sides, and light admiralty grey (BS381C/697) on undersurfaces. Due to the necessity to fly 40-45 minute-long CAPs for most of the October 1973 War, Egyptian MiG-21M/MFs were usually configured with two or three drop tanks and only two R-3S missiles. (Artwork by Tom Cooper)

Another aircraft of the el-Mansourah-based No. 46 Squadron was this MiG-21MF, serial number 8447. As well as receiving the same stylised 'Vulture of the Goddes Nekhbet' applied on the forward fuselage as the MiG-21M shown in the preceding artwork, it also wore a large letter 'E' in black, outlined in white, on the fin – which was used for easier identification during air combat training. Other known examples of similar markings included letters A, B, C, and D. The 'sand and spinach' camouflage pattern was applied before delivery to Egypt and consisted of beige (BS381C/388), dark green (BS381C/641), and light admiralty grey (BS381C/697). (Artwork by Tom Cooper)

Libyan-owned Mirage 5Ds 'borrowed' by No. 69 Squadron in the 1972-1974 period all retained their standardised camouflage pattern in Brun Café (sand), Gris Vert Fonce (dark green), and either Terre de Sienne (dark brown) or Kaki François (brown-green, which rapidly oxidised into dark brown). The aircraft originally retained their big serials applied in black on the rear fuselage, too – and, no matter if operated by Egyptians or Libyans, wore the same set of national markings (fin flashes and roundels in six positions). The serials of the six Mirage 5Ds involved in the strike on el-Arish airfield remain unknown; this example is shown in the same configuration as during that operation, including two 400kg SAMP Type 21C bombs under the centreline, and a pair of 1,300-litre drop tanks. (Artwork by Tom Cooper)

One of the few Libyan Mirage 5Ds known to have been operated by No. 69 Squadron during the October 1973 War was this example, serial number 443. Like all other aircraft of that unit it had its full serial repeated in Arabic digits on the cover of the front undercarriage. This illustration shows it as loaded with 10 French-made SAMP 25CE 250kg bombs (including two under the centreline, and four on each of two drop tanks), as during the attack on Fayd AB. The inset shows a JL.100: a combination of a Matra F4 rocket launcher for 18 68mm rockets and a 250-litre drop tank. This saw widespread use by Mirage 5Ds of No. 69 Squadron during the fighting for the Deversoir Gap. (Artwork by Tom Cooper)

As of October 1973, all Israeli F-4Es wore a standardised camouflage pattern including light sand (FS33531), tan (FS30219), and light green (FS34227) on upper surfaces and sides, and light blue (FS35622) on undersurfaces. This Block 39 aircraft belonged to the first group of 44 Phantoms delivered to Israel and was assigned to No. 201 'The One' Squadron. It was upgraded through addition of the 'Midas' gun-blast-diffuser before the October 1973 War, but did not receive the LES modification. It is shown in the standard configuration for attacks on air defence positions of Egyptian (and Syrian) air bases, including an AN/ALQ-101(V)-3 twin-band ECM-pod, an AIM-9D and a pair of SUU-30H/B CBUs on the left inboard pylon. These were usually complemented by three CBUs on the right inboard pylon and three drop tanks. Drop tanks carried on outboard underwing pylons are not shown. (Artwork by Tom Cooper)

Shown in a similar weapons configuration – though with an AN/ALQ-71(V)-2 twin-band ECM-pod in the left forward Sparrow bay – the F-4E with serial number 160 was assigned to No. 119 'The Bats' Squadron. Like most Phantom IIs of that unit, it was decorated with a red arrow and the unit crest on the fin, but also received national markings of a slightly smaller diameter than those applied on earlier F-4Es of No. 201 Squadron. This F-4E is known to have survived combat damage over Syria on 11 October: it was repaired in time to take part in the final strike on Tanta AB on 15 October 1973, but was then shot down whilst climbing prior to attacking its target. Pilot Yigal Livneh was captured but his RIO, Rachamim Sofer, was murdered by Egyptian civilians. (Artwork by Tom Cooper)

The F-4E serial number 122 was the aircraft flown by the CO of No. 107 'Knights of the Orange Tail' (also 'Tigerheads') Squadron, Iftach Spector, into the attack on Tanta AB on 14 October 1973. It is shown in the configuration for that mission, including an AN/ALQ-71/(V)-4 four-band ECM-pod in the forward left Sparrow bay, one AIM-9D or AIM-9G and two 750lb (340kg) M117 general purpose bombs under the left inboard underwing pylon, and AIM-7E-2s in the rear Sparrow wells. Visible on the front fuselage below the forward part of the cockpit are five kill markings applied to commemorate aerial victories scored by different crews flying the aircraft during the October 1973 War. Notably, this was one of about 25 Israeli F-4Es equipped with LES by the time. (Artwork by Tom Cooper)

A very rare, in-flight photograph of the MiG-21F-13 serial number 5824 from No. 26 Squadron, taken shortly before the October 1973 War. Notable is the camouflage pattern in beige and olive drab, and the underside painted in light admiralty grey. (Gallal el-Bassel Bassily Collection)

Another shot from the same series, showing a pair of MiG-21F-13s, including an unidentifiable example in foreground, and the Nile Valley-pattern-wearing serial number 5916 in the background. (Gallal el-Bassel Bassily Collection)

One of relatively few MiG-21MFs to enter service with the EAF shortly before the October 1973 War received the serial number 8620, and wore one of the least well-known insignia applied to any of Egyptian MiG-21s: apparently a stylised, white-headed eagle that also decorates the official EAF crest. (Albert Grandolini Collection)

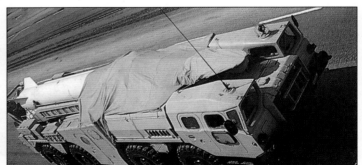

A pair of MAZ-534 TEL of the 65th Missile Brigade – both loaded with R-17E missiles – as put on display during a post-war parade in Cairo. (Tom Cooper Collection)

A top view of a MAZ-534 TEL of the 65th Missile Brigade, as seen on the same occasion. (Tom Cooper Collection)

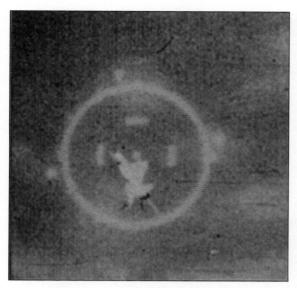
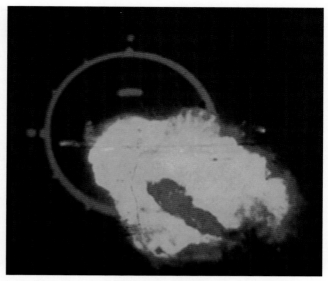

Colour gun-camera films were still relatively rare as of October 1973, and were used by Israeli F-4Es only. These two sequences show the downing of the MiG-21MF flown by Ahmed Yusuf el-Wakeel by the F-4E serial number 119, flown by Asher Snir and Aharon Katz, over Tanta AB on 15 October 1973. (Iftach Spector (left) and Tom Cooper Collection (right))

A splendid study of an early Israeli F-4E: notable is the early, short gun-blast-diffuser visible under the nose, and national markings applied on intakes that were almost twice as large as those applied on examples delivered in 1971 and afterwards. (Albert Grandolini Collection)

A formation of F-4Es from No. 107 Squadron – also known as 'Knights of the Orange Tail' or 'Tigerhead' squadron. The Phantom with serial '101' – only the fin of which is visible on the right side of this photograph – was the aircraft flown by Naftaly Maimon during the strike on Tanta AB, on 14 October 1973, after which he was officially credited with two confirmed kills and highly decorated. (IDF via Albert Grandolini)

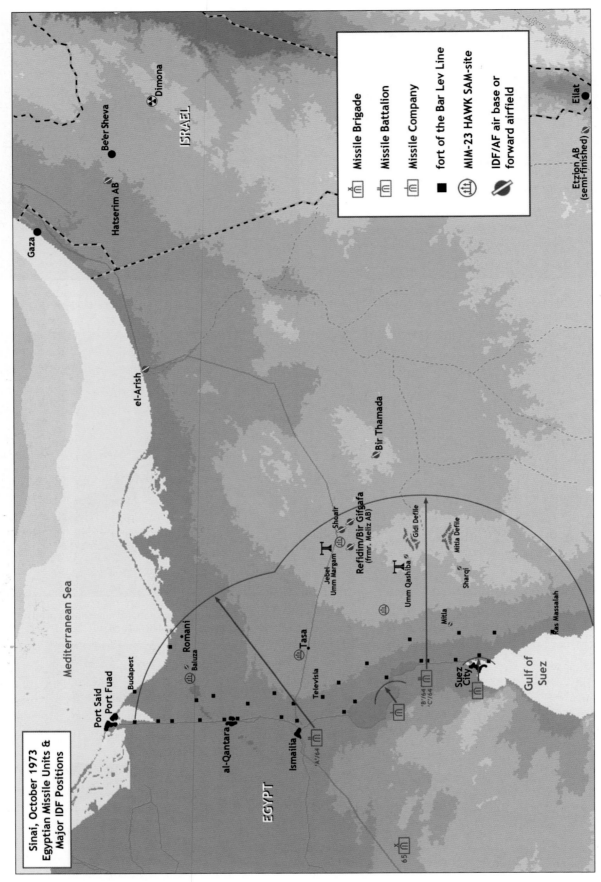

Based on a US intelligence report, this map depicts major installations of the IDF/AF on the Sinai, the approximate positions of Egyptian missile units at the start of the October 1973 War, and their maximum ranges. (Map by Tom Cooper)[1]

1   DIA, *Scud B Study*, August 1974.

send a signal to the former, triggering a response: if this was correct, the aircraft was identified as friendly; if not, it was identified as enemy. As the ADC was built-up during the late 1960s and early 1970s, it became heavily reliant on the proper function of IFF-transponders installed into EAF aircraft: its SAM and anti-aircraft artillery-crews had no other means of distinguishing own from enemy aircraft from dozens of kilometres away and on time without the help of the Soviet-made Kremniy system, which in turn relied on SRO-2 IFF-transponders installed in aircraft.

However, during the Cuban Crisis of 1962, the National Security Agency (NSA) of the USA discovered that it was capable of not only reading transponder codes from the SRO-2 but also to emit the signal necessary to trigger a response from the Soviet transponder. This discovery was followed by the development of the ability to read codes from two further Soviet-made transponders, the older SRO-1 and SOD-57. Despite the NSA's reluctance to share this intelligence with any of the US armed services, the resulting technology – the 'enemy IFF-interrogators' – soon found their way into service with the USAF, which installed them into its Lockheed EC-121 Warning Star airborne early warning (AEW) aircraft. In 1966, in the course of the Project College Eye, a unit of these was deployed in support of the US offensive operations against North Vietnam where they quickly proved capable of detecting MiGs from as far as 250 kilometres away – even if these were still parked on the ground, all provided they had their IFF-transponder either set on active, or on passive (of course, the College Eye could not track MiGs that turned their IFF-transponders off). Indeed, the SOD-57 IFF-transponders were even providing information on speed, flight altitude, and remaining fuel. Moreover, by 1970, the USAF introduced to service a small number of F-4D Phantom IIs equipped with a miniaturised enemy IFF-interrogator: the APX-80 Combat Tree. This proved to be a true game-changer, enabling Phantom-crews of the USAF to trigger responses from enemy aircraft as far as 80 kilometres away, and thus – reliably – detect 'MiGs' even if not actually acquiring them with their own radars. In the 1970-1972 period, Combat Tree proved instrumental in at least 50% of aerial victories achieved by the USAF's crews over North Vietnam: with its help, the crews of Tree-equipped F-4Ds were capable of not only detecting MiGs very early, but also of deploying the primary advantage of their aircraft – their superior firepower in the form of AIM-7 Sparrow missiles – from long range. Unsurprisingly, by 1972, the APX-81 – a slightly advanced variant of the Combat Tree – was installed into USAF F-4Es, too. While the IDF/AF received no APX-80-equipped F-4Es before October 1973, its ground control intercept sites are meanwhile known to have all been equipped with IFF-interrogators of US origin.[21]

Although the Soviets eventually discovered that the Americans had cracked the Kremniy system, and launched a crash project to replace the same not only with the upgraded Kremniy-2 – and then the much more advanced Parol (the first to include encryption) – the availability of enemy IFF-interrogators remained a tightly guarded secret in the Middle East until only recently: indeed, not one of the Egyptian pilots that served during October 1973 and was interviewed by the authors over the years had ever heard of such technology before.

CLOSING

The availability of enemy IFF-interrogators and of favourably-positioned radar stations was of crucial importance for the next phase of nearly all of the air combats fought between the EAF and the IDF/AF in October 1973: the closing phase is the logical result of the detection phase (or the failure to detect the opponent), and usually resulting in one side reaching a favourable position from which to initiate an attack.

At the operational level of aerial warfare, the most important requirement is to have sufficient numerical strength to match the enemy in the air: in theory, an aircraft type can be vastly superior to its opponents, but this does not matter if one lacks the numbers of such aircraft necessary to actually fly the sufficient number of combat sorties in order to counter those flown by an opponent. Unsurprisingly, while the mass of accounts about Arab-Israeli air combats fought over the last 70 years creates the impression of the 'hopelessly outnumbered' Israeli pilots fighting 'hordes' of Arab aircraft, and winning only thanks to their superior training and skills, in reality, the IDF/AF always went to great extents to secure numerical superiority – in general, and in every specific combat operation. For example, during the opening air strike on Egyptian air bases on 5 June 1967, it simultaneously attacked with nearly three times as many fighter-bombers as there were interceptors standing alert on Egyptian air bases. The logical consequence was that, even if the latter would be able to scramble on time, they would still have been hopelessly outnumbered. Similar conclusions can be drawn from all the air combats staged by the IDF/AF during the following five years: even though regularly initiating an engagement through the appearance of the 'decoy' section of 'only' 2-4 aircraft, the Israelis would then always 'reinforce' through the addition of between two and four further flights, thus nearly always achieving at least local numerical superiority.

This is of critical importance for what is actually the second most important moment in every air combat: the factor of surprise. A pilot preoccupied with flying and navigation, not to mention combat, is near certain to become surprised by the appearance of a new, additional opponent. Unsurprisingly, any detailed examination of aerial victories achieved ever since 1914 reveals that the crews of at least four out of five aircraft shot down in air combats had never seen their opponent – if at all. Indeed, most so-called 'aces' were specialists in stalking and then taking their opponents by surprise. Therefore, the most important attribute of a modern fighter jet is not only to take the enemy by surprise, but also to avoid being taken by surprise.

At long range, there is no doubt that the crew of an F-4E was capable of regularly achieving surprise against any MiG-21: supported by the ground control that could rely on enemy IFF-interrogators for early detection of enemy interceptors, and by remaining outside radar and visual range, they could detect the opponent with their own radar and regularly set up an attack from a favourable position. Furthermore, the Phantom's higher cruise speed at low altitude – the highest possible speed that can be sustained without deploying fuel reserves too rapidly, which in the case of the F-4E was above Mach 0.9 – was of immense advantage: this was high enough to force MiG-21 pilots to operate their aircraft at near maximum speed most of the time, further depleting their non-existing fuel reserves.[22]

At least in theory, the situation was diametrically opposite at short range: the F-4E was not only much bigger than the MiG-21, but also powered by two engines that emitted plenty of smoke (which also made them easier to identify). Unsurprisingly, if knowing where to look for them, MiG-pilots frequently sighted Phantoms from as far as 8 nautical miles (15 kilometres) away. On the contrary, anybody who ever saw a MiG-21 with their own eyes in action knows that the type is nearly invisible from a range of less than two nautical miles (3.2km) even in crystal clear weather from the ground.

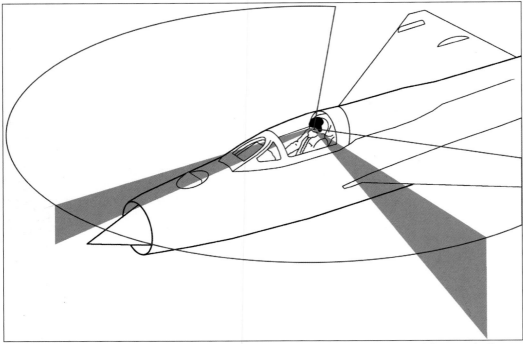

A diagram illustrating the limited view outside the cockpit of the MiG-21PF/FL/PFM/M/MF. (Diagram by Tom Cooper)

However, this is when the next important factor conspired against the MiG-21: it had only very poor visibility from the cockpit. The MiG-21's cockpit was not only narrow, but also characterised by a thick windshield and framing, resulting in all the variants suffering (and, as for those still in service: still suffering) from a poor view out of the cockpit towards the front and the rear. The pilot had a field of view of less than 270 degrees, and almost no sight at all to the area below and behind the aircraft. The view towards the front was further hampered by the instrumentation installed directly behind the windshield. In front of the cockpit was a relatively long and wide nose, which hampered visibility to the front and below the aircraft: unsurprisingly, MiG-21 pilots often lost track of their target precisely when in the perfect position to open fire – when behind and slightly above. This weakness was recognized quite early and thus tactical manuals for this type from the early 1960s began recommending an approach so that the pilot would be able to visually acquire the target through the side of the front section of the main cockpit hood. Of course, in reality, and for reasons explained earlier, achieving such 'ideal' positions proved extremely problematic. Worse yet: the cockpit of all the variants that entered service after the original MiG-21F-13 enabled no view towards the rear at all. Indeed, the majority of pilots flying versions like the MiG-21PFS, MiG-21PFM, and MiG-21M/MF could not even see the wingtips of their aircraft. Attempts to solve this problem through the installation of a rear-view mirror atop the cockpit hood were never fully satisfactory. Overall, although small and thus theoretically hard to detect, and no matter what a pleasure to fly in peace – even during serious exercises – the MiG-21 was a clear underdog in the skies over the Middle East of October 1973, and this not only with regards to detection, but also during the closing phase of every air combat.[23]

ATTACK

Conditioned by the relative position of the opponents and the performances of their fire-control systems and weaponry, attack is the phase dominated by the combination of firepower and precision. In an ideal world, a fighter aircraft would be invisible to the human eye, electronic- and infra-red detection, equipped with sensors providing it with a full 360x360 degrees of coverage – and armed with autonomous weapons ascertaining something like one-shot-one-kill capability. Obviously, such capabilities were a far cry as of October 1973. Nevertheless, the F-4 Phantom IIs were 'at least close to something similar' – especially when compared to the MiG-21: they were capable of dictating an engagement to their opponents, and then by a wide margin – by the virtue of their superior speed, avionics, armament, and endurance. Certainly enough, in the IDF/AF of the early 1970s there was still a big emphasis upon the ethos of the fighter pilot as a 'warrior', the sole decisive factor in an air combat. The concept of the 'guy in the back' – the radar intercept officer (RIO) – was still new: indeed, the RIOs were often ignored by Israeli Phantom-pilots of the time, at most considered useful only to provide an additional pair of eyes. The Israelis also considered the Sparrow missile as too complex, unsuitable, and unreliable for air combat, and emphasised the deployment of shorter ranged air-to-air missiles like Sidewinder instead.

Therefore, most air combats were joined within visual range. Even in this discipline, the F-4E was superior to the MiG-21: although bigger and thus easier to detect and track, its radar and a two-man crew meant that it was more likely to detect and track its opponent first. Moreover, and as described above, the Israeli Phantom IIs from October 1973 were far better armed than Egyptian MiG-21s, resulting in a situation where – even if 'only' flown by pilots of equal skills – they were more likely to score kills.

LOFT-BOMBING TACTICS AND HARDENED AIRCRAFT SHELTERS

In air-to-ground discipline, for air strikes deep inside Egypt, the primary Israeli methods of penetrating enemy defences usually included a mix of sophisticated means of enemy detection and reporting through the command and control network – i.e. intelligence – extremely careful planning based on exploiting every possible weakness within the enemy's air defence system, and full exploitation of every advantage provided by the terrain. This went as far as that avoiding losses (while inflicting them to the enemy) became the second most important operational aim of the IDF/AF. Correspondingly, in order to carry out their task the Israeli pilots had to satisfy three conditions: penetrate enemy air defences (both outbound and on the return leg), locate and correctly identify the target, and aim as accurately as possible. However, the establishment of powerful air defence systems in Egypt and Syria, and the lack of suitable ECM, resulted in a situation where during the October 1973 War IDF/AF pilots had to fly into the centre of an envelope of multiple, overlapping and very diverse weapons systems operated by their enemies. This resulted in heavy losses, which in turn necessitated new solutions for their attack profiles: typical bombing attacks from low and medium altitude as flown during the War of

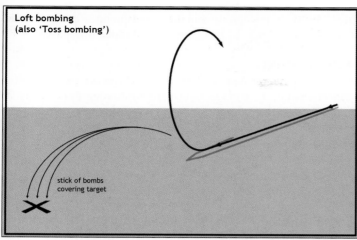
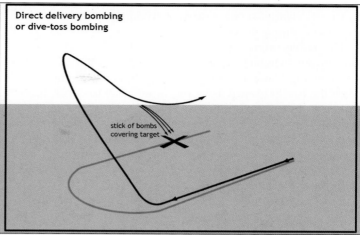

Two diagrams illustrating the principal bombing tactics of the IDF/AF's F-4E crews in 1973. The left diagram shows Loft- or Toss-bombing: the attacking aircraft would approach its target at a speed of up to 600kts (1,110km/h) and an altitude between 100 and 200ft (31-61m), before entering a full-power climb at 45 degrees and releasing its bombs while still climbing, usually from an altitude of about 2,000ft (607m). The aircraft would then dive back to low altitude as soon as possible. The right diagram shows the tactics frequently applied for attacks on Egyptian and Syrian air bases: this saw the aircraft initiating a climb while passing aside of the target, then climbing and diving while executing a 180° turn to either deliver its bombs in a direct delivery- or dive-toss bombing method. Because they were including sharp turns in the vertical axis, which missiles like SA-2 and SA-3 could not follow, both of these attack methods proved highly effective for self-protection, too. (Diagrams by Tom Cooper)

One of over 500 aircraft shelters constructed on Egyptian air bases between 1967 and 1973. (photo by M. P. H.)

coordinates, enabling the crew to approach the target and then let the computers in their aircraft release weapons automatically. A crucial factor for the success of any loft-bombing attack was precise navigation: once such an attack was initiated, the pilot had to fly the climb manoeuvre in an extremely precise fashion. Even a slightest deviation in speed, g-force and angle could result in significant errors: entering the climb a friction of second too early or too late, or a climb at the wrong angle, easily resulted in bombs missing their target by several kilometres. This problem was partially solved through the method of bomb release itself. Namely, in order to avoid possible collision of bombs upon their release (which was likely to lead to their catastrophic detonation directly below the aircraft), the normal procedure was for bombs to be dropped one after the other, at intervals between 0.2 and 0.5 seconds. This resulted in a 'stick' of bombs released by the Phantom or Skyhawk reaching the target zone in 'column formation'. While most were almost certain to miss, at least one was very likely to hit the actual target.

Attrition offered a reasonable compromise between fuel economy, endurance, mutual protection from enemy interceptors and SAMs, and enabled accurate target location. However, such operations usually resulted in extended exposure to enemy weapons. The solution of the IDF/AF was to make use of loft-bombing tactics, which promised to expose the aircraft to enemy defences for only a minimal period of time. Originally developed for delivery of nuclear weapons, and designed to enable even heavy bombers to avoid the highly destructive blast from nuclear bombs, loft-bombing transformed into a method of stand-off bomb delivery during the Vietnam War. Facing massive Egyptian and Syrian air defences, the Israelis began deploying it during the afternoon of 6 October 1973, and continued doing so for the rest of the war.[24]

The capability to employ loft-bombing tactics was made possible through the availability of – for their time – very advanced navigational and attack (or 'fire control') systems, centred upon inertial navigational systems (INS) and micro-computers of aircraft like the F-4E: these could be pre-programmed with target

Immediately after releasing bombs, the pilot was free to fly evasive manoeuvres – which usually consisted of him turning away to escape outside the engagement envelope of enemy weapons. In this fashion, the IDF/AF fighter-bombers were exposing themselves to Egyptian and Syrian air defences for only a few seconds. An additional advantage of the loft-bombing tactics was that the pilot could also fly evasive manoeuvres while approaching and before entering a full-power climb. As far as is known, the Egyptian and

Syrian air defences had not found any working solution to counter these tactics during the October 1973 War.

The results from this 'switch' from the tactics of close-in, pinpoint dive-bombing to pop-up and lofting techniques resulted in disappointing accuracy: in turn, accuracy was of crucial importance when the Israelis wanted to hit one of over 500 hardened aircraft shelters that the Egyptians had constructed on 27 of their air bases between 1967 and 1973. This even more so because even a direct hit on one was no guarantee of success: not only that the shelter might have been empty, but post-war US intelligence assessments have also shown that, 'the Arab aircraft shelters are much harder than US and allied shelters in Europe'.[25]

Therefore, during the October 1973 War, the usual Israeli method of attacks on enemy airfields was to bomb and crater the runways, much bigger targets, easier to hit, in turn blocking the airfield at least for a few hours – until the enemy could fill the craters, clean the debris, and repair the surface of the runway.

CBUS AND S-60S

Because even the loft-bombing tactics proved not particularly effective, the IDF/AF sought to compensate the decreasing accuracy of its air strikes. As a result it put ever greater emphasis on the deployment of cluster-bomb units (CBUs): containers dispersing smaller submunition – usually explosive bomblets designed to kill personnel and/or destroy vehicles – over a wide area. A post-October 1973 War US intelligence report dramatically illustrated this development: while the Israeli pre-war stockpile of US-supplied ordnance consisted of 83% general-purpose (GP) bombs (like Mk.81, Mk.82, Mk.83, Mk.84, M117 and M118) and 12% of CBUs by weight, the ordnance actually expended during the October 1973 War consisted 66% of GP-bombs and no less than 32% of CBUs. The CBUs – foremost US-made containers like SUU-30/A, CBU-58/A and CBU-59/A – thus became the weapon of choice to compensate for reduced delivery accuracy.[26]

The use of cluster bomb units was of particular importance for attacks on enemy air bases: obviously, the submunition dispersed by them was too light to cause damage to hardened facilities or even to runways – even more so when it turned out that a high percentage of bomblets usually failed to detonate. However, precisely the latter factor became particularly important: unexploded submunitions could still kill or maim personnel or damage aircraft and other equipment. Correspondingly, the use of CBUs had an indirect effect of de-facto creating 'minefields'.[27]

Another reason for an increased use of CBUs were their effects upon the enemy anti-aircraft artillery (AAA): aw well as large air defence networks equipped with SAMs, Egypt and Syria also operated a large number of AAA-pieces. These included 14.5mm heavy machine guns (like ZPU-1 and ZPU-4), and light automatic 23mm cannons (like ZU-23), up to Soviet-made 100mm KS-19 air defence guns. Especially the radar-directed, self-propelled variant of the ZU-23 – the ZSU-23-4 Shilka – gained notoriety during the October 1973 War for its effective operations in the defence of Egyptian (and Syrian) frontlines. However, away from the frontlines, and especially when it came to the defence of their air bases, the Egyptians depended on ADF air defence regiments usually totalling at least 16, sometimes 20, older, Soviet-made AZP S-60 towed 57mm anti-aircraft guns. Indeed, the S-60 was something like an 'unrecognized star' of this conflict: firing much heavier shells that tended to cause much more damage than those of 23mm, it proved highly effective at ranges between 400 and 1,500 metres. During the October 1973 War, such units caused a number of painful losses to the IDF/AF, in turn prompting the Israelis to open every air strike on an enemy air base by bombing their positions with CBUs.

MANOEUVRING

Depending on the outcome of the attack phase, an air combat can degenerate to a degree where re-positioning is necessary in order to re-attack: this results in the best-known, certainly the 'most glamorous', and wildly over-rated phase of an air combat: manoeuvre.

The manoeuvring phase of an air combat is entirely depending on man-made machines, all of which have their limitations – in regards of their relative position and their performances. This is why all combat aircraft contain plenty of high technology, but also why their design is actually a result of thousands of compromises: after all, they are expected to fly and to fight, to have a good acceleration and speed, at least good endurance and a manoeuvrability necessary for their task – and all of this in very diverse atmospheric conditions, which in turn vary according to the altitude, local climate, season, and weather.

The essence of flying is the 'lift'. Lift is created by the wing, the upper surface of which is curved slightly more than the lower surface. As the wing moves through the air, low-pressure areas form above the wing, while the air pressure underneath remains normal or slightly higher than normal. The lift increases if the angle at which the wing meets the airflow – the 'angle of attack' (AOA) – is increasing: the higher the AOA, the more lift is created and the more the aircraft is going to climb. However, if the wing meets the air at too steep AOA, the air will burble and disturb the low-pressure area over the wing, thus disturbing the lift: if lift is lost, the aircraft will stall and depart controlled flight. This is why every aircraft has a minimum speed, the speed at which its wing ceases creating sufficient lift: due to the density of the air, minimum speeds increase with the altitude.

The other factor contributing to the amount of lift created is the shape of the wing: a narrow, thick wing creates more lift, but also more resistance to the air – 'drag' – which is constantly increasing in proportion to the speed. Therefore, fighters usually have thin wings in order to achieve higher speeds.

The essence of *jet* fighters is their engine: brought to the point, this sucks air in the front, compresses and mixes it with fuel, burns the resulting mix and exhausts the superheated gases out at the rear, thus producing thrust. The more thrust an engine produces, the better. The engines are packed into an aerodynamically shaped fuselage: 'cleaner' aerodynamics results in better acceleration, higher top speeds, and lower fuel consumption.

Thrust and drag decrease at higher altitudes as the oxygen content of the atmosphere diminishes and the air density lessens. They increase the lower that the aircraft flies, and then to a degree where the structural strength of the airframe and the engine becomes a crucial issue: not only that the kinetic heating caused by the friction of the air tends to create temperatures high enough to weaken metallic alloys from which the aircraft and their engines are constructed, but an airframe travelling through the denser air at lower altitude is subjected to higher structural stress and stronger vibrations, too. This is one of the least-well known factors in air combat, although resulting in a logical conclusion: at low altitude, rugged aircraft can operate at higher speeds than delicate ones.

The essence of air combat is the energy state of the involved aircraft. Every aircraft contains two forms of energy: positional and kinetic. Positional energy is the weight of the aircraft multiplied by its altitude, while the kinetic energy is the dynamic motion and usually depending on the thrust to weight ratio of the aircraft. The total energy of an aircraft is thus variable and generally measured in 'energy state': obviously, aircraft flying higher and faster are always going to have a better energy state than those flying slower or lower.

The energy state is directly related to acceleration: the basic ability to accelerate depends upon the combination of aerodynamic configuration of an airframe and the thrust produced by its engine. An aircraft with a cleaner aerodynamic configuration is creating less drag and thus certain to have superior acceleration even in comparison to an aircraft with a similar thrust to weight ratio.

Over time, pilots have developed multiple methods to increase acceleration. The most common is called 'unloading': using the fact that the gravity is accelerating all objects that are falling, a pilot can nose down the aircraft into a shallow dive, thus increasing the acceleration.

The combination of all the factors listed above results in the aircraft's ability to manoeuvre – i.e. fly turns, which are important for the aircraft's ability to re-attack as necessary. The aircraft capable of re-pointing its weapons at a target in a quicker fashion is more likely to win the manoeuvring phase of an air combat.

There are three measures of turn: radius of turn, rate of turn, and 'g'. The radius of turn and rate of turn are usually used to compare the manoeuvrability of diverse fighter aircraft types. However, this is a massive oversimplification: radius and rate of turn are a function of speed, while g is centrifugal force expressed in terms of the acceleration of gravity: nearly all the fighters of the early 1970s were limited to turns up to 6-6.5gs. Turns at higher acceleration were possible, but tended to cause damage to the aircraft structure: in the worst case, they could result in the disintegration of an aircraft.

The amount of gs pulled in a turn is dependent on the AOA and the angle of bank: however, the harder a fighter turns, the more drag and less lift its wing is creating. Without excess thrust from the engine to overcome the total drag, the energy is lost and, due to the resulting loss of lift, the aircraft will depart controlled flight. Therefore, hard turns can only be attempted when there is sufficient energy on hand, and their execution is heavily dependent on the thrust to weight ratio. Contrary to the widely available impressions, comparison of the data from flight manuals has shown that the LES-equipped F-4E not only possessed a higher thrust to weight ratio than even the improved MiG-21M/MF, but – at lower altitudes – actually had a slightly higher turn rate, too.[28]

The conclusion is thus: the Phantom was not only more likely to detect its opponent first, but also more likely to hit it in the first attack, or at least that it was more likely to re-position and re-attack before the enemy aircraft could do so, and then hit with help of such superior weapons as the AIM-9D and AIM-9G.

DISENGAGEMENT

The final phase of any air combat is disengagement: far more often than generally known, this phase is dictated by one factor as common as it is crucial for every air force, and every combat aircraft, no matter where on the World and in what conflict: the fuel state. Once again, this was a discipline in which the F-4E was clearly outmatching the MiG-21: while Phantoms were able to reach out of Israel deep over the Mediterranean Sea before turning south to strike targets deep in the Nile Delta, and then fight a swirling dogfight before disengaging, following a high-speed chase at low level, the average MiG-21 was short on fuel already 10-15 minutes after taking off. Indeed, during some of the bigger air battles of October 1973, Egyptian MiG-21 pilots would scramble, take part in an air combat with the first wave of the Israeli air strike, land, refuel

and scramble again to intercept another incoming wave.

4

SHOCK, BLUNDERS, PANIC, NUKES – AND LIBYAN MIRAGES

The first three days of the October 1973 Arab-Israeli War saw Egypt and Syria advancing and sent Israel reeling. Although eventually receiving the crucial information about an Arab attack, and launching an emergency mobilisation at 0930hrs in the morning of 6 October, the Israelis expected the Arab assault to start at 1800hrs. Indeed, the Israeli government briefly contemplated a pre-emptive strike at Arab air bases and air defences by the IDF/AF – which was already in a state of advanced readiness when the war began – but, under pressure from the USA, decided against this initiative for political reasons. Thus, when the Arabs attacked at 1400hrs, the IDF was caught by surprise, and still at least 48 hours from being fully mobilised.[1]

What happened next caused a series of shocks – and not a few defeats – for the Israelis. On the Golan Heights, three Syrian infantry divisions and two armoured divisions assaulted positions of a single division of the IDF, destroying one and mauling another Israeli armoured brigade, achieved a major break-through and nearly overran the local headquarters (HQ). In the south, two Egyptian field armies crossed the entire length of the Suez Canal in one of the best-orchestrated obstacle-crossing operations in history, neutralizing one Israeli brigade in the process. Countless counterattacks by the sole IDF regular division defending this frontline resulted in the catastrophic loss of two thirds of its tanks.

From the standpoint of the Egyptian 64th and 65th Missile Brigades, the war began with the involvement in the opening strikes for the former, and 'just' further training of the latter; similarly, from the standpoint of the pilots assigned to two EAF-brigades subordinated to the ADC, and to SAM-gunners defending the Egyptian skies, there was little action early on. On the contrary, the Israeli F-4 crews found themselves in the middle of the war, right from the start.

THE FROG-STRIKE[2]

During preparations for the October 1973 War, officers of the 64th and 65th Missile Brigades were given very specific tasks. On receiving the order to move out of its base the 64th was to split into three battalions: one was to deploy west of Ismailia and operate in support of the 2nd Field Army; another south of the Great Bitter Lake, and assigned to the 3rd Field Army. These two units were to use between four and six rockets each to strike targets selected by field commanders. The third battalion of the 64th Missile Brigade, and the entire 65th Missile Brigade (based inside an underground facility constructed 10 kilometres south-east of Cairo), were kept under the control of the Minister of War. Correspondingly, officers of both units reconnoitred potential launching sites at diverse spots west of the Suez Canal – all outside the range of Israeli artillery – and their personnel undertook necessary geographic and geometrical processing, before carefully concealing these. All the related construction work and training were run by night, under conditions of utmost secrecy: Most of the time, even the commanders of neighbouring units were never informed about their presence.[3]

For commanders of the 64th and the 65th Missile Brigades, the October 1973 Arab-Israeli War began at noon of 5 October 1973, when they were summoned to the office of the Director of the

Table 8: Known Targets of 64th Missile Brigade's FROG-7-Strikes on 6 October 1973

Geographic Area	Target
Jebal Umm Khushayb (Gidi Defile)	HQ Southern Command IDF (Unit 511), COMINT/SIGINT/ELINT-, ECM- and radar site
Umm Margam	HQ Northern Sector IDF
Umm Mekhassa	reserve HQ
Romani & Baluza	airfield & MIM-23 HAWK SAM-site
Tasa Defile	HQ Central Sector IDF, airfield, camp of a mechanised battalion
Bir Gifgafa	Shoair airfield (part of the complex designated 'Refidim AB' by the IDF
Mitla Defile	HQ Southern Sector IDF & airfield

A still from a documentary film released by the Egyptian Ministry of Defence, showing one of the ZIL-135 TELs of the 64th Missile Brigade in position, shortly before firing a Luna-M ('FROG-7') rocket during the October 1973 War. (Albert Grandolini Collection)

Another still from the same film, showing the same TEL in the process of firing a Luna-M (or FROG-7) rocket. According to the War Diary of the sister unit, the 65th Missile Brigade, the 64th continued firing Luna-Ms against diverse Israeli positions on the Sinai until 20 October. In total, it launched 80 such rockets during the war. (Albert Grandolini Collection)

Artillery Corps, in Cairo, and assigned their tasks. On return to their units, the commanders ordered the crews to inspect and load selected rockets and missiles, while scouts were sent to inspect all of the prepared launch sites. Starting at 1800hrs, all the elements of the 64th Missile Brigade moved into their combat positions, heavily camouflaged their vehicles and, by the dawn of the next morning, reported their readiness. The final order to start the war was issued at 1130hrs on 6 October: as the EAF flew the opening strike at 1405hrs, the gunners of the 64th Missile Brigade removed the camouflage from their TELs and prepared these to fire. At 1440hrs, they unleashed 12 Luna-M rockets against major Israeli military installations in the western Sinai. The 65th Missile Brigade was still kept back. After reloading, at 2220hrs the 64th Missile Brigade fired six additional missiles at the HQ at Um Margam, and another six missiles against Israeli armoured concentrations near Romani and Baluza. Just as the available Egyptian documentation is incomplete with regards to exactly what target was attacked at what point in time (for list, see Table 8), so also the results of these strikes remain largely unknown. However, according to the same Egyptian report, the Israeli COMINT/SIGINT/ELINT and ECM-site at Jebeal Umm

Khushayb (also 'Umm Qashiba') fell silent at 1442hrs, and it was not to reactivate for at least a week longer.[4]

Brigadier-General Ahmad Sadik, former officer of the Intelligence Directorate of the Iraqi Air Force, explained:

…The attacks on Umm Qashiba could not have knocked out the extensive underground facilities because we were lacking suitable warheads. But, the conclusion of our post-war studies was crystal clear: attacks on Umm Qashiba on 6 October 1973 had caused enough damage to put this strategically important post out of business until 13 or 14 October 1973. That meant that the IDF was blind and deaf: it could not collect intelligence and relay it to Israeli commanders. Arrogant about Arab military capabilities as they were, Israeli commanders thus lacked timely information about intentions, dispositions, and capabilities of the Egyptian Army. They could not receive such information in advance, and thus began making the same mistakes everybody else is doing in every war.[5]

Further hits may have disabled an Israeli MIM-23A HAWK SAM-site at Baluza, and badly damaged a camp of an Israeli mechanised battalion 'opposite to the Deversoir area'.[6]

MIRAGES IN ACTION[7]

At 0100hrs of 7 October 1973, Colonel Ali Zien al-Abideen Abdul-Jawwad, commander of No. 69 Squadron, woke up four pilots of his unit and ordered them into one of the hardened aircraft shelters at Tanta AB. He was ordered to dispatch two Mirage 5DRs – each armed with two 250kg bombs and 240 rounds for their 30mm cannons – for an armed reconnaissance sortie to find a column of Israeli armoured personnel carriers underway in the Romani area, in north-western Sinai. Together with his pilots, Abdul-Jawwad selected a route from Tanta via Ras el-Bar, then east to a point north-east of the Lake Bardavil, then south, and then west along the coastal road. Such a circumnavigational course was necessary

Colonel Ali Zien al-Abideen Abdul-Jawwad, commander of the Mirage 5-equipped, (independent) No. 69 Squadron, EAF, during the October 1973 War. (EAF)

for two reasons: the Mirages still lacked an IFF-system that would have made them recognizable as friendly to ADC SAM-sites, and thus had to avoid these by flying well to the north before entering the airspace controlled by the enemy. Furthermore, approaching the Israeli ground forces from the east was certain to take the enemy by surprise. The two Mirages – the first flown by Lieutenant-Colonel Sharif ash-Shafei, with Major Hussein Ezzat as wingman – launched at dawn despite light fog: flying at only 15 metres altitude (50ft), they passed Lake Bordavil, turned south and then west before finding a column of armoured vehicles in the process of refuelling.

One of the Libyan Mirage 5Ds as seen during the training in that country, before No. 69 Squadron re-deployed to its home-base at Tanta AB in 1972. (Albert Grandolini Collection)

On sighting two Mirages approaching from the east, the Israeli troops waved at their pilots – and were certainly surprised when the jets then dropped four bombs on them. Rifaat commented:

> It was funny to listen to the Israeli radio chatter after such attacks, because they were neither used to get attacked by our air force, and even less so by Mirages!

Unknown to Abdul-Jawaad, ash-Shafei, Ezzat and Rifaat – and indeed to most of the IDF/AF pilots they were to confront over the following days – this attack set an entire chain of events into motion.

OPERATION CHALLENGE 4

The brief action of two 'Libyan Mirages' early that morning was over before the IDF/AF was able to react. However, the Israeli Air Force would not let the EAF wait for much longer. Indeed, although the Israelis repeatedly stressed the necessity of occupying the Sinai as a giant 'buffer zone' to 'keep themselves safe from Egyptian attacks' in the period 1967-1973, this idea ceased playing a role in the minds of their commanders as soon as the October War began. During the night of 6 to 7 October 1973, the High Command IDF had assessed the situation on the Golan Heights as 'stable', and thus ordered the IDF/AF to set in motion its plan for a 48-hour-long air superiority battle against Egypt – Operation *Challenge 4*. Unable to run an enterprise involving all of its squadrons on two frontlines simultaneously, the air force decided to hit Egyptian air bases first, and then to destroy the SAM belt along the Suez Canal in three successive waves. The first wave of *Challenge 4* thus launched around 0625hrs Israeli time (one hour ahead of the Egyptian time) on the morning of 7 October 1973 with the aim of striking Jiyanklis, el-Mansourah and Tanta in the Nile Delta, Qutamiyah east of the Egyptian capital, and Beni Suweif and Bir Arida AB south of Cairo. It included 87 aircraft: foremost F-4Es and McDonnell-Douglas A-4 Skyhawks, but also KC-97s that acted as airborne command posts, and S-61 helicopters that deployed stand-off electronic countermeasures. However, it lacked the support of No. 200 Squadron's UAVs: a day earlier, these were deployed to the Dalton airstrip in northern Israel with the aim of taking part in the pre-emptive strike on Syria, and there was no time to re-shuffle the unit to the Sinai.[8]

The first to reach their targets were A-4s that attacked SAM-sites in the Port Said area: two were shot down and several damaged without achieving anything in return. About 20 minutes later, the main wave of the attack force converged on the area between el-Mansourah in the north and Beni Suweif in the south: seven F-4Es from No. 69 Squadron went for Jianklis; four F-4Es from No. 119 Squadron targeted el-Mansourah AB and Qutamiyah; 12 F-4Es from No. 201 Squadron went for Tanta AB; a part of No. 107 Squadron for Beni Suweif and another for Bir Arida. The ADC detected the first formation of F-4Es as these were approaching Jiyanklis and directed four MiG-21s led by Major Reza Saqr to intercept:

> I led a flight of four on a combat air patrol at an altitude of 3,000 metres above el-Mansourah, with Major Hussein Sidqi as Number 2. The ground control directed us towards the Mansour Channel, when my Numbers 3 and 4 reported Phantoms underneath us, and promptly attacked. I followed together with Sidqi, who then reported a problem with his engine. Then I saw a Phantom approaching: I dove, locked on and pressed the trigger, but the missile failed to launch. Until today I don't know why. The Phantom unleashed its bombs upon our air base before turning north-east at a relatively slow speed. I followed in the direction of Kfar el-Sheikh, approached within range and fired again. The missile scored a direct hit, and the aircraft blew up, crashing into the local sports stadium: one of the crew was killed in the crash, the other after ejection. Turning back towards my home-base, I decreased the speed to conserve fuel. With el-Mansourah AB still being busy, I considered landing at Tanta to refuel, but there was no reply from their control tower. Eventually, I landed at Qwaysina AB.[9]

As the Israeli formation continued its attack it nearly caught the flight led by Medhat Zaki – and including Reda el-Iraqi, Mohy Fahad, and Mamdouh Moneib – still on the ground. El-Iraqi recalled:

> The ground control advised us of two formations of Israeli aircraft approaching from the north. Then I heard a call from two MiGs that were airborne as they manoeuvred behind the enemy and counted 12 Phantoms before attacking them. They complained that the enemy was very hard to see because of their camouflage colours against the backdrop of many farms below…

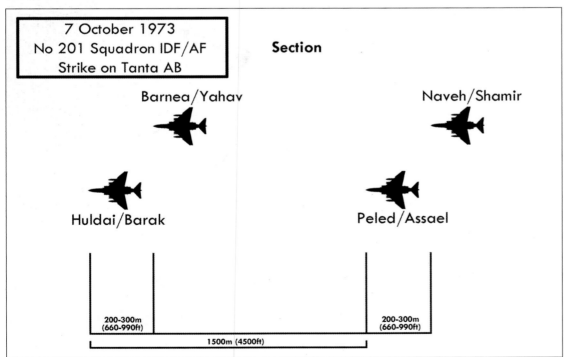

A diagram showing the composition of the No. 201 Squadron's flight detailed to strike Tanta AB, on the morning of 7 October 1973. This formation encountered no MiG-21s, but also caused no damage to its target. (Diagram by Tom Cooper)

While accelerating down the runway, we were able to see the first two Phantoms above, climbing, rolling out and diving to attack as we were still on the ground but moving in their direction. Their bombs exploded next to the MiG flown by Monib, forcing him to eject. Then the Phantoms flashed by while the rest of us quickly tucked in our undercarriage and continued to accelerate on afterburner.

Then I saw additional Phantoms approaching from the north: realising their attack had failed they jettisoned their bombs on farms below, killing civilians and causing a large number of fires. We passed by and then turned around to attack them. A minute later, the airspace over Jiyanklis was full of aircraft: 12 Phantoms against three, then seven of us as another flight scrambled (including Mamdouh, who had run to man another MiG and scramble within five minutes for the second time)…

Back over Jiyanklis, I looked up and saw Medhat climbing behind a Phantom, reaching a good position for a missile attack. He fired and there was a brilliant explosion, but at the same time two Phantoms appeared from behind and fired missiles at him. I warned Medhat to

Medhat Zaki in the cockpit of one of No. 26 Squadron's MiG-21F-13s. (Medhat Zaki Collection)

Mamdouh Moneib was shot down by the detonation of Israeli bombs on 7 October 1973 while scrambling from Jianklis AB. He ejected safely and was back in action only five minutes later. The MiG-21F-13 behind him on this photograph wore the serial number 5590. (Mamdouh Moneib Collection)

break hard, then engaged the nearest Phantom and out-turned him. Rolling out, I put my sight on him and fired a burst from my cannon. Then our AAA opened fire, and the sky was quickly full of smoke… My opponent turned away, trailing a thick trail of black smoke. Then his co-pilot ejected. I didn't see the pilot eject but I doubt he could reach Israel… short on fuel after flying on afterburner all the time, I returned to base.[10]

Magddin Rifaat confirmed Saqr's recollection:

During that attack, our MiG-21s clashed with Phantoms and Major Saqr shot down one, while Captain Hani Issa hit another before he was shot down and forced to eject. I took a jeep and drove out to pick him up, because he came down with the

parachute near Shubrakhet AB. I found him there under attack from local peasants – who were beating any pilot that fell from the sky, no matter if Egyptian or enemy. Indeed, hardly that I scattered the farmers when they told me they have beaten and killed another 'enemy', few minutes before. Joined by few Military Police soldiers, I went there only to find the smashed body of the Israeli pilot...

Samir Aziz Mikhail recalled the attack on el-Mansourah:

Around 0730, we went to our aircraft and that's when the Israeli attack came. I spent it next to my MiG-21 inside a hardened aircraft shelter. A fragment from one of the bombs passed next to my ear, but the only problem caused by that attack was an Israeli

A still from a video showing the MiG-21F-13 serial number 5258 from No. 26 Squadron, armed with a pair of R-3S missiles, emerging out of a hardened aircraft shelter. (Albert Grandolini Collection)

bomb that embedded itself next to one of the runways after failing to detonate. Squadron Commander Magdy Kamal led a team that disarmed the bomb by removing the fuse, but operations never stopped.[11]

… while Nassr Moussa summarized:

The enemy attack on el-Mansourah on 7 October neither caused serious damage nor slowed our operations. On the contrary, Qadri Abdel Hamid shot down a Phantom, and Kamal Magdi shot down a Skyhawk that day.[12]

Citing from the War Diary of the Mirage-equipped No. 69 Squadron, EAF, Okasha found the Israeli attack on Tanta barely worth mentioning:

Early that morning four enemy fighters penetrated our air defences and bombed Tanta. We were not ordered to scramble but the Israelis caused no damage and there was no interruption in normal operations.

Overall, pilots from Air Brigade 102 claimed two Phantoms and a Skyhawk in exchange for Monib's MiG-21F-13 serial number 5911, and the MiG-21 from which Issa ejected, while pilots from Air Brigade 104 claimed two Phantoms for no loss. The Israelis credited crews from No. 107 Squadron with two MiG-kills over el-Mansourah AB, without any friendly losses. Reportedly, the participating Israeli crews returned 'optimistic and reassured', expecting to achieve 'total supremacy' over Egypt during their next mission.[13]

The reasons for such optimism are completely unclear because – with the exception of the strike on Jiyanklis – the Israeli attacks actually caused minimal damage and left next to no lasting impression upon the Egyptians. Moreover, there are strong reasons to doubt that related reports satisfied any commanders of the IDF/AF: too many of the involved aircraft were forced to jettison ordnance well before reaching their targets.

RED LINES

Challenge 4 had hardly begun, when the Israeli Minister of Defence, Moshe Dayan, ordered the commander of the IDF/AF, Major General Benjamin Peled, to change the priority and switch attention to the situation on the Golan Heights. Re-routed in a mad rush, the involved IDF/AF units thus launched their next wave towards the north – without the necessary reconnaissance and planning – and flew straight into the airspace effectively sealed by the Syrian air defences. The result was the worst loss the Israeli air force ever experienced in one day: by the end of 7 October 1973, at least 13 Israeli jets were shot down over Syria, and another dozen damaged. The total combat loss of at least 22 aircraft on that day left the air force in a state of deep shock, and the ground forces without urgently necessary air support.

Worse was to follow on 8 October 1973: instead of easily scything through the Egyptians, one of two reserve armoured divisions of the IDF committed to counter-attack the Sinai was badly mauled, while the other spent the day with chaotic and useless manoeuvring behind the frontlines. Meanwhile, the ADC caused the IDF/AF additional losses in aircraft and aircrews, effectively preventing all their attempts to knock out pontoon bridges on the Suez Canal. With their ground forces retreating in shock and confusion, the Israelis became concerned that the Egyptians might launch an advance on the three crucial passes in central Sinai. Moreover, by the afternoon of the same day, Syrian tanks were approaching the hills overlooking the Jordan River Valley and the Sea of Galilee: all that stood in their way were battered remnants of three regular brigades and a miscellany of ad-hoc mobilised reservists, all exhausted, and some showing signs of panic: instead of quickly winning the war as expected just a few days earlier, the IDF was on the way to losing it. During the afternoon of 8 October, Meir met Dayan and the Chief of Staff IDF, Major-General Elazar, to discuss the situation. Finding no other solution, they decided to use the air force for an attack on 'the Syrian depth' – major power plants, refineries, and bridges deep inside Syria. The Israeli prime minister then asked Dayan and Elazar about the expected Egyptian response to such an action: relying on AMAN's reporting, both concluded that the threat was low, because the Scud was not yet in service and the Egyptians thus lacked the means of attacking central Israel. Immediately afterwards, Elazar set up a press conference: seething with anger, he bluntly threatened Syria promising that Israel shall, '…strike them, we shall beat them, we shall break their bones'. Reportedly, at the time of that conference, Elazar was not in possession of the facts about the disastrous defeats and losses of the day. Moreover, by the end of 8 October 1973, Major-General Peled was forced into realisation that the IDF/AF had meanwhile lost nearly 40 aircraft shot down and at least 20 others badly damaged: it was well on the way to reaching its 'Red Line' – the lowest number of operational aircraft with which it could still operate effectively.[14]

It is doubtful if anybody in Israel expected the Syrian reaction to Elazar's announcement, though it is unlikely that this improved the mood within top ranks of the IDF by any degree: at 0335hrs on 9 October 1973, three Luna-Ms fired by the 115th Missile Brigade of the Syrian Arab Army rocked the Ramat David AB in northern Israel. The Syrians had fired Lunas at Ramat David already twice before: during the nights of 6 to 7 October, and 7 to 8 October, but – at least according to Israeli sources – failed to hit their target and only caused 'some material damage to the nearby settlement of Migdal HaEmek'. However, one of three rockets that hit Ramat David AB on 9 October smashed the residential house for bachelor officers, killing an A-4 pilot from No. 110 Squadron IDF/AF, and injuring two others. Another Luna hit the nearby barracks, causing additional injuries.[15]

NUCLEAR BLACKMAIL[16]

The – unexpectedly precise – Syrian strike on Ramat David AB took the Israelis completely by surprise. Foremost, it prompted the AMAN into changing its related estimates and an assessment that the Soviets might order the deployment of Egyptian Scuds 'if they have to'. The option of striking Egypt's 'depth' was thus out of the window before it was ever exercised.[17]

Still, that report was a mere 'dot on the i', because meanwhile there was just no end of bad news for Israel: especially reports about heavy losses on the Golan, followed by the shocking defeat of the counter-attack on the Sinai had created the impression of an imminent collapse of the IDF. The situation drove Dayan to the point of despair: he began announcing apocalyptic consequences

for Israel – 'unless something drastic would be done'. Eventually, the panic reached such proportions that Meir later wrote of having nearly 'gone to pieces' after hearing Dayan's descriptions. Although not sharing the worst visions of her military commanders, she was concerned enough to take steps aimed at putting on alert not only No. 150 Squadron, IDF/AF, but also alerting the Nixon administration in Washington.

With the help of communication intercepts, the US intelligence learned of the 'defensive' measures prepared by the Israeli government even before Meir's message reached the White House. Still, the Nixon administration was surprised by the flood of bad news that began arriving already during 7 and 8 October. Perfectly aware of Israel's clear military superiority over all Arab militaries, before the war the Americans expected the IDF to swiftly counterattack and achieve another easy victory within a week (or even less) without any kind of external assistance. Moreover, the Nixon administration was preoccupied with the so-called Watergate affair as of October 1973: therefore, it was up to Nixon's National Security Adviser, Henry Kissinger, to run the affairs related to the war in the Middle East at his own discretion. Bad news prompted Kissinger into a series of meetings with Israeli representatives. Early on 9 October (US Eastern Standard Time) the Israeli ambassador to the US, Simcha Dinitz, informed him that the counteroffensive in the Sinai had failed, the Israeli forces had suffered heavy losses and were in a difficult position. Perplexed, Kissinger asked, 'Explain to me, how could 400 tanks be lost to the Egyptians?'

Dinitz's reply remains unknown. Instead, he took Kissinger to the side for a 'private and off the record' meeting. In order to underline

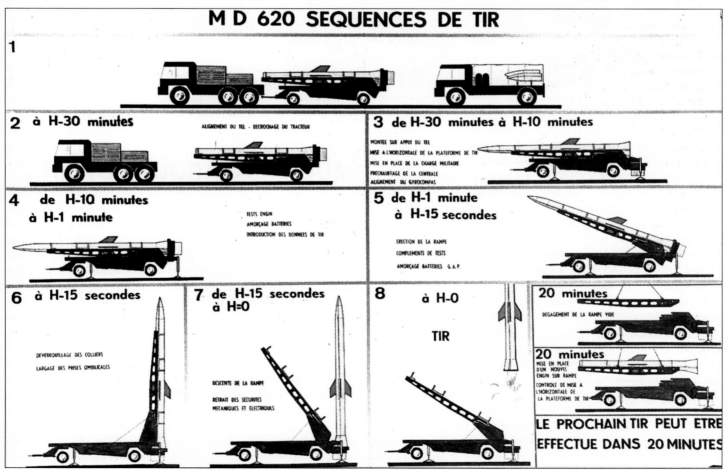

A diagram describing the sequence and duration of deployment of the MD.620 for combat. On 8 October 1973, the Israeli political leadership ordered No. 150 Squadron, IDF/AF, based at Sdot Micha AB, to pull its Jericho missiles out of their shelters, and undertake exactly this procedure – and that in view of US reconnaissance satellites. (Dassault, via Albert Grandolini)

A prototype MD.620 as seen in erected position, together with its launcher/trailer, during pre-delivery testing in France. (Dassault, via Albert Grandolini)

the urgency of the situation, the Israeli then introduced what even the historians of the National Security Archives in Washington refer to as 'an element of nuclear blackmail'. Accordingly, the failure of the Israeli counterattack in the Sinai on 8 October caused such panic within the Israeli cabinet that during a late morning meeting on the same day Moshe Dayan recommended to Golda Meir that Israel must prepare its 'ultimate weapon'. Following a briefing by the nation's nuclear chief (head of the IAEC), Shalheveth Freier, the ministerial forum decided to 'arm and target the nuclear arsenal in the event of total collapse', or at least a 'nuclear demonstration', but also to 'inform Washington of its unprecedented action' – and then demand initiation of an 'emergency airlift to supply Israel with the arms and ammunition required to continue waging an all-out war effort'. Correspondingly, several MD.620s of No. 150 Squadron were pulled out of their shelters and armed with nuclear warheads, while nuclear bombs were loaded on six modified F-4Es at Tel Nov AB, 'at least to influence Washington'.

Dinitz was apparently not the only one to report the activation of the Israeli nuclear arsenal to Kissinger: US intelligence warned the US National Security Council (NSC) about this fact too. However, meetings between Dinitz and Kissinger seem to have been crucial in so far as that Israel agreed not to use its nuclear arsenal *if* the US would resupply it with whatever was needed to drive back the Arab forces, and because Kissinger assured that the US would replace all Israeli losses.

The first result of this agreement was the permission for Israeli transport aircraft arriving in the USA to launch a – discrete – airlift of armament like the latest AIM-9G Sidewinder and AIM-7E-2 air-to-air missiles, additional AGM-45 Shirke anti-radar missiles CBU-30H/B CBUs, and ECM-pods directly from the stocks of US armed forces, nearly a week before the USA then launched its public air-bridge with similar purpose.[18]

Whether it was Kissinger's agreement – or 'promise' – to resupply Israeli stocks of aircraft, tanks and ammunition, or something else that eventually prompted the Israelis to de-activate their Jerichos, remains unclear. What is certain is that despite alarming news from the battlefield Washington was not convinced that Israel's security interests were seriously threatened: to the Americans, the Egyptian capabilities and intentions were clearly much too limited for more than to cross the Canal and then entrench – which is precisely what these did between 6 and 9 October.[19]

However, according to other US intelligence sources, Kissinger's promise to resupply Israeli stocks of aircraft, tanks and ammunition made it possible for the IDF/AF to disarm its nuclear-capable Phantoms and use them for conventional tasks: instead of being held back, standing quick reaction alert, six precious F-4Es and their crews were thus free for offensive operations. Indeed, combined with the fact that the IDF/AF meanwhile managed to repair nine Phantoms damaged during the first three days of the October 1973 war, Kissinger's promise resulted in what amounted to a 'near-instant recovery' of the Israeli F-4 fleet, through the influx of 15 operational airframes to daily operations.[20]

5

MUCH ADO ABOUT NOTHING?

As chaos, panic and disagreement continued to dictate the decisions made by its commanders, the IDF/AF continued excelling at wasting time, fuel, ammunition, and precious aircraft and aircrews to achieve next to nothing in return – and for a few days longer. Despite countless urgencies elsewhere, it still found the opportunity to continue flying ever bigger strikes on the Port Said and Port Fuad area. This operation attracted little attention in Israeli and Western publications, and remains insufficiently explained. While at least as poorly researched, this campaign is not only well-recalled in Egypt, but indeed: the subject of several legends.

PORT SAID FRACAS

Constructed at the north-eastern side of the entry into the Suez Canal, surrounded by Lake Manzala and the extensive salt marshes, Port Said is geographically isolated from the rest of Egypt: as of 1973 it could be reached only via a narrow causeway stretching south along the strategic waterway. On the opposite, eastern, side of the Suez Canal is Port Fuad, the only town on the Sinai Peninsula that remained under Egyptian control after the June 1967 War. Indeed, most of the triangle-shaped area further east and south of Port Fuad was under Egyptian control as of October 1973: 'Budapest' and 'Orkal' – the two northernmost fortifications of the Bar Lev Line – marked the limits of this marshy zone. The area was important for Egypt not only as a matter of pride, but also because it contained at last one launch site selected by the commander of the 65th Missile Brigade for possible operations against Israel. Correspondingly, it was heavily protected – not only on the ground: the ADC squeezed the entire 98th Air Defence Brigade of the 10th Air Defence Division – a unit including four SA-2 and SA-3 SAM-sites – into the little dry terrain that was available.[1]

As mentioned earlier, initial AMAN reports on FROG-7s and Scuds in Egypt indicated that this was not a particularly precise system. Indeed, the available intelligence indicated a CEP of between 480 and 1,300m (0.25 and 0.7nm). Unsurprisingly, the majority of top Israeli military commanders essentially ignored the preparations of the two Egyptian missile brigades. The reason for this is that, relying on rather patchy US intelligence reports, the AMAN produced a technical report discussing the missile's specifications, and not its military importance. Because it had no clear information about its range, the Israeli military intelligence estimated that the Scuds could reach only the region south of Netanya *if* fired from the Port Fuad or Port Said area and then that the missile's behaviour when fired over the maximum range would be much too unpredictable to expect it to hit any 'important target'. However, and just like the Americans, the AMAN was unable to identify who exactly was responsible for the unit operating Egyptian Scuds – the Soviets or the Egyptians? Curiously, it simply concluded that Moscow would not let Cairo deploy the weapon in combat at its own discretion, and that for a while longer. Probably for the same reason, Israeli intelligence did not arrive at the idea to warn about any kind of deployment of these missiles in combination with nuclear warheads provided by the USSR: considering the mental status of diverse top Israeli officials at the time, this was probably a very reasonable decision.[2]

The reason is that Moshe Dayan remained insistent on considering Egyptian Scuds a 'serious threat'. Indeed, on an as of yet unknown date – almost certainly 8 October – he 'recommended' the Chief-of-Staff IDF, Major-General David Elazar, to 'intensify aerial operations around Port Fuad'. At least according to Israeli sources, it is unclear if Elazar followed Dayan's recommendation: it is certain only that Peled did – even if subsequently exposing himself to fierce critique from Elazar, who began demanding that he attack the SAMs further south. The IDF/AF thus flew its first air strikes on the 'concentration of SAMs in the Port Fuad area' (with the official intention of 'clearing the path for the ground attack'), and on the Egyptian air defences in the Port Said area (with the intention of 'testing these', or, 'because it could').[3]

The first Israeli air strikes on the Port Said area took place late in the morning of 8 October 1973, when F-4Es from No. 119 Squadron bombed the early warning radar site at Baltim, and those from No. 201 Squadron dive-bombed a similar site at Damietta. The official Egyptian account of this action cited the following:

…Our radar screens picked up Israeli aircraft approaching from the east at medium and high altitudes. Immediately, the Port Said air defence commander assigned part of his defensive effort to deal with these targets, should they enter the operational area. At the same time he ordered the major part to be prepared to attack the planes approaching from the south and to concentrate reconnaissance efforts towards the north and east.

The aircraft approaching from the east lost altitude to give the impression that they were about to attack. This manoeuvre deceived no one…Soon the main enemy attack was detected, approaching Port Said from the south. The aircraft were in two groups, one heading towards the northeast to attack the missile positions there, the other northwestward to attack the other defensive positions.

Some small SA-7 personnel-borne weapons were positioned on the line of approach of the attacking aircraft. As these missiles were launched, the aircraft were forced to zoom up quickly, exactly as planned. Thus, they were in the most convenient positions for our SA-2 and SA-3 batteries to destroy them.[4]

According to the Israeli accounts, none of the aircraft involved was shot down, although the, 'Port Said SAM-network fired 15 missiles alone at the first Phantom to pop-up for its attack'. Both sides are in agreement that the IDF/AF repeated the exercise during the afternoon, and – largely – about its results. Israeli sources cite the same two F-4 units targeting the SAM-sites in the Port Said area around 1630hrs. The IDF/AF post-strike analysis assessed this operation as having 'inactivated' all of these for the next two days, in return for no loss of their own.[5]

The official Egyptian position largely confirms this, though differs in regards to Israeli losses:

The Israelis sent over a total of 94 aircraft. Defending against such a number was beyond the capacity of our four batteries, which could face only one aircraft at any one time. Any aircraft in addition to the four being engaged could thus bombard the missile positions and evoke no counteraction. Using these tactics, the Israelis were able to silence all four missile batteries. But, in return they lost 12 aircraft.[6]

While the Israelis provided very few details, there is no doubt that this was a major operation and that the F-4Es involved were protected by at least two flights of Mirage 5s of No. 101 and No. 144 Squadrons, IDF/AF. As the ADC scrambled two flights of MiG-21s of the 104th Air Brigade from el-Mansourah AB, an air battle ensued, which Samir Aziz Mikhail recalled as follows:

Early that morning our squadron CO, Magdy Kamal, approached me requesting to replace him because he caught influenza and was exhausted. I accepted and took over the responsibility for our unit and his aircraft. Running the operations of our squadron, which was launching one CAP after another the whole day, kept me busy, so when the time came for me to fly a mission too, I encountered a problem. Magdy Kamal was a big bloke in comparison to me, but in my rush to scramble I forgot to re-adjust my seat belts. I took off, nevertheless, together with Salah as my Number 2, Qabbany as Number 3, and Abdel Muneim Hammam as Number 4. While accelerating and climbing, I was hoping to find a few seconds to attempt and adjust my belts, but there was no time: the ground control ordered us to accelerate towards Port Said and said the enemy was already attacking. Approaching the combat zone, I ordered my wingmen to jettison their drop tanks and prepare for combat. But, my tanks hung up because of an electrical failure. I was flying with three tanks but, since I was in the lead, I continued on…Then I saw four Mirages above us and diving towards Qabbany and Hammam. I decided to make a head-on pass and began to manoeuvre, but then four

An F-4E from No. 201 Squadron, IDF/AF, releasing a M117 bomb from high-altitude. (Albert Grandolini Collection)

Samir Aziz Mikhail in the cockpit of a MiG-21MF. Notable is how the headrest of the ejection seat limited the pilot's ability to turn his head around, and see to the side or behind him. (Samir Aziz Mikhail, via Abdallah Emran)

well and fought themselves between the Israelis in my direction, forcing two to break off their attacks upon me. They all descended to very low altitude and were manoeuvring at very low speeds. I decided to exploit this moment, made a steep dive down towards the sea to accelerate and turned in the direction of el-Mansourah. But after pulling out I said to myself, why did you leave Qabbany and Hammam alone? I made a combat turn towards them, rolled out… and then noticed a Mirage next to my right wing. Before I was able to turn left, I felt an impact like a bus hitting a bicycle. A missile hit me very hard. My aircraft began to spin out of control. While falling towards the sea, I looked into the overhead mirror and could not see the fin, while the fuselage and wings were on fire. As the aircraft began to rotate, I ejected, but felt a terrible pain in my back: my belts were not tightened and I was not in the right position to eject…I crashed into the water in severe pain, inflated my life jacket and tried to remain conscious.

other Mirages appeared from below and behind and hit Salah. He was dead about 30 seconds later: they shot him with a cannon.

My world darkened then: rather than entering the battle with four aircraft, we were only three, against eight enemies, two of which were coming to shoot me with their cannon. I made a very hard turn to the right, forcing them to overshoot: one of the Mirages came out in front of me and I reversed my turn to left to shoot him. I pressed the trigger, but there was no response. I tried to change the missiles, but to no avail: there was a failure in the electrical circuit for the armament. I thought, something is very wrong with my aircraft; the tanks won't separate, the gun doesn't work, and the missiles don't fire. Without armament, my aircraft was just a useless piece of iron…

I knew they would kill me for sure; everywhere I looked I saw a Mirage. I decided to crash into one of them. If I'm sure to die, I will take one of them with me. So I tried to hit Mirages twice, but they were very clever at evading. Qabbany and Hammam did

Nassr Moussa summarized the outcome:

…we nearly lost Samir Aziz in an air combat near Port Said, but Abdel avenged him by dropping one of Mirages. Samir Aziz was rescued and several of us visited him in the hospital in Cairo, the same evening, where we found him suffering excruciating pain from spinal injuries. Even then, he was all the time giving us tips about how to fight the Israelis and warned us to remain disciplined. His lessons remain in my head ever since.[7]

Captain Abdel Moneim Hammam, Mikhail's Number 4, was officially credited with one Mirage 5 as shot down before recovering safely at el-Mansourah AB. The IDF/AF credited its pilots with a total of three MiG-21s shot down in this combat, for no loss in return:

officially, its sole loss of that afternoon – the Mirage 5 serial number 93, flown by Eitan Carmi – was caused 'by anti-aircraft defences' during an engagement with multiple MiG-17s of the EAF, forcing the pilot to eject over the Lake Bardavil.[8]

FROM BLUNDER TO BLUNDER

From the Egyptian point of view, the situation regarding Port Said was of utmost importance. Unsurprisingly, the commander of the ADC, Major-General Fahmy received the order to reinforce local air defences and acted accordingly. Indeed, already by the morning of 9 October, the Egyptian air defences were bolstered to a degree where the next Israeli air strike ended in disaster: two A-4 Skyhawks were shot down, including the aircraft flown by the CO Ramat David AB, Colonel Arlozor Lev. When the IDF/AF deployed an F-4E, Bell 205 and a S-65 helicopter to search for Lev, the Phantom and one of helicopters were damaged, too.[9]

Meanwhile, in the wake of the Syrian

A MiG-21MF (serial number 8691) from the 104th Air Brigade, as seen several years after the October 1973 War. While generally considered 'highly reliable' by air forces that never flew it in combat, a jet of this variant suffered several malfunctions while flown by Samir Aziz Mikhail in the air combat over Port Said, on 8 October 1973, resulting in the downing of this highly experienced pilot. (Albert Grandolini Collection)

Fin of the Mirage 5 serial number 93, as 'fished' by Israeli sailors out of Lake Bardavil. The Egyptians claim the aircraft was shot down by Captain Abdel Moneim Hammam, flying a MiG-21MF from No. 46 Squadron; the Israelis credited its loss to (the Egyptian) 'ground-based air defences'. (Albert Grandolini Collection)

FROG-strike on Ramat David AB, the IDF/AF continued dissipating its efforts. On the morning of 9 October 1973, it first attacked a dysfunctional radar station in Lebanon, before sending two of its Phantom-squadrons to bomb the HQ of the Syrian Arab Air Force in Damascus. While frequently famed in Israel and the West as a 'highly successful operation undertaken against all odds', the latter action can hardly be described even as 'symbolic': not only that the HQ compound was empty or barely scratched in this attack, but most of the Israeli bombs randomly massacred up to 200 civilians anywhere between the Soviet Cultural Centre in downtown Damascus, in apartment buildings neighbouring the HQ-compound, and at the Umayyad Square in the west. Moreover, the IDF/AF again suffered losses in precious Phantoms and their aircrews.[10] Major-General Peled then ordered the balance of his force into an all-out attack on the Egyptian air defences along the Suez Canal, only to lose at least

five additional aircraft while achieving exactly nothing. Finally, 18 F-4Es from No. 119 Squadron were sent to strike el-Mansourah AB, while 13 from No. 201 Squadron went for Qutamiyah AB, in Egypt. Nassr Mousa recalled:

That, second Israeli attack took us by surprise. Israeli Phantoms came in as Mohammed Suleiman and Medhat Arafa were underway to their aircraft in a jeep. One of the bombs hit next to their vehicle and this overturned: Arafa broke his shoulder in the process, while Suleiman received shrapnel injuries. … we scrambled but the Phantoms ran away. This made us so mad, Magdi, Qadri and me began planning an attack on el-Arish airfield: we wanted to fly there at low altitude and bomb. It turned out this would be a suicide mission. Our MiG-21s lacked the necessary range for us to get there and return if carrying bombs

The F-4E from No. 201 Squadron seen while rolling out of a hardened aircraft shelter at Hatzor AB, loaded with 10 CBU-30H/B CBUs, during the October 1973 War. (IDF via Albert Grandolini)

and flying at low altitude. Unsurprisingly, our commanders cancelled that plan.

Magddin Rifaat recalled the message that arrived at Tanta AB, shortly after:

At 0900, a report arrived about enemy aircraft dropping CBUs at the entrances of the hardened aircraft shelters of el-Mansourah AB. The bomblets in the size of a hand grenade would then roll and enter from under the doors to hit our aircraft. They also acted as booby-traps for personnel, just like many of the 250- and 1,000kg bombs that failed to detonate….A soldier positioned on the water tank of the nearby village of Mahhallat Marhum then hit one of enemy jets with a Strela missile, as this was leaving the combat zone. He jumped in joy but fell from the tank and broke a leg. Nevertheless, he continued chanting Allah-u-Akhbar all the time!

Overall, not only the Egyptian air defences, but both of the attacked air bases remained operational. Indeed, to demonstrate his determination, Lieutenant-General Mubarak then ordered the Mirages from No. 69 Squadron into their second combat sortie of the war, as recalled by Rifaat:

At the hour of Asr [early afternoon; authors' note], four aircraft led by Majors Hamdi Akl and Abdul Hadi Gad al-Mawla – each armed with JL.100 drop tanks that had launchers for 68mm unguided rockets at their front – flew the second combat sortie of our unit. They attacked a MIM-23 HAWK SAM-site near Romani. Although facing a hell of hostile anti-aircraft fire, Hamdi carried out three strafing runs. I asked him why, and he replied, "I meant, why return if I still have ammunition. I'm telling you, I burnt those sons of bitches!"[11]

418TH TO THE RESCUE

Meanwhile, the ADC issued the order for the 92nd Air Defence Brigade to dispatch one of its SA-2 battalions in the direction of Port Said. This is how the 418th Air Defence Battalion came to receive the order to march north, as recalled by its commander, Major Hob el-Din:

On 8 October, the enemy knocked out SAM-battalions protecting Port Said *and the site selected for Scud-B attacks on Israel*. At 1600 of 9 October, I received the order to mobilise my unit, move it from its position near Cairo International to Port Said, to take over the control of local air defences and to protect the launching sites for Scud missiles.[12]

Hob el-Din's men scrambled to disassemble and load their equipment, and get moving: by the last light of the day, a convoy of 84 darkened vehicles started its long voyage towards the north. This re-deployment was anything other than easy: the unit spent most of 10 October concealed next to the road connecting el-Mansourah with Damietta, as – in order to keep this re-deployment secret – further movement closer to the combat zone was limited to small groups of three vehicles. Even this was particularly problematic because the road and the causeway carrying it were heavily cratered by bombs, and the amount of damage was such that the local engineers could not keep up with repairs. Hob el-Din recalled his arrival in the effectively besieged Port Said:

Our air defences counted 214 Israeli aircraft attacking Port Said on 8, 9 and 10 October, and claimed 21 of these as shot down. On 10 October, 122 enemy aircraft attacked the previous SA-2 battalion in Port Said, and destroyed it completely. Then the Israelis hammered at the other three SAM-sites and when these were knocked out, they continued bombardment by night, with help of flares to prevent us from repairing damaged equipment. Several times they bombed our occupied sites and decoy-sites at the same time as they hit the causeway: they wanted to make sure that we could not replace SAM-equipment that was knocked out and there would be no positions from which we could operate. As well as using general-purpose bombs, they were dropping plenty of CBUs filled with mines, trying to deny our crews even the movement around their positions.

Continuous Israeli air strikes eventually provoked several air combats with MiG-21s from el-Mansourah AB. Around 1530hrs on 10 October, Lieutenant-Colonel Mamdouh el-Malt claimed a Mirage 5 as shot down in the Port Said area: the Israelis denied any such loss, while stressing that a 'Nesher' that crashed while trying to return to Refidim AB after its pilot ejected safely, was hit by 'anti-aircraft fire'.[13]

Without any breaks or hesitation, late in the evening of 10 October the officers and other ranks of the 418th Battalion went into a position previously occupied by a destroyed SA-2-unit: this was a completely bombed out site in between Port Said (east), the coastal highway and the sea (north), Lake Manzalah (south) and Gamil airport (west). While clearing the wreckage of destroyed equipment and unexploded Israeli ordnance by moonlight, and reconstructing the four metre high and four metre wide circular blast pens around their vehicles and launchers, the crews found the bodies of several colleagues killed in earlier attacks. At 0600hrs in the morning of 11 October, the 418th Air Defence Battalion reported as ready for action. The Israelis did not let them wait for very long: the first air raid alert was sounded slightly over an hour later. Hob el-Din continued:

Once the Israelis recognized our presence, their reaction was near-instant. At 0738, we detected about 16 enemy aircraft approaching along the coast, from the direction of el-Arish. After a while, our radar sorted them out: there were four "finger four" formations, separated by about 1,000m (1,093yds), underway at an altitude of 3,000 metres (9,842ft) – above the envelope of our SA-7s. At 0745, we fired two missiles on the first target. There was no reaction: the enemy formation continued along a steady course. The first missile scored a direct hit, exploding one of the targets at a range of 15 kilometres (8nm). We promptly fired a second missile towards another target, and again, there was an explosion in the sky. Our visual observation posts confirmed both hits. We were delighted: two hits within a dozen of seconds!

We hardly re-loaded our launchers when another formation of 16 aircraft approached, around 0930. This time we waited until they came closer then took them by surprise and opened fire and hit two. The others fired several television-guided missiles, but our soldiers set on fire barrels filled with oil and sand, creating a dense smoke barrier, and all of these missed.

From the Egyptian point of view, this time the EAF interceptors did not become involved for reasons explained by Reda el-Iraqi:

We were well-informed about developments in Port Said, and could hardly believe the ferocity of enemy attacks on this city. We were eager to hit back, but saw no combat. After air battles on 8 and 9 October, the Israelis were extremely careful to avoid getting intercepted by us. By 11 October, they would repeatedly hit our early warning radar stations and jam them with electronic countermeasures, then quickly approach to drop their bombs, and disappear. We were scrambled very often, but always came too late. Even so, Port Said cost them dearly: during every attack they would lose two or three aircraft.

RELENTLESS ASSAULT

As far as the Israeli sources are concerned, IDF/AF attacks on Port Said of 11 October 1973 were either not worth mentioning, or did not take place: instead, the air force was preoccupied with supporting a counteroffensive against Syria, and launched only one significant air strike against Egypt. Eight F-4Es from No.

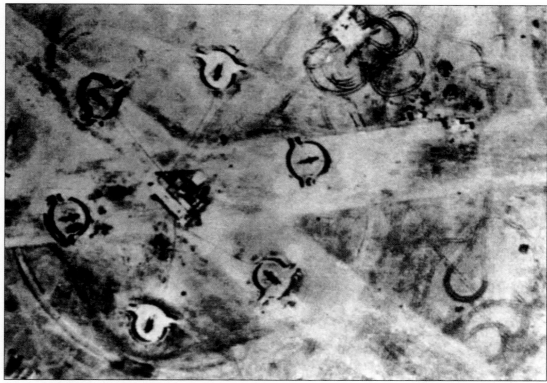

This reconnaissance photograph of the first Egyptian SAM-site constructed on the former Gamil airfield, west of Port Said, was taken during the War of Attrition. (IDF via Albert Grandolini)

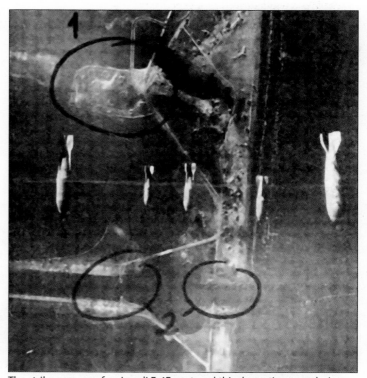

The strike-camera of an Israeli F-4E captured this dramatic scene during one of the attacks on targets in the Port Said area. Notable are M117 bombs released by the Phantom, SA-2 SAM site of the ADC (marked with 1), and multiple craters in the causeway and the road-bridges connecting the port with the mainland (marked with 2). (IDF via Albert Grandolini)

201 Squadron were ordered to bomb a bridge south of the city of Benha in the Nile Delta, carrying a military cable communication system, around the noon. Although – reportedly – completing their mission successfully, the Phantoms were then caught by 16 MiG-21s scrambled from el-Mansourah, Abu Hammad and Inchas ABs. Medhat Arafa, who served with No. 46 Squadron, recalled how

eagerly the Egyptian pilots exploited this opportunity:

> After my jeep overturned during the Israeli attack on el-Mansoura on 7 October, I felt no pain and made an air strike in Sinai that evening (my main mission was attacking ground targets by night). I felt no pain after landing but my colleagues advised me to go to the hospital. There, my shoulder was X-rayed and showed some torn tissues: the doctor advised me to take leave. I promised him to do so as soon as I arrived at the air force hospital in Cairo. As usual, I didn't. Three days later, we were scrambled and this time I got a pay-back for my shoulder: I managed to shoot down a Phantom over the Nile Delta with one missile.[14]

Nassr Mousa provided the details about the second claim:

> Lieutenant Mohammed Adoub shot one Phantom down with his MiG, but he was so close to the exploding enemy, his MiG was damaged too. The Israeli and Mohammed ejected very close to each other. Farmers almost killed the Israeli pilot but it was Mohammed who saved him and the Israeli was taken to a hospital and rescued. He had a visitor the next day: it was Mohammed Adoub.[15]

The Israelis credited one of their F-4E crews with a confirmed MiG-21: even if, this was certainly a meagre compensation for the confirmed loss of two precious aircraft and four crewmembers, two of whom were killed.[16]

FROG'S IMPACT

In the meantime, the combination of main defeats on the battlefield, and the precise Syrian FROG-strike on Ramat David AB, on 8 and 9 October 1973, prompted the Israeli military intelligence agency AMAN into a complete reversal of its original assessments about the usefulness of Scud missiles delivered to Egypt shortly before the outbreak of that conflict. Indeed, during the night from 12 to 13 October, it reported 'strange movements on the ground' making it 'clear that the Soviets were mobilising and re-deploying Scuds in the region of Port Said'. This caused 'enormous' unrest amongst Israeli military commanders, even more so because the newest

reports had indicated that even the crucial oil refinery of Haifa was within Scud range.[17]

Nevertheless, this unrest should have not been the reason for reinforced Israeli air strikes on Port Said on 12 October, for which the IDF/AF concluded to have 'knocked out all SAM-sites' in the area. According to the Egyptians, the 418th and the 425th Air Defence Battalions were the only such units left, and both operated just one SA-2 site. Indeed, the Egyptians stress that all the Israelis had managed on that day was to knock out two out of its six launchers of the 418th Battalion – in exchange for three additional Egyptian claims. Nevertheless, the IDF/AF was back to bomb the place on 13 October again: two air strikes on the 418th Air Defence Battalion were launched between 0803 hrs and 0805 hrs, and the unit claimed two of the Israelis at shot down. At 0855 hrs, its P-12 radar detected an enemy formation approaching from the north-east and another, at very low altitude, from south-west, over Lake Manzala. Hob el-Din promptly called the CO of the 425th Air Defence Battalion – which was still holding out in the Port Fuad area – to provide cover for his unit, and then ordered his gunners to turn their launchers around and open fire. However, the Israelis came in much too fast: the first A-4 Skyhawk missed its target, but the other two deployed at last six CBUs with devastating effects:

- 1 crewmember was killed and 9 injured;
- the horizontal reflector of the RSNA-75 Fan Song radar was damaged, decreasing its detection range to 25km (13.5nm)
- the radar control cabin for the P-12 was badly damaged
- the cable-connection between the P-12 radar and the UV fire-control station was cut off;
- 3 out of the remaining 4 SM-63 launchers were destroyed;
- a missile loaded on the last SM-63 was damaged, causing a leak of dangerous oxidiser fuel;
- the entire position was full of bomblets that failed to detonate.

The crew scrambled to initiate repairs, and the 418th Battalion was – at least nominally – operational again within 20 minutes: henceforth it had to operate with a greatly diminished capability to localize the target, without the usual cable connection between its early warning radar and the command post, and with only one SM-63 launcher.[18]

Of course, the Israeli attacks went on. At 0925 hrs, an enemy aircraft that approached from the north flying low over the sea was engaged by a single missile, and claimed as shot down. At 1320 hrs, two Israeli aircraft approached from the west, and the battalion launched another missile: a big fireball was observed as the weapon scored a direct hit, apparently destroying the second target, too. Shortly after, additional Israeli aircraft were tracked west of the battalion's position, but the sole remaining launcher suffered a technical malfunction and they could not be engaged. Nevertheless, Hob el-Din ordered his Fan Song crew to mimic the firing of a single missile with their radar: reportedly, after several

Crew of an Egyptian air defence battalion as seen in the process of reloading an SA-2 missile from its PR-11 transporter/loader to the SM-63 launcher. Barely visible in the right upper corner of the photograph is a P-12 early warning radar of the site. (Albert Grandolini Collection)

times rapidly changing his direction, the Israeli pilot eventually ejected over Lake Manzala. Overall, the 418th Battalion claimed five IDF/AF aircraft as shot down that day.

REASONS?

Considering the ferocity of the sustained Israeli attacks on Egyptian air defences in the Port Said area, it might appear that the reasons for this aerial onslaught published by Israeli sources so far are entirely unsupportable. After all, the above-described attacks were flown at a time of great urgency on the Golan Heights, at the time the IDF/AF was stumbling from one blunder into another, and suffering heavy losses. This poses the question: would the top Israeli political and military leaders really order their air force to fly air strikes 'on some unimportant place' for such reasons as 'for testing purposes', or because 'they could'? Were they as arrogant as to gamble with the fate of the entire nation at the time of great peril? Or, were air strikes on the Port Said Area related to AMAN's reporting on the Egyptian Scuds, and run along requests by Moshe Dayan?

Another photograph showing the next phase of the re-loading process. Average re-loading time for most of ADC's SA-2 battalions was down to just five minutes: even this proved insufficient during prolonged Israeli air strikes. Furthermore, the massive launcher with the big missile took time to train around its axis and was thus vulnerable to surprise attacks from unexpected directions. (Albert Grandolini Collection)

Nassr Moussa and his ground crew getting some rest in between two combat sorties underneath a fully armed MiG-21M during the October 1973 War. Notable are the R-3S missile and an underwing fuel tank in the right upper corner of the photo. (Nassr Moussa via Abdallah Emran)

Available Israeli publications indicate a positive answer to the first two questions. Although never involved in operations against Port Said, Iftach Spector, the CO No. 107 Squadron, explained:

The area in question was close to our bases. Its importance was small, and thus it was good to serve the purpose of testing diverse tactics and weaponry. Moreover, the last surviving fortification of the Bar Lev Line, Fort Budapest, was in front of Port Said. It was isolated and in need of support. The commander of the IDF/AF had to react to the demands of the authorities, of the public, requests for help from his comrades, and to his own conscience. He had to do something. That fortress survived the war still under Israeli control. These were all good reasons for attacking Port Said continuously.[19]

However, well before the latest research of Israeli historians was published in that country, Egyptian points of view were entirely different, and supportive for a positive answer to the third question.

Not one of the interviewed Egyptian veterans has ever arrived at the idea of Israeli air strikes on the Port Said area being in connection with Fort Budapest. Instead, none has any doubts about this affair being directly related to the concerns of Israel's political leadership about possible deployment of Egyptian Scuds – *perhaps armed with Soviet-made nuclear weapons* – either in the case that Israel would launch air strikes on 'Egypt's depth', or deploy its own nuclear weapons against Egypt. Unsurprisingly, their understanding is that the destruction of the Egyptian capability to operate Scuds from the Port Said area would have been a 'priority number 1' for the IDF/AF.[20]

The authors consider it perfectly possible that all the 'versions' in question are the truth. Although not providing any kind of official documentation in support of their statements, multiple Israeli sources are – independently from each other – consistent in their reasoning for these attacks. In the light of the fact that the interviewed US intelligence sources never mentioned No. 107 Squadron as of 1973 in connection to Israeli nuclear weapons, nor in relation to Port Said, there is no reason to have doubts about

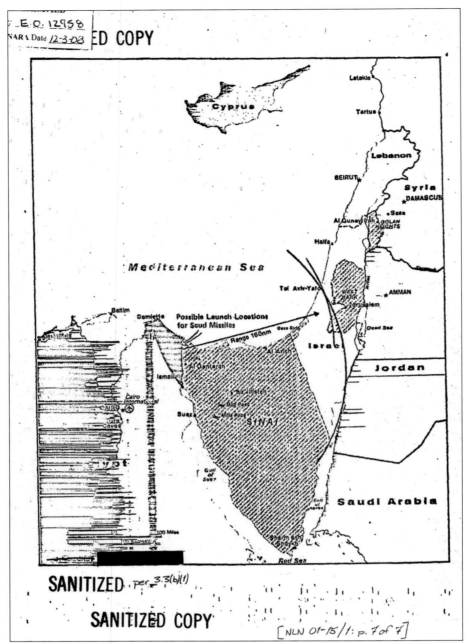

This map from a DIA 'Scud B Study' (prepared in 1974) seems to confirm the Egyptian notion according to which the continuous Israeli air strikes on the Port Said area were motivated by the fact that the same was the 'only point' from which R-17 missiles operated by the 65th Missile Brigade could have reached targets in central Israel. (DIA)

A quartet of MiG-21MFs from No. 46 Squadron (104th Air Brigade) as seen on a post-war parade over Cairo. (Albert Grandolini Collection)

what they say. That said, due to the general rule that the military personnel are provided only the information it 'needs to know', the majority of Israeli veterans are entirely unlikely to know what was going on in the minds of – and between – various of their military and political superiors, foremost Dayan, Elazar, and Peled. Finally, given the above-described Israeli policy of 'nuclear ambiguity', and experiences from such affairs as the fate of Mordechai Vanunu, expecting any other kind of official explanation – especially some that might confirm the Egyptian thesis – is, currently and for the foreseeable future, little more than an illusion.

6

MYTHS OF 14 OCTOBER

By 10 October 1973, the crossing operation of the Suez Canal was completed and the Egyptian Army entered the 'consolidation phase': having achieved the crucial aim of limited war by establishing a firm foothold on the Sinai and repulsing Israeli armoured attacks, it stopped further offensive operations and instead took care to consolidate its positions. Meanwhile, the Israeli counterattack on the Golan Heights reversed the Syrian advance and returned the situation to what it had been before the war. Moreover, on 11 and 12 October, the IDF ran an offensive that brought it to within 40 kilometres (24.9nm) of Damascus. Simultaneously, the IDF/AF subjected the crucial economic installations in Syria to a systematic aerial assault. The Iraqi expeditionary forces began appearing on this battlefield on 12 October, but their mass still required days longer to arrive, while the MiG-21s of the Iraqi Air Force deployed in Syria had the same problem as those flown by the EAF and the SyAAF. Overall, the Syrians proved unable to tackle the Israeli onslaught. In the eyes of political and military leadership in Damascus, the only option left was to demand Egypt to honour its commitment and develop its attack towards the Sinai passes in order to put Israel under pressure and force it to stop advancing.

Much too slowly, Cairo then did launch an offensive – on the morning of 14 October – and ever since this day has been exaggerated as a kind of 'special day' by both Egypt and Israel. More or less in accordance with each other, nearly all sources on both sides maintain that early that morning the Egyptian Army launched a large-scale offensive on the Sinai, aimed at lessening Israeli pressure upon Syria. Not only nearly all of the Israeli sources, but nearly all of the ones released in the English language, maintain that this offensive resulted in the 'biggest tank battle since Kursk in 1943', in which 'thousands of tanks' became involved and the IDF won a clear-cut victory, de-facto destroying the Egyptian armour as result.[1] Egyptian sources usually confirm a 'big tank clash', though adding the aerial 'Battle of el-Mansourah' as another high point, supposedly involving more than 200, perhaps 300, or even 400 combat aircraft from both sides and ending in a major victory for them – even more important because this should have, at least indirectly, 'secured' the Port Said area as a suitable launching point for Scud-attacks on Israel. As so often, a closer look at both of these affairs reveals an entirely different picture.

MYTHICAL EGYPTIAN OFFENSIVE

After crossing the Suez Canal and beating back dozens of minor and then the major Israeli counterattack, on 7 and 8 October 1973, the Egyptian Army entered its 'operational hold' phase of the war: except for some 'creeping advance' by the Third Field Army and frequent artillery barrages, it limited itself to developing positions

on the Sinai reached during the first two days. The longer this stage lasted it became ever more apparent that it was missing the point – because the Israelis did not renew their counterattacks and thus did not continue to suffer as debilitating losses as earlier. Nevertheless, Egyptian president Sadat remained insistent on accepting Soviet, British, and US offers for a mediated cease-fire only on conditions well-known to be 'unacceptable' for Israel: an unconditional withdrawal from all territories occupied during the June 1967 War. Unsurprisingly, although initially showing some interest in an early cease-fire, as the IDF stabilised the situation on both the Sinai and the Golan Heights, the Israeli mood began to change. At this point in time, Damascus began pleading with Cairo to renew the offensive, arguing the obvious: should the Israelis rout the Syrians, they would be free to transfer their forces to the Sinai and rout the Egyptians, too.

Such demands prompted a fierce debate in Cairo, which Sadat proved unable to ignore. On 11 October, he issued the order for the Egyptian Army to launch a new offensive. Unable to withstand Sadat's pressure, Ismail ordered Shazly to attack. Perfectly aware of the low success potential of such an operation, Shazly fiercely opposed the idea. He was not alone: the commander of The Second Field Army, Major-General Sa'ad Ma'moun, even went as far as to offer his resignation rather than carry out Sadat's order.[2]

Officially at least, what happened after that point 'is history': orders were orders and all of the Egyptian commanders eventually had to do what Sadat wanted. Only a closer examination of the Egyptian military documentation subsequently captured by the IDF reveals that Sadat, Ismail, Shazly, Ma'moun and others found a compromise in the form of a 'quasi-offensive', an operation nowhere near as large as usually reported. Indeed, such documents captured by the Israelis as The War Diary of the Third Field Army show no army- and no division-sized attacks, but only the local and half-hearted involvement of single brigades: indeed, instead of deploying two field armies for an all-out attack, as widely reported – by Egypt and by Israel – only a total of five brigades became involved in a very limited attack on more than three Israeli armoured divisions.[3]

Considering the nature of this 'offensive', all the dozens of studies of it published ever since were an entirely futile exercise. Nevertheless, because Tel Aviv was in need of good news about 'easily defeating Arabs at minimal costs', and because it prematurely concluded that the Egyptians failed because Israeli commanders expected them to fail, the Israelis quickly adopted the Egyptian legends about the involved forces, the ferocity of the fighting, and losses. Vice-versa: because Cairo needed publicity about its supposed 'offensive launched to decrease Israeli pressure upon Syria' – to satisfy its own public, and allies in Damascus and elsewhere – it was more than happy to accept the Israeli-launched story of 'the biggest tank battle since Kursk in 1943', and then bolster the resulting legend by adding diverse fabrications. The resulting myth was rapidly circulated to the media on both sides, reaching such proportions that even top Egyptian military commanders and commentators (including Shazly) rushed to adopt the exaggerated number of 250 of their tanks knocked out – as claimed by the Israelis. With the exception of a few little-known sources in Egypt and Israel, both sides have maintained this legend ever since.[4]

Overall, hard facts about the Egyptian offensive of 14 October that have become available in recent years permit only three conclusions: even this half-hearted show-attack was much too costly, and it not only failed to force Israel to switch any of its resources from Golan to Sinai, but foremost emboldened the IDF into a counterattack that ultimately brought Egypt to the verge of a defeat.

Moreover, subsequent reporting about this affair by both sides is a clear illustration of both Egypt and Israel being more than happy to exploit each other's propaganda for their own purposes. Indeed, along with what subsequently happened in relation to further events from 14 October 1973, it is obvious that Cairo went a step further by adding another myth about that day.

'AIR BATTLE OF EL-MANSOURAH'

The affair in question is related to an air strike launched by the IDF/AF during the same afternoon – that of 14 October 1973 – against a major EAF air base in the Nile Delta. Because official and unofficial Egyptian sources claim that the EAF MiG-21 pilots had shot down a large number of Israeli Phantoms during that operation, while the Israelis flatly deny having suffered even one loss, the story has become a matter of massive controversy ever since, and even one or two conspiracy theories.

As usual, the first issue is that of the Israeli reasoning for – and the objective of – the operation in question. Not only the Egyptians, but foremost the Israelis argue that if this was supposed to suppress the EAF's support for the (show-)offensive of the Egyptian ground forces on 14 October, it was launched much too late. If it was undertaken in support of the IDF's ground counteroffensive planned for 15 October, then it was not only flown too early, but also hit the wrong target: el-Mansourah was the home of two MiG-21 units with minimal ground-strike role, while – as described above – the Mirages from Tanta had hardly participated in the war by that point in time. Foremost, the majority of Egyptian publications argue that the objective of this Israeli operation was el-Mansourah because that air base was responsible for the defence of Port Said, for the defence of the 65th Missile Brigade, and with that, for the defence of the sites selected for Scud-attacks on central Israel. On the contrary, the Israelis stress that their actual target was Tanta AB, home-base of the 'Libyan Mirages'. With Cairo subsequently declaring 14 October as the day of the Egyptian Air Force, this affair is presented in the local media in terms that can only be described as fantasy: according to one recently published version, in the course of a '53 minute-long clash, the largest of that kind during the October 1973 War', the EAF shot down 'at least' 15, 17, or 20 enemy aircraft, and that although 'outnumbered', 'at least', '62 to 160', and 'Israel had erased that event from its history'.[5]

Irrespective of their reliability, claims of this kind impose numerous questions, including not only those related to losses on one or the other side, but about Israeli intentions and about the number of their aircraft involved.

THE TARGET AND THE F-4ES INVOLVED

Iftach Spector, the former CO No. 107 Squadron, IDF/AF, leaves no doubts about the aim of the operation in question and units involved:

> The air force ordered an attack on Tanta AB, located in the Nile Delta, roughly half-way between Cairo and the coast of the Mediterranean Sea, and a home-base of one MiG-21 squadron and two Libyan Mirage squadrons. The aim was to suppress their operations, because they looked like our Mirages and thus caused confusion whenever appearing. This operation was to involve three Phantom-squadrons: the task of the No. 201 was to 'open' the way by a diversion against el-Mansourah AB, from where Egyptian interceptors have operated; No. 119 Squadron was to suppress air defences at Tanta, and my unit, No. 107 Squadron, to deliver a direct attack with 12 aircraft. The organisation of this

operation proved exceptionally problematic and its timing was repeatedly postponed: it was only around 1500 in the afternoon that the crews left the briefing-room for their aircraft.[6]

Spector's recollection is supported by reports from US sources with intelligence backgrounds:

> By 14 October 1973, all the Israeli F-4E Phantoms were equipped with new ECM-pods delivered from the USA on board of El Al passenger aircraft converted to serve as transports, starting with the fourth day of the war. The old ECM-pods had proven unreliable. By 12 October it was known that these new systems could at least blind Soviet-made SA-2s and SA-3s, although they couldn't jam newer SA-6s.
>
> The main objective for the air strike on Tanta on 14 October was to put the Egyptian armed forces on the defensive and keep them there. The IDF/AF had maintained overall air superiority over both fronts and shot down many Arab fighter bombers. But, since the start of the war, the Egyptian and Syrian air forces were flying air raids on the front against Israeli forces. These were having little effect on the war but had been causing a surprising number of deaths and injuries. Yes, the 104th Air Brigade at el-Mansourah was also tasked with providing air cover for the Egyptian Army's Scud missile batteries, and the MiG-21s from el-Mansourah also damaged two F-4Es on 7 October (their warheads failed to explode), and shot down two F-4Es on 11 October. But, for the Israelis it was more important to make sure that Mirages from Tanta could not provide close air support for the Egyptian ground forces.
>
> The Israelis knew they couldn't destroy hardened aircraft shelters: they targeted runways, equipment and storage depots nearby instead. Moreover, the sheer vehemence of their air strikes on 14 October took the Egyptians somewhat by surprise, as their generals said everybody was ready to hear that the IDF/AF had been run down, shot down, or damaged beyond repair for the most part.[7]

All the available Israeli sources cite the same composition of formations from the three involved units, as listed in Table 9. Notable is that, contrary to the doctrine developed before the war, the F-4Es in question were to fly this mission entirely on their own, without any backing from combat-support platforms like S-65 helicopters equipped with stand-off jammers, or UAVs of No. 200 Squadron, IDF/AF. Israeli Mirages provided top cover for F-4Es only on the way into the combat zone and on return from the same: lacking ECM-systems that could protect them in high-threat areas, they remained well outside the reach of Egyptian SAMs, already peeling off north of Port Said. While it is possible that the IDF/AF deployed one or two of KC-97 Stratocruisers or Noratlas transports to act as radio relays well north of the Egyptian coast of the Mediterranean Sea, the involved Phantoms were not refuelled in the air, as suggested by some Western sources. Indeed, with the planners hoping to take the Egyptians by surprise, all three F-4E-formations went into the combat zone protected only by ECM-pods installed on individual aircraft. Even then, according to Spector, there were not enough of these for every Phantom. Correspondingly, only 27 F-4Es from three units of the IDF/AF were involved in this operation, and then entirely on their own – which in turn means that it is out of the question that the Egyptian claims for an attack by 100, 160, 200, or even 300 Israeli aircraft might have been based on fake radar picture caused by, for example, diversionary moves of IDF/AF aircraft prior to the attack,

Table 9: Composition and Targets of IDF/AF Units for Strike on Tanta AB, 14 October 1973

Unit	Number of Aircraft	Task and Time on Target
No. 201 Squadron	8 F-4Es	diversionary attack on el-Mansourah AB, 1535
No. 119 Squadron	7 F-4Es	suppression of enemy air defences at Tanta AB, 1540
No. 107 Squadron	12 F-4Es	main strike on Tanta AB, 1545

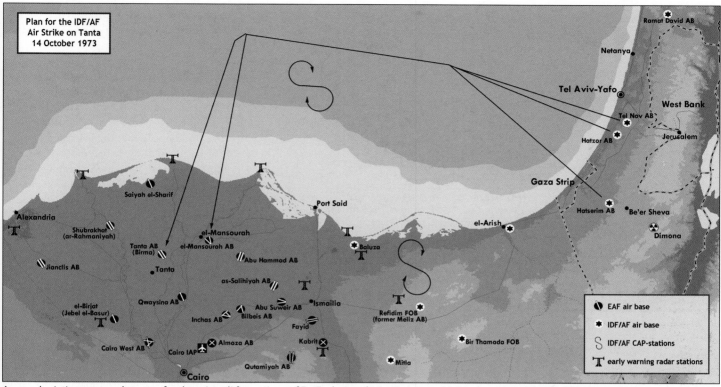

A map depicting approach routes for three Israeli formations of F-4Es during their mission on 14 October 1973. (Map by Tom Cooper)

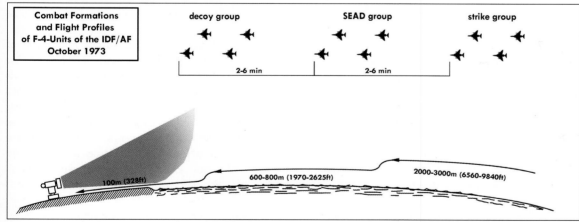

Nearly every single Israeli air strike against targets in the Nile Delta during the first 10 days of the October 1973 War, saw the F-4Es involved approaching operating in three waves, including the decoy group, a group for suppression of enemy air defences (SEAD), and the strike group. The aircraft were usually underway at 2,000-3,000m altitude (6,560-9,840ft) over the Mediterranean Sea, until turning south and then entering a gradual descent to 'below the horizon' of Egyptian radar stations and approaching the combat zone at 100m (328ft) or less altitude. (Diagram by Tom Cooper)

or such electronic countermeasures as deception jamming.

DIVERSIONARY ATTACK ON EL-MANSOURAH

According to the official Egyptian version of the following engagement, it was already around 1515hrs when the visual observation posts along the coast of the Mediterranean Sea notified the ADOC of the ADC that about '20 Phantoms' were coming from the sea and heading towards Port Said:

Air Marshal Hosni Mubarak received the signal and gave orders to General Jamal Abd al-Rahman Nassr, commander of the 104th Fighter Brigade to scramble 16 MiG-21s to create an aerial umbrella only and not to engage the Israeli planes....The Egyptian high command reacted in such a way because of what had been learned from Israeli aerial tactics. Their tactics depended on doing an air attack in three stages:

1) A wave of fighter escort having the job to drag the interceptors away from the target
2) Suppression wave with escort
3) Main attacking force heading straight to the target zone.

55

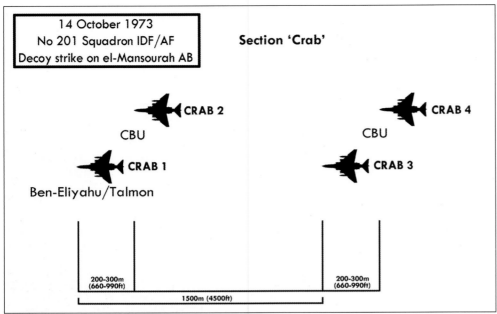

A diagram describing the first flight from No. 201 Squadron to enter the combat zone over the Nile Delta on 14 October 1973, which had the call-sign 'Crab'. The Phantoms from this formation were all armed with CBU-30B/Hs and their task was to divert the attention of Egyptian air defences towards el-Mansourah AB. (Diagram by Tom Cooper)

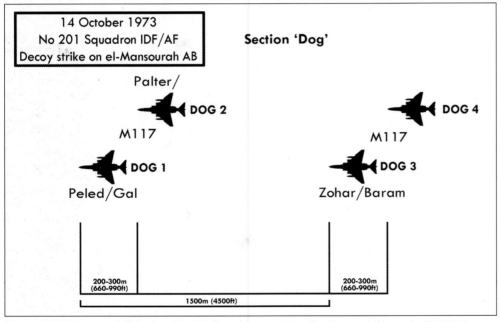

Phantoms of the second flight from No. 201 Squadron – call-sign 'Dog' – were all armed with M117 bombs, and also had the task of bombing el-Mansourah AB. (Diagram by Tom Cooper)

... From this, the Egyptian high command knew that these Israeli Phantoms were just a decoy to drag the air umbrella away to make clear for the main body to attack its target and therefore, orders were given for the MiGs not to intercept. The Phantoms went in circles for some time until retreating towards the Mediterranean Sea.

Around 1530hrs, Egyptian radar signalled a warning that around 60 Phantoms were approaching from different areas such as Baltim, Damietta and Port Said. Then and only then did Air Marshal Hosni Mubarak give the order to intercept...[8]

According to the same version, the ADC's radars and ground observers thus detected no fewer than 116 'Israeli Phantoms' either 'circling off the northern coast' or 'in the process of approaching', between 1515hrs and 1530hrs: none of the aircraft actually crossed

the coast. Therefore, around 1530hrs, the ground control at el-Mansourah granted permission for a flight of MiG-21s that was short on fuel to return to the base and refuel. At that point in time, and – seemingly – 'out of nowhere', the Egyptian sources report the appearance of no less than three incoming Israeli formations, which prompted Mubarak to order the scramble of additional MiG-21s:

...Meanwhile, the air umbrella that was already airborne, around 16 MiG-21s, was ordered to intercept at once the three Israeli formations simultaneously, so that they could be dispersed and easily attacked by the rest of the brigade.... orders were issued for another 16 MiG-21s from the Mansourah air base and another 8 MiG-21s from Tanta air base to scramble....around 15.38hrs, the Egyptian radar signalled that there is another wave, around 16 Phantoms, coming in low from the same previous direction. Orders were given for the last 8 MiG-21s at el-Mansourah to take off and intercept while orders were given to MiG-21s from Abu Hammad air base to intercept too.

Correspondingly, by around 1540hrs, Lieutenant-General Mubarak should have had 64 MiG-21s airborne and underway anywhere between el-Mansourah, Tanta, Abu Hammad and the coast of the Mediterranean Sea. Nevertheless, all the available recollections of involved Egyptian and Israeli pilots are in agreement in one regard: the first Israeli formation – eight F-4Es from No. 201 Squadron – approached el-Mansourah AB entirely undisturbed and attacked as planned. Moreover, it did so right at the moment when at least a flight – probably more – of MiG-21s were about to land, as recalled by Qadri Abd el-Hamid:

We were coming from a combat air patrol and I was short on fuel. A wave of F-4s was coming to strike our base. They used to come and the first two would pull up and drop cluster bombs on us to keep the ack-ack gunners down. Then these F-4s were clean and we got into a severe dogfight right over the base ...

It was a hell of a fight. Wherever I turned I saw a Phantom behind a MiG and MiG behind a Phantom. Eventually, I pulled behind a Phantom and attacked with my gun – at the same time my engine stalled. I tried to restart but it would not, because of a lack of fuel. I had engaged in this combat for three or four minutes, which is a long time. To be frank, I didn't watch because I fired and hit, the Phantom exploded and I had my own problems.... My cannon shells hit the Phantom, and it exploded like the sunlight right over the field near the maintenance shops....I wanted to make a forced landing to save the airplane, but I was crazy. If I had done it, I would have been killed because other Phantoms had hit the runway and it was full of holes. At 50 metres height I ejected. I got compression fracture and was in the hospital for four or five days. Then I went back to the squadron, but I could not fly for the rest of the war.

Abd el-Hamid was not the only one whose recollection deviates from the official Egyptian version. Indeed, Nassr Moussa reported taking off only seconds before the Phantoms released their bombs:

The F-4E serial number 620 from No. 201 Squadron taking off for a combat sortie during the October 1973 War in almost the same configuration as used by all three units involved in attacks on el-Mansourah and Tanta AB on 14 October 1973: loaded with an AN/ALQ-101(V) ECM-pod, a single AIM-9D or AIM-9G Sidewinder air-to-air missile, and eight M117 general-purpose bombs. For strikes against targets in the Nile Delta, the MER with five M117s on the centreline was replaced with a third drop tank. (IDF via Albert Grandolini)

I returned from a CAP around the noon and was preparing for the next one. Around 15.00hrs, the alert was sounded and the order came for 12 aircraft to make 'Red Scramble' – meaning to provide protection for our base. All 12 MiGs launched within the following three minutes. Led by Magdi Kamal, my flight was the last to take off from Number 2 runway, when a Phantom appeared above. No sooner than my and the wheels of Hassan Saqr's MiG have left the runway, there was a tremendous detonation behind us: the enemy missed us but by few metres! While keeping that Phantom in sight, I jettisoned all three drop tanks and made the tightest possible turn. The Phantom refused to fight but fled in full afterburner: I was unable to catch him but determined to try. While my aircraft was still accelerating, I attempted to set my sight on the enemy when the words of Samir Aziz came to my mind: always check your six! I took a look at the rear-view mirror in the periscope above, and saw another Phantom lining up with me! It was a dread moment: I was converted form an attacker into a prey in a matter of seconds. I broke right so hard, I nearly fainted, but I did see a detonation behind me. The enemy missile missed me. The Phantom did not try to follow but acted like the first one and attempted to accelerate away in full afterburner. Accelerating again, I chased him down the full length of our air base, all the time listening to radio messages from our ground controller, Colonel Hassan Khadr, who remained in the control tower during the enemy attack and continued providing advice and warnings. As the Phantom in front of me began to descend, I fired one missile. I expected the Israeli pilot to turn and avoid, but instead he continued on. There was a bright flash and the Phantom began emitting smoke – and then it exploded. In excitement over my victory, I shouted "Allah-u-Akbar, Allah-u-Akbar!" over the radio...

The 'Crab' formation from No. 201 Squadron reached el-Mansourah AB undisturbed by EAF's MiG-21s, and hit the base with multiple bombs, as obvious from this strike camera photo shot during the attack on 14 October 1973. (IDF via Albert Grandolini)

According to Israeli accounts, the Phantoms from No. 201 Squadron engaged in a 'wild fight… on the deck'. The CO of No. 201 Squadron, Eitan Ben Eliyahu, attacked a MiG-21, the pilot of which 'manoeuvred wildly, trying to buy time as his wingman came to his rescue': moments later, Ben Eliyahu's RIO spotted that second MiG behind them. Instead of breaking off, the Israeli squadron commander opened fire with his 20mm cannon and the MiG exploded in flames. With his RIO shouting, 'Break! Break! Ben Eliyahu then turned hard, which the MiG behind him 'could not follow': it spun out of control and crashed. No. 201 Squadron

did not suffer any losses in this attack: instead, it was credited with victories against two MiG-21s.[9]

Whether the Egyptians lost any MiG-21s in this clash remains unknown: at the time of writing, not one related report has ever surfaced. It is possible that the aircraft the Israelis reported as 'crashed' was Abd el-Hamid's. However, contrary to the Israeli version, it was not that it 'could not imitate…the manoeuvre and crashed': Qadri Abd el-Hamid ejected because he ran out of fuel and could not land while the base was under attack.

Indeed, there is no evidence for most of what was claimed about this engagement, regardless of by which side. On the contrary, it is obvious that despite the – supposedly – timely warning, the ADC failed to detect the first ingressing Israeli formation, and that Mubarak was late in scrambling his interceptors and then vectored most of these in the wrong directions, thus depriving them of an opportunity to engage. In turn, this is also confirming the Israelis who stress they did not deploy stand-off jamming in support of this operation, because if they had done that, the Egyptians would have been alerted much earlier, and Mubarak would have reacted by scrambling his interceptors at an earlier point in time. With this, the Egyptian version with the involvement of '160 Israeli aircraft' in this air battle collapses on its own.

Finally, there is no doubt that all eight F-4Es from No. 201 Squadron not only managed to reach el-Mansourah AB, but also bombed their target at the most inconvenient moment for two flights of Egyptian MiG-21s – when one was short on fuel and in the process of landing, and another in the process of rolling for take-off. Nevertheless, there is no evidence that the Egyptians lost more than one MiG-21, and there is no evidence that any of the involved F-4Es was shot down by any of the Egyptian interceptors.

ATTACK ON AIR DEFENCES OF TANTA AB

If the appearance of No. 201 Squadron's F-4Es over el-Mansourah caught Mubarak and the ADC on the wrong foot, the commander of the Egyptian Air Force was certainly determined not to be outdone: as mentioned above, he continued ordering additional MiG-21s into the air all the time between 1535hrs and 1540hrs. Where exactly he sent each formation remains unknown: what is certain is only that at most eight Egyptian interceptors actually engaged the second incoming Israeli formation – that from No. 119 Squadron – and that they did so as this was already close to the actual target for the mission: Tanta AB. The only related Egyptian account of the following engagement was provided by Medhat Arafa, who flew although having his broken shoulder bandaged, and caught up with seven Phantoms as these were engaged in an air combat with between four and eight MiGs directly over this Egyptian air base:

I was with a Readiness Rate I flight of four MiG-21s...and was given the order to take off immediately, at about 15.30hrs. The battle had already started when we arrived two minutes later to see a frightening sight because I've never seen so many airplanes in one area and we were not only dogfighting but also warning other pilots that there is a Phantom on his tail and many pilots were saved.

At least a few of the Israeli fighter-bombers thus managed to bomb air defences of Tanta AB, although they caused next to no damage, as recalled by Okasha:

Very few Phantoms came through and even fewer managed to drop their bombs within the perimeters of el-Mansourah and Tanta. Detonations of their weapons threw plenty of

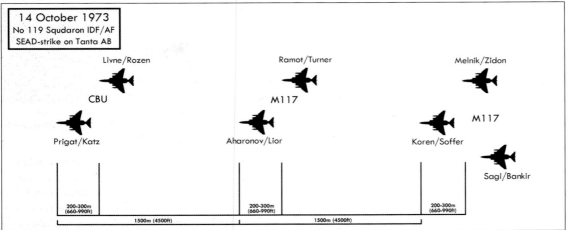

No. 119 Squadron, IDF/AF, deployed 'just' one big formation for the 14 October 1973 strike on Tanta AB: this consisted of seven F-4Es, the leading two of which were armed with CBU-30H/Bs, and the rest with M117s. Their task was SEAD. (Diagram by Tom Cooper)

One from a series of photographs showing F-4Es from No. 119 Squadron, famous for being taken while they were overflying the city of Jerusalem. Notable are aircraft with serials 114 (foreground) and 132 (right lower corner), but also their excellent camouflage: this made them hard to visually acquire for Egyptian MiG-21 pilots, during the afternoon of 14 October 1973. (IDF via Albert Grandolini)

sand on our runways but that was ineffective and both bases remained operational.

Ahmed Yusuf el-Wakeel who served with No. 42 Squadron did not fly on that day, but monitored the developing action from the ground. He recalled seeing a Phantom, 'crashing closely outside the base perimeter'. From the Egyptian standpoint, after that one Phantom was shot down, the rest of the engagements with retreating Israelis remained fruitless, and the EAF suffered no losses at all. For comparison, the Israelis denied any losses while a crew from No. 119 Squadron was credited with a kill for a MiG-21 that 'crashed while breaking hard to evade'.[10]

BUFFETS AND BEDS

The third Israeli formation consisted of 12 F-4Es from No. 107 Squadron – six in the formation with call-sign 'Buffet', and six in the formation with call-sign 'Bed' – all tasked with bombing Tanta AB. Each aircraft was armed with five M-117s, 2 AIM-7s and a single AIM-9D, and carried three drop tanks. In the lead was the CO of No. 107 Squadron, Iftach Spector. The original plan called for his formation to follow those of No. 201 and No. 119 Squadrons by flying well to the north and west over the Mediterranean Sea before turning south and striking its target from north-western direction. However, after hearing on the radio about multiple air combats ahead of him, Spector ordered his crews to 'cut the corner': turn south earlier than planned, engage afterburners and accelerate to a speed at which no MiG-21s could follow them at low altitude. Naftaly Maimon flew as Bed 2:

It was afternoon and we flew west into the haze, visibility was not good. We planned to outflank Tanta and to arrive from northwest but our squadron attack tactic was to fly really fast with afterburners, and pull-up really high. Fast as we were no one could intercept us, but there wasn't enough fuel to fly like this to Tanta along the route planned for us. We rounded corners: we didn't outflank but we turned south much earlier than planned, to arrive at Tanta from the northeast or almost north.

Two results of Spector's decision were unavoidable: his formation first ran into Phantoms from No. 119 Squadron returning from their attack on Tanta, and narrowly avoided several frontal collisions as a result, but also passed much too close by el-Mansourah over which dozens of MiG-21s were meanwhile airborne.[11]

Before long, several Egyptians were at deep six of the ingressing Phantoms and at least two fired R-3S missiles. Maimon continued:

While Mubarak – and thus the ADC – was late in detecting the first incoming Israeli air strike of 14 October, over the following minutes they scrambled more than 60 MiG-21s in the skies over el-Mansourah. This post-war photograph shows a pair of MiG-21PFMs (foreground) and a pair of MiG-21PFS from No. 44 Squadron of the 104th Air Brigade. (Albert Grandolini Collection)

This pre-war photograph shows a quartet of MiG-21F-13s (including the serial number 5843, third from the camera) from the Inchas-based No. 26 Squadron. Pilots from this unit rushed to aid the defenders of el-Mansourah AB, but arrived much too late to take part in action. (Gallal el-Bassel Bassily Collection)

The MiGs appeared just as we crossed the coastline, but we didn't see them yet. Spector was really aggressive in his briefing. He stated that a crew who would not bomb would face court martial! I took him very seriously and so did others: thus we simply pressed on although having MiGs on our tails and shooting. Luckily, no one was hit but it was a narrow escape. Then pilots began to ask for permission to break.

Threat of jail or none, under pressure from an ever larger number of aggressively-flown MiGs, one by one, Phantom-crews were left without a choice but to jettison their bombs and turn to avoid or engage, as recalled by Wakeel:

… we intercepted six Phantoms, so we split into two sections of two planes each and attacked the enemy. The Phantoms had to drop their bomb-loads to be able to dogfight with us. I hit one Phantom with my cannon because he was too close for me to use my missiles. There were two parachutes.[12]

Amir Nahumi, who flew as Number 5 in the Buffet formation, was one of the pilots forced to jettison his bombs and drop tanks:

We were intercepted by two MiG-21s, one of them chased Most and the other chased me. We had to break and I decided to go after the MiG that chased Most. I launched an AIM-9D from a range of 1,200 metres, the AAM hit, the Egyptian pilot ejected and we passed very close to his parachute.

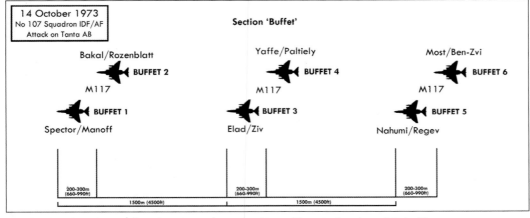

No. 107 Squadron, IDF/AF, flew the main strike against Tanta AB on 14 October 1973. Its Phantoms were organized into two flights: the six aircraft with call-signs 'Buffet-1' through 'Buffet-6' were in front. Each F-4E was armed with 10 M117s, one AIM-9D, two AIM-7E-2s, but not all carried ECM-pods. (Diagram by Tom Cooper)

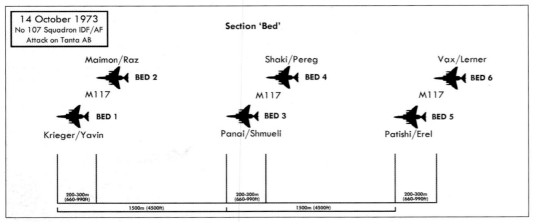

The rearmost formation of the 14 October 1973 Israeli air strike on Tanta AB consisted of six F-4Es from No. 107 Squadron, with call-sign 'Bed'. All were armed like the 'Buffet'-section, which is with 10 M117s and air-to-air missiles. Their objective was to bomb the runways of the crucial Egyptian air base. (Diagram by Tom Cooper)

Bits and pieces of recollections by various Egyptian participants indicate that the Egyptians who intercepted the Phantoms from No. 107 Squadron flew MiG-21MFs from Hassan Khadr's No. 44 Squadron. The fact that this unit flew this advanced variant – the only one capable of keeping up with low and fast-flying F-4Es – might be the reason why they managed to intercept at all. According to unofficial Egyptian sources, MiG-21s from No. 44 Squadron should have claimed two aerial victories in the course of this engagement. However, while the Israeli accounts leave no doubt that the F-4E crews from No. 107 Squadron found themselves subjected to sustained attacks well before reaching their target, they also stress that not one Phantom was shot down. On the contrary, according to the Israelis, it was their pilots that scored a series of victories. Watching the situation around him unfold, Maimon concluded:

It was like an onion: pair after pair the six Phantoms ahead of us and the four Phantoms trailing behind us broke to engage the MiGs. It was crystal clear to me that we alone were pressing towards Tanta and that every minute we flew onwards was actually worth two minutes, as we would have to return the same way too.

We flew very low and the windshield was covered with insects. Visibility became poorer and poorer. I kept on looking for the MiGs but I didn't dare looking behind as we flew that low. Then I saw a MiG. I could judge by his behaviour that he saw us and that he was targeting Krieger. I shouted "break" using the wrong call sign but Krieger understood and broke. I pushed the "panic"

button to jettison everything to clean the aircraft. I then heard a boom and the aircraft started to skid, behaving in an abnormal fashion. For a moment, I thought that we were hit, only after we landed I realized that when I pushed the "panic" button only the external stores under the left wing were jettisoned. The external stores hanging below the right wing were not jettisoned and from that moment on I was flying an asymmetrical aircraft that I thought was damaged.

Shortly after, another MiG appeared behind Krieger's Phantom and in front of Maimon: easing his throttles in order to avoid overshooting his target, the pilot of Bed 2 pressed the trigger but nothing happened: within the following seconds, and while trying to maintain his favourable position behind the MiG, Maimon went through all the 14 safety switches on his armament control panel, re-selecting them one after the other – then he pressed the trigger again. The AIM-9D jumped off its rail and went straight for the MiG, reportedly scoring a direct hit.

With this, the ingress of the last two Phantoms still loaded with bombs was spoiled: free of their load, both turned around and accelerated. Not waiting to see what was going on behind him, Krieger retreated at Mach 1.1, with Maimon following him at Mach 0.9 – the highest speed his aircraft could make with drop tanks and bombs still attached to his right wing. Moments later, another MiG appeared. Once again, the Egyptian attacked Krieger in front, thus exposing himself to a counterattack from Maimon. Ignoring the two Sparrows still in the rear under-fuselage wells of his Phantom, the Israeli selected 'gun':

…I had to use the cannon: the teamwork with my navigator was far from perfect so we didn't lock on the radar and there was no range or firing solution to feed the sight. When no radar lock on was achieved the sight was set to 300 metres and I estimated the range at 700 to 800 metres. I opened fire, a short burst but it was crystal clear to me that I would hit him. Only when I was right behind him, when no deflection was needed except for a compensation for the effect of gravitation, I placed the pipper slightly above the MiG and squeezed the trigger. I knew my aim was good so I gave him a really long burst but even for the cannon rounds it took about a second to cover 800 metres. For a moment nothing happened and then the rounds hit the MiG. It didn't explode in a fire-ball but it simply stopped flying in a high-g pitch-up. I noticed a parachute and there were reports that the pilot ejected…

According to Spector, several pieces that broke when the MiG

While taken later during the conflict in 1973, this photograph of the F-4E serial number 172 from No. 107 Squadron shows a very similar weapons configuration to that carried by Phantoms of the formation with call-sign 'Bed': an AN/ALQ-71(V)-1 ECM-pod, one AIM-9D or AIM-9G Sidewinder, and up to 11 M117 general purpose bombs. During the mission against Tanta, on 14 October, the five M117s under the centreline were replaced by a drop tank. (IDF via Albert Grandolini)

was hit, hit Maimon's jet as this flashed by. However, whether any Egyptian pilot was really forced to eject in this air combat remains unclear: no recollection either confirming an ejection or the death or injury of any Egyptian pilot in an air combat of this kind – and thus the victory for the Israeli F-4E pilot – or confirming a safe return of any MiG-21 – is available. What is certain is that all 12 Phantoms from No. 107 Squadron failed to reach their target. Instead, they fought a series of frantic air combats in the course of which their pilots claimed no fewer than six MiG-21s as shot down. Indeed, the last three of these should have taken place as the Egyptians pursued the retreating Israelis all the way to the Mediterranean Sea – and then under circumstances indicating that several of the IDF/AF crews were lucky that the Soviet-made R-3S missiles were as poorly manufactured as they were. Nahumi recalled:

Nassr Moussa inside the cockpit of a MiG-21MF from No. 46 Squadron, decorated with a stylized 'Vulture of the Goddess Nekhbet' (for details on this aircraft, see the Colour Section). Moussa flew three sorties on 14 October 1973, and was officially credited with one aerial victory against an Israeli Phantom. (Nassr Moussa collection)

We already crossed the coast flying at 15,000ft over the sea when suddenly I saw a shadow overtaking me. It was an AAM that for whatever reason passed very close to us but didn't explode. Right behind the AAM came the MiG-21 that launched it. My fuel state was terribly low but I had to engage him in a 1v1 combat. I broke hard and pulled up so he overtook me at a very close distance, perhaps 50 metres, and I could see the pilot in the cockpit looking at me. He climbed about 3,000 or 4,000 feet above us and he was very aggressive: he rolled over to re-attack me so I pulled a ruse. At 200 knots I dropped my nose (as through I lost all of my energy) and as he waited for that moment he came in. The moment he came in, I lifted my nose abruptly. That surprised him, he overtook me and it was my moment to attack. I opened fire with my cannon, a long burst. I expended all my cannon rounds in that burst. He didn't explode but he lost all of his energy so I overtook him and then I had to concentrate on our very own recovery (from the dive). We recovered very close to the water surface and then we looked back and we saw a huge splash. The MiG crashed.

No such Egyptian loss is known. The only available recollection related to this part of the battle was provided by Nassr Moussa:

I followed another Phantom and opened fire with my 23mm cannon. He avoided with hard manoeuvres but by that time we were already over the Mediterranean Sea and I was out of fuel. I disengaged and returned to el-Mansourah, landing into an excited crowd and a warm welcome from the base commander. My ground crew congratulated and then painted a white star on my plane to indicate a Phantom kill.... Later that evening, we received greetings and appreciation from President Sadat. Everybody was congratulating us for success in defence of our airspace.

Meanwhile, additional MiG-21s were approaching the combat zone after being scrambled from air bases much too distant to arrive on time. Reda el-Iraqi led a flight of four MiG-21F-13s from the Inchas-based detachment of No. 26 Squadron:

As so often, we arrived too late to take part in this battle, and thus only CAP-ed overhead while locally-based units were refuelling...

Medhat Arafa confirmed:

I landed when my fuel became low and took off again and joined the chase with other MiGs when the Israelis were retreating towards the east.

NO RESPITE

The retreating Phantoms of No. 107 Squadron were still entangled with MiG-21s, when the final drama of this afternoon unfolded, as recalled by Spector:

... already over the Mediterranean and right after the second air battle with MiGs, my own Number 2 was shot down by a Mirage. The crew bailed out over the Mediterranean Sea and was rescued. They returned to fly and fight a day later.

Worse yet: while one of the Mirages from No. 144 Squadron, IDF/AF shot down the F-4E with the call-sign Buffet 2, another went for the Phantom with call-sign Bed 6 and fired at last one missile. Only a timely radio warning ordering the crew to break prevented the downing of the second Phantom: the crew of the same became convinced it was attacked by one of the 'Libyan Mirages', in turn adding weight to the Israeli explanation according to which the aim of the entire attack on Tanta was to suppress operations of the No. 69 Squadron. Spector explained:

The reason was a mistaken identification by our Mirage-pilots: it was late afternoon, and the light was bad. We were entangled with MiGs over there, they joined the battle, weren't careful enough and... well, such things happen at war.

Ironically, because they had followed this action with their radars, the Egyptians saw their success as confirmed by the Israeli confusion, as explained by Nabil Shuwakry:

They denied to have lost any Skyhawks to our MiGs in earlier attacks but then took them off airfield attacks. One of the captured Israelis told us their commanders finally decided the losses were too great for the results. Another told us about bad morale and unrest amongst their pilots, about them disobeying orders and jettisoning bombs rather than facing our air defences. We had already noticed that their bombing accuracy was even poorer than during the War of Attrition. Therefore, our primary aim became to force Phantoms to jettison their bomb loads: without bombs, they could not damage our bases or hit our aircraft on the ground. Then they began jettisoning not only their bombs but also their bomb racks on sighting us [airborne MiGs, authors' note]: that was no professional conduct but a sign of panic. By 14 October, they were so confused they shot down several of their own aircraft over Port Said too.

CONSPIRACY THEORIES

At least one of the published Israeli sources about this mission indicates that the entire attack on Tanta AB was a 'huge ruse', intended to provide Egyptians with a mix of correct and wrong information in the case that some of the involved aircrews were shot down, captured and interrogated.[13] Iftach Spector confirmed something of this kind:

Indeed, before that mission, I was ordered to tell my pilots some specific pieces of untrue information – and have them believe it – so that if any of us gets shot down, captured, and interrogated, these stories might be extracted from him. I was told that nobody wanted us to get shot down and this was "just in case": I am not aware of where this idea came from, nor if the same order was issued to other squadrons.

Upon receiving that order, it looked to me as quite a crooked idea, and I hated it. But, the time was too short to argue. I obeyed and provided that information to my crews during the pre-flight briefing. Of course, I lied to them, I couldn't disclose to them why. During that specific briefing, I fed them that information together with "general information on the war".

According to the version about a 'huge ruse', the reason why the Mirages from No. 144 Squadron then attacked the returning Phantoms, shot down one and narrowly missed the other was that this was the final attempt to get at least one of the involved F-4E crews captured by the Egyptians. However, Spector left no doubts about actual circumstances:

...During the post-mission briefing, and lo and behold, I realized that nobody (except for me) could recall a word of my lies. In the many technicalities briefed before that mission they simply didn't listen to my blah-blah. It was "out of context", unnecessary information. Thus, even if any of them would have been shot down and captured, the lie would have been lost on him. A lesson in itself...Moreover, there is no connection whatsoever between that stupid lie I had to tell my pilots before the mission, and this accident. The Mirage-pilot certainly wasn't shooting at brothers: nobody would have obeyed such an order – the issuer of which would, most likely, be jailed on the spot. Such stories are conspiracy theories, and rather stupid ones.[14]

BEAN COUNTING

For all practical purpose, the Israeli air strike on Tanta AB from 14 October 1973 was a failure: although the official history of the IDF/AF stated that the base was, 'closed for 24 hours', this was incorrect: no damage at all was inflicted and aerial activity continued all the time. Indeed, even the – much more successful – diversionary strike on el-Mansourah was a failure: combat activity resumed shortly after the attack. Certainly enough, the involved Israeli Phantom-crews were quite satisfied with their performance. The usual cross-examination of their gun-camera films and intelligence about activities of Egyptian interceptors – most of which was based on comparing the number of those that were scrambled from specific air bases, with the number of those that returned to the same bases – the IDF/AF credited the Phantom-crews involved with nine 'confirmed' kills. Maimon was highly decorated for downing two MiGs while flying a Phantom asymmetrically loaded.[15]

Whether the Israeli figures are strictly accurate, remains unknown. Because not all of the involved F-4Es were equipped with gun-cameras, because gun-camera films are not considered 'ultimate proof' of an aerial victory (numerous cases from other engagements are known where MiGs declared and 'confirmed as shot down' landed safely and were subsequently repaired), the IDF/AF is unlikely to ever be able to provide definite proof for every single kill credited to its crews.

Ironically, on the Egyptian side the number of 'confirmed' aerial victories was 'clear' well before all the claims could ever be cross-examined – indeed, even before all of the involved pilots were able

On 14 October 1973, MiG-21s from 102nd and 104th Air Brigades managed to force nearly all of the F-4Es from No. 119 and No. 107 Squadrons to jettison their bombs before reaching Tanta AB. This was a success even veteran Israeli pilots grudgingly admit. US sources credit the Egyptians with scoring a number of hits with their cannons and R-3S-missiles. However, there is no evidence for even a single Israeli F-4E being shot down over the Nile Delta that day. This pair of MiG-21Ms (serials 8214 and 8444) from 104th Air Brigade's No. 42 Squadron was photographed after the October 1973 War. (Albert Grandolini Collection)

to land! Reda el-Iraqi explained:

> [While CAP-ing el-Mansourah immediately after the battle]...on the wireless we could hear first reports about that clash: over 160 Israeli aircraft came in, 17 were shot down while we've lost seven planes of which four or five actually ran out of fuel. El-Mansourah remained operational. We were overjoyed by this success.

At 2200hrs that evening, Radio Cairo broadcast 'Communiqué Number 39', announcing 'several air battles' that day and '15 enemy aircraft' shot down by Egyptian fighters for the loss of three of their own. Supposedly, following a more detailed analysis after the war, the EAF returned to the original figure of 17 Israeli aircraft confirmed as shot down for the loss of six MiGs. Two of the latter crashed because they ran out of fuel, and one blew up after flying through the debris of an exploding Phantom which it had just shot down. Two EAF pilots were killed (their names remain unknown), while others ejected safely.[16]

With hindsight, it is clear that the Egyptian figures are vastly exaggerated. Moreover, it is meanwhile certain that nothing of any possible evidence is ever going to be released: according to a well-positioned source in Cairo, the entire EAF documentation about the 'Air Battle of el-Mansourah' was destroyed by accident, 'several years ago'.[17] Participant recollections are thus all that is left, and in this regards the conclusion is that although at least two F-4Es were claimed as shot down directly or at least very close to over el-Mansourah AB, and although even some US sources cite numerous Israeli Phantoms as hit and damaged during this action, until the time of writing all the available Egyptian sources remain unable to provide authentic and undisputable evidence for their claims.[18]

WHY THE 'AIR BATTLE OF EL-MANSOURAH'?

After all that is known about the Israeli attack on Tanta AB from the afternoon of 14 October has been presented, one issue remains open: why have the Egyptians subsequently styled this affair into the 'Air Battle of el-Mansourah'?

Some of the exaggerations by both sides are understandable: visibility over the Nile Delta was rather poor that afternoon. With pilots under immense combat stress – pulling g-s while flying at high speed and low altitude through haze and around obstacles, with their windshields covered in insects, while being fired upon not only by enemy jets but Egyptian flak too – plenty of what they think they had seen was not what it seemed to be. However, exactly why Cairo decided to style this affair into an 'Air Battle of el-Mansourah' is much harder to explain: it becomes obvious only once a closer look is taken at events from November 1973, when president Sadat began distributing rewards (and punishments, in cases like that of Shazly) to the Egyptian military commanders responsible. Amongst others, he appointed Hosni Mubarak as his Vice President. It is unlikely that this happened without quite a dose of political manoeuvring in the background, and it is unlikely that Sadat's decision took Mubarak by surprise. On the contrary, it is more likely that the commander of the EAF was well-aware of his prospects for climbing to the top levels of political power already before the October 1973 Arab-Israeli War. With other top Egyptian military commanders being able to show the success of the crossing operation and beating back all of the Israeli counterattacks, Mubarak was in need of a similar major success – even more so because he had actually botched up at least one operation at the start of the war, resulting in catastrophic losses of EAF helicopter squadrons and army commandos, and a large-scale failure of most of the subsequent commando raids behind the Israeli lines.[19]

Therefore, it is apparent that when his pilots claimed 17 kills over el-Mansourah and Tanta, Mubarak – whom the official EAF version of events in question is personally crediting as commanding this battle – grabbed the opportunity. Beloved and acknowledged within the EAF for his skills as an administrator, caretaker, organizer and motivator, and in control of a highly centralized force, he certainly experienced no problems when deciding to ignore the need for in-depth studies of what happened on that afternoon and instead launched the legend of the 'Air Battle of el-Mansourah'. Henceforth, 14 October was declared as the 'Day of the Air Force' in commemoration of a supposed success without any further cross-examination, and in honour of not only the EAF, but also the man who was to dominate the political scene and rule Egypt from 1981 until 2011.

7
SECOND NUCLEAR ALERT

Irrespective of the outcome of the IDF/AF's air strike on Tanta AB from the afternoon of 14 October, by the following morning it was clear that the Israeli armed forces had shifted their attention from Syria to Egypt. Indeed, by the end of 15 October, the IDF was on an all-out offensive against Egyptian positions on the Sinai, which would result in the counter-crossing of the Suez Canal, followed by a drive deep into the rear of The Third Field Army. Nevertheless, and although by that time nothing changed with regards to Egyptian positions and capabilities – or precisely because of that – the IDF/AF was then not only ordered to repeat the air strike on Tanta AB, but also to deliver the final blow against the defenders of the skies over the Port Said area.

FINAL STRIKE ON TANTA AB

Early on the morning of 15 October, a detachment of eight MiG-21MFs from No. 42 Squadron forward deployed at Luxor IAP, was ordered to re-deploy to Tanta AB. The decision of the EAF headquarters proved correct, because hardly had the aircraft in question reached their destination, when the IDF/AF hit once again.[1]

Concluding that the attempt on the afternoon of 14 October was unsuccessful, the Israeli air force decided to re-attack Tanta, and this time in a different fashion: all of the 28 F-4Es involved (for their break-down, see Table 10) were to target this base only. The only change in the plan was the addition of two flights of F-4Es well to the north of the combat zone, over the Mediterranean Sea: their task was to 'de-louse' egressing formations. Furthermore, the first pair of Phantoms to enter the target zone – tasked with the suppression of enemy air defences – was to provide cover for others once it was free of bombs. Finally, the primary formations of all involved units were decreased in size to flights of four aircraft, because earlier experiences had shown that these are easier to manage.[2]

Such adaptations proved perfect enough, because although taking place only at noon, and although anticipated by the ADC, the new Israeli attempt caught the Egyptians by surprise – once again. Indeed, approaching at the usual speed of 600 knots, the leading flight from No. 119 Squadron bombed as planned, even though without the intended results. On the contrary: the flight arriving right behind it was engaged by a volley of three SA-3s. According to the Israelis, one of these damaged one Phantom, while another was hit as it was climbing for a toss-attack, forcing the crew to eject. According to the Egyptians, this happened just around the time that the first of several MiG-21 flights finally converged on Tanta and Nassr Moussa claimed a Phantom shot down by two R-3S missiles: Moussa could not recall seeing any SAMs in the sky at all.[3]

The number of MiG-21s airborne over Tanta further increased by the time the next Israeli formations – two flights from No. 201 Squadron – arrived. Engaging their enemy in dogfights, the Egyptians managed to spoil this attack, but, according to the Israelis lost one MiG-21 in return. Together with other pilots from No. 69 Squadron, Magddin Rifaat witnessed the action from the village of Mahhallat Marhum, about one kilometre outside Tanta AB:

Alarm sirens sounded and Reza Saqr led four MiG-21s into a scramble from the other side of the runway. As far as I recall, the other four MiG-21s took off only seconds before the enemy attack. The first flight of MiGs engaged as the first Phantom began to drop its bombs, and a fierce air combat ensued. I saw Reza Saqr's jet firing its guns on one of the Israelis until he lost control of his aircraft and ejected: the Phantom crashed right next to our air defence batteries. Another aircraft crashed near the road to Birma, throwing up a big plume of mud. Then I saw two parachutes: right away, it was clear that at least one of them was an Israeli.'

Ahmed Yusuf Ahmed al-Wakeel flew one of four MiG-21s that scrambled early:

On take-off, my flight was directed towards el-Mansourah to intercept incoming enemy bombers. We barely exited the perimeter, when the ground control ordered us to turn around and engage the enemy directly over Tanta! We arrived just in time to see a series of detonations on the ground, and then the four Phantoms that caused them. Our formation split and each went after one Phantom. I engaged one in front of me and followed him into a break. I got really close and fired with my cannon, hitting his tail and fuselage, but the Phantom continued to fly and take shots as if nothing happened. Then I felt two hits in the rear of my plane, my cabin started filling with smoke and I smelled fuel through my oxygen mask. When I took a look into my rear-view mirror, I could not see the rear of my aircraft because it was aflame. I ejected and landed safely near Tanta.

While this creates the impression of the SA-3s and then MiG-21s engaging and shooting down multiple Phantoms, the Israelis insist that by this point in time, only one of their aircraft was lost, and another damaged. On the contrary, Asher Snir shot down the MiG-21 flown by Wakeel. Indeed, Spector recalled that No. 107 Squadron – the third formation to reach the target – encountered no resistance at all:

Unlike what happened on the 14th, [the attack on] Tanta of the 15th worked for No. 107 Squadron like greased lightning: cool and nice. We bombed our targets (mine was a group of hangars), with no opposition, and egressed nicely and organized.

On our northbound exit, I saw a MiG behind Elad, one of my wingmen. It was so close I did not fire out of fear I might hit a friendly aircraft. But, shortly after, the MiG separated enough for me to open fire: it broke very hard up and disappeared. I did not try to re-attack: just passed underneath and continued towards north. I did not claim a kill, but after the war, our intelligence reported that this MiG subsequently crashed.

Rifaat continued his recollection:

Together with two officers of the military police and Lieutenant Sherif Shafei, I jumped into a jeep and we rushed to the scene. Military policemen were armed with sub machine guns, we with pistols. We followed the landing of the two parachutes: the Israeli pilot landed in a garden near Mahhallat Marhum, while the Egyptian landed in the town of Shubra el-Namla. I decided to rescue the Egyptian pilot first and we rushed there at mad speed, until we found him amidst a large crowd of local farmers. The pilot was Captain Hany Issa: he was white with blond hair

Table 10: Composition of IDF/AF's Units for Strike on Tanta AB, 15 October 1973

Unit	Number of Aircraft	Task
No. 119 Squadron	12 F-4Es	suppression of enemy air defences at Tanta AB & top cover
No. 201 Squadron	8 F-4Es	main strike on Tanta AB
No. 107 Squadron	8 F-4Es	main strike on Tanta AB

A pair of Egyptian V-601 missiles of a Neva/Pechora SAM-system (better known by its ASCC/NATO-codename as SA-3 Goa) as carried on a PR-14AM truck. According to the latest Israeli publications, it was one of such missiles fired by the defences of Tanta AB that scored the first – and only – kill against any of the Phantoms involved in air strikes on that air base on 14 and 15 October 1973. (Tom Cooper Collection)

and blue eyes. They grabbed and beat him, took off his shoes and hung him in a tree. Everybody was convinced he was an Israeli and they were about to lynch him when we arrived. My group and me fired several shots in the air to disperse the mob, and then managed to get to Hany. Then we decided to find the Israeli pilot… We entered the garden where he had landed and cautiously got out of the car. Some farmers were still around and I asked them if a pilot landed there. One answered, full of pride, "Yes Sir, and we have arrested and finished him off with an axe!" I asked why, and another replied, "But Sir, he took out his gun and shot at us hitting a child. So I tricked him and came from behind, hit him with my axe and he died instantly!" I sarcastically replied, "Brilliant, brother: he would have been useful as a prisoner of war! Where is he now?" They pointed us towards a heap of food bags: the sight was scary and disgusting. The biggest piece of the smashed body was the size of a kebab. I left the two military police officers behind, to guard the remnants of the Israeli until the arrival of our military intelligence, and returned with Hany to the base hospital.

The only pilot definitely confirmed to have been shot down in air

combat by that point in time, al-Wakeel, passed through Mahhallat Marhum shortly after:

On my landing with a parachute, I ran into a group of our air defence soldiers. They took me to the military zone in Kfar el-Sheikh, and then with a car back to Tanta. Underway there we were stopped by military police. I jumped out of the car and inquired what is going on. They told me that a Phantom was shot down and the crew ejected: the navigator died, but the pilot was alive. I went to the pilot and shook his hand. He was showing clear signs of extreme fear and fatigue: I spoke to him in English very quietly until he was assured that he will be OK. Then I left him and returned to Tanta.

The 'pilot' murdered by farmers of Mahhallat Marhum seems to have been Rachamim Sofer, the radar intercept officer (or 'weapons system officer', in USAF jargon) of the F-4E piloted by Yigal Livneh, shot down at the start of this attack (Livneh is known to have been captured alive and subsequently returned to Israel in an exchange of prisoners of war). If so, then Rifaat's and Wakeel's recollections are related to the only Phantom the Israelis admit as

קרב אויר ליד שדה התעופה טנטא

מיג-21

טיס צונח

The strike camera on Asher Snir's F-4E caught this dramatic scene over Tanta AB, as Wakeel's MiG-21 went down in flames. (Iftach Spector Collection)

lost during operations against the Tanta AB, on 14 and 15 October 1973. In turn, the IDF/AF credited its F-4E crews with two MiGs as shot down over Tanta on 15 October, while denying any losses to EAF MiG-21s.[4]

Indeed, Tanta was badly hit this time, even if the damage to the heavily fortified base remained limited, as recalled by Rifaat:

The enemy hit Tanta with between 100 and 130 bombs of different weight (later on, we counted all the craters with help of

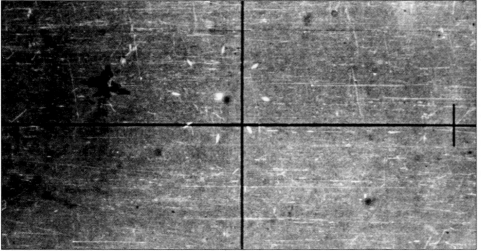

This is one of several stills from an Egyptian gun-camera film often associated with the 'Air Battle of el-Mansourah'. Actually showing a shot that went high and to the right of a Phantom still carrying at least the two underwing droptanks, precise date and circumstances of the taking of this photograph remain unknown. (David Nicolle Collection)

reconnaissance photographs shot by one of our Mirage 5DRs). A 1,000lbs bomb scored a direct hit on the Bunker 4 as Captain Galal Abdul Wahab Hafez was inside, sitting in the cockpit of his MiG-21. The bomb went through three metres of reinforced concrete, punching a hole one metre wide, but caused no other damage. Not one of the other bombs hit the runways, even though they fell quite close to it and the taxiways, covering all of them with lots of clay debris. Many additional bombs landed in the nearby agricultural areas, without detonating. To our amazement, except for few air defence gunners hit by the debris of the Phantom that crashed next to them, nobody was wounded: Galal Abdel Wahhab and his ground crew were all evacuated and sent to the base hospital, but none was injured.

Our base engineers quickly surveyed the runways before restoring them to operational status by the last light. The wounded were evacuated to the military hospital in Tanta. That said, the base remained full of bombs that failed to detonate. Although all were removed from the proximity of the runway, they continued causing lots of trouble as they detonated randomly through the night. One of the bombs went off just 80 metres away from me, as I was inspecting the bunkers with our Mirages inside, that evening: it killed one of our NCOs, Hussein, and damaged the car I used to drive around the base…Eventually, we were forced to evacuate all the remaining personnel from that area…. The base was back to operational status by the following morning.

MISSILE GAMES

Through all of this time, the IDF/AF also continued pounding Port Said. As of 15 October, Hob el-Din's 418th Air Defence Battalion was still fighting back with its last operational SM-63-launcher:

We used smoke generators to cover our position. Moreover, we used our last remaining launcher and our well-camouflaged Fan Song radar to fake electronic missile launches: we would acquire a target with the radar and switch its working mode to the one for guiding missiles, thus simulating a launch. This repeatedly deceived the Israelis, forcing them into evasive manoeuvres. We would wait for them to approach to the optimum range of 14-16km (7.5-8.6nm) before actually firing a missile. Repeated losses made them overcautious: whenever our radar powered up, they would start flying hard manoeuvres in attempt to break our lock-on. Nevertheless, obviously unaware of what kind of damage they had already caused to us, they kept coming in and bombing.

For all practical purposes, the 418th Air Defence Battalion was 'finished'. Early on 16 October, the ADC ordered Hob el-Din's crews to pack their surviving equipment and withdraw from Port Said. After nearly a week of almost uninterrupted, high intensity combat operations, the unit left the combat zone towards Inchas, to rest its crews and repair equipment.

Considering that there are no reports about the 418th Battalion being replaced by another unit, and the importance of this area from the Egyptian standpoint, this is still surprising – even more so because the unit was withdrawn at a fateful point in time.

During the same morning the High Command in Cairo received the first reports about activity of an 'Israeli raiding party' on the western side of the Suez Canal. Uncertain about what was going on, the Egyptian commanders were slow to react until, later during the day, the Soviet Prime Minister Aleksey Kosygin arrived in Cairo, bringing with him satellite photographs showing a dangerous Israeli counter-crossing of the Canal in between The Second and The Third Field Armies. However, when Kosygin attempted to persuade Sadat to accept a cease-fire the Egyptian refused. Nevertheless, a few hours later Kosygin was granted the honour of standing beside Sadat as he was delivering a well-known speech to the Egyptian Parliament, in the course of which – amongst others – the Egyptian president stated that any Israeli attack on the Egyptian depth would be confronted by an Egyptian attack on the Israeli depth. Moreover, Sadat announced that the 'Zafir' missiles would be 'ready on their launchers in Port Said and waiting for the signal' to be fired against the 'deepest depth of Israel', before concluding that part of his appearance with, 'an eye for an eye, a tooth for a tooth, and a depth for a depth'. Cautiously studying this speech, the Israeli leaders realised not only that the Egyptian president was actually speaking about Scuds, but also interpreted Kosygin's presence next to Sadat as Moscow granting a green light for their use against Israel.[5]

Perhaps the most famous set of photographs of the 'Air Battle of el-Mansourah' was taken by a strike-camera of an F-4E from No. 107 Squadron over Tanta AB on 15 October 1973. This shot was taken as the jet was pulling up after releasing its bombs on a group of hardened aircraft shelters. (IDF/Spector Collection)

Seconds later, a well-known photograph showing one of the accompanying Phantoms over Tanta AB was taken, as both jets were descending in a turn. A few moments later, they became involved in a short but sharp clash with multiple MiG-21s. (IDF/Spector Collection)

DEVERSOIR GAP

Later on 16 October, Sadat presided a meeting of his top commanders, aimed at finding a solution for the Israeli presence west of the Suez Canal. When Shazly demanded the withdrawal of four armoured brigades from the Sinai and their re-deployment for a strong, concentrated counterattack on the Israeli troops west of the waterway, Sadat angrily dismissed the Israeli crossing as a 'television operation', and ordered a pincer attack from northern and southern bridgeheads on the Sinai instead. Until this could be launched, it rested with the EAF to attack and contain the Israelis in what soon became known as the 'Deversoir Gap', named after a disused former base of the Royal Air Force near the Israeli crossing site. This was to become the area over which the mass of air combats between the

EAF and the IDF/AF was to be fought over the following eight days.

As expected by Shazly and his commanders, the Egyptian counterattacks on the eastern side of the Suez were easily beaten back by the IDF on 17 October. Indeed, they caused so few concerns in Israel that the IDF/AF continued pounding Port Said and then a concentration of SAM-sites protecting Abu Suweir AB (only used for emergency landings during this war), further south-west. Realising that the sustained Israeli air strikes were about to break the coverage of the 10th Air Defence Division of the ADC over the northern portion of the battlefield, the EAF scrambled to re-deploy several of its MiG-21 units closer to the combat zone.

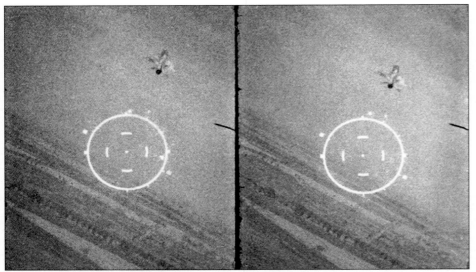

A series of stills from Iftach Spector's gun-camera, showing the results of a fleeting engagement with a MiG-21 over Tanta AB on 15 October 1973. (IDF/Spector Collection)

Magddin Rifaat in the cockpit of a Mirage from No. 69 Squadron, shortly after the October 1973 War. Based at Tanta, Rifaat was a first-hand eyewitness to nearly all of the actions described in this volume. (Magddin Rifaat Collection)

Ahmed Yusuf el-Wakeel served with the MiG-21M/MF-equipped No. 42 Squadron during the October 1973 War, and participated in several air combats with Israeli Phantoms. On 15 October, he claimed one as shot down shortly before his MiG received a hit that forced him to eject. (Ahmed Yusuf el-Wakeel Collection)

EGYPTIAN STRIKE ON EL-ARISH AIRFIELD

If the top Egyptian and Israeli military and political leaders were fighting their own, indirect missile games – indeed, an 'indirect nuclear war' – as of mid-October 1973, the EAF and the IDF/AF continued fighting their own battles. Amongst others, the Egyptian air force was meanwhile informed that on 14 October the USA had launched a major airlift effort to re-supply the IDF with armaments and ammunition. Ultimately, this resulted in Cairo ordering No. 69 Squadron to fly the mission the unit wanted to fly on the first day of the war – and which the Israelis expected with great of anxiety. Magddin Rifaat recalled:

We had received the information that the enemy was using the airport of el-Arish to land US transport aircraft that brought in replacement armament. This was a brazen violation of Egyptian territorial integrity, and offence to our pride. From that moment onwards, el-Arish received priority in our further planning. That evening, we went to bed hoping we would receive the order to execute that mission.

....On 18 October 1973, following the noon prayers, the CO of our squadron gathered us in a closed meeting, then said, "Today at 1800, we are going to fly the sortie against el-Arish airport where the enemy is receiving US supplies. Six aircraft are going to take part. Two others are going to be prepared as spares. Each aircraft is going to be armed with 238 rounds of 30mm for internal cannons, two 1,300 litre drop tanks, and two 400kg bombs. The formation is going to reach el-Arish along the route from Tanta via Ras al-Bar, to a point 20 nautical miles northeast–east over the sea, then to a point 20 nautical miles north of el-Arish before turning south, at a speed of 420 knots [777km/h] and an altitude of 66ft [20m]. On approach to the target, they are going to accelerate to 560kts [1,036km/h] and climb to 210ft [70m]: target will be the runways of el-Arish. The mission is going to be led by Major Hayder Dabbous, with Captain Rifaat Mabarz as wingman; second pair Major Mohammed Amin Bassoumi, with Captain Rida Musharraf; third pair Major Moheb Shehab, with Captain Mohammed Fathallah Rifaat. The formation is going to self-escort itself against enemy fighters: we do not have any air-to-air missiles and if they get intercepted, Moheb and Fathallah are going to jettison their ordnance and provide cover for the front two pairs with their cannons to make sure they can reach the target. The formation is going to return to the base along reciprocal course via Baltim, along the pre-determined corridor safe from our interceptors and air defence. This is what we have trained for years. The success of this mission is going to deliver a painful blow and deprive the enemy of a precious airport close to the frontlines. This mission is necessary and we should have flown it already on 6 October. Any questions?"

After the squadron intelligence officer added that the enemy was protecting el-Arish with interceptors and ground based air defences, Major Dabbous observed, "Don't worry, Sir, we will execute this mission even if we do not come back".

Rifaat watched the formation take off, and remained behind in anticipation. An hour and 20 minutes later, two aircraft returned, flown by Moheb and Fathallah. They landed at last light. Then a third Mirage appeared, flown by Rida Musharraf, Number 4, who recalled:

We proceeded as planned until about one minute before reaching the point north of el-Arish, where we wanted to turn south and accelerate. The visibility was very low due to the fog prior to sunset. Then we were surprised to see Mirages attacking the front pair. This forced us to jettison our load and engage the enemy. I could not see Haider Dabous and he did not make any calls on the radio. I only saw that Rifat Mabarz continued at low altitude before coming under attack: then he made a sharp turn and jettisoned his bombs and drop tanks, but lost the control of the aircraft and crashed into the sea. I separated from Bassoumi who was manoeuvring hard but was then hit by the enemy and fell into the sea. The visibility continued to worsen and I kept manoeuvring with an aircraft that was chasing me. There were lots of Mirages around me and it was impossible to distinguish friend or foe. I called Moheb to inform him we are under attack, but he did not respond. Fathallah answered as I got rid of the assailant behind me and then turned back towards Baltim. I switched to the channel used by el-Mansoura and heard them scrambling interceptors; I kept calling them to announce a friendly aircraft, but there was no response. This forced me to take a route further north, and worry about my remaining fuel. Only in the last moment did I turn south towards Tanta, and landed on my last drops of fuel.

An exceptionally rare photograph of a Libyan Mirage 5Ds taken during their tour of duty with No. 69 Squadron in Egypt: it shows the example with serial number 445 in front of a hardened aircraft shelter at Tanta AB. Notable is the damage atop of the hardened aircraft shelter in the background: this was caused by one of the Israeli bombs during the strike on 15 October 1973. (Albert Grandolini Collection)

MiG-21s from 102nd and 104th Air Brigades remained operational for the rest of the conflict, and reacted aggressively to every appearance of the IDF/AF's fighter-bombers. This still from a video released by the Egyptian Ministry of Defence shows a pair of fully-armed MiG-21F-13s from No. 26 Squadron rolling for take-off. (Albert Grandolini Collection)

MiG-21PFS' from No. 44 Squadron – like the example visible here, serial number 8025 – saw plenty of action over the Deversoir Gap during the final days of the October 1973 War, when their primary task was the protection of Egyptian fighter-bombers in attacks on Israeli pontoon bridges over the Suez Canal. (Albert Grandolini Collection)

Fathallah's recollection was similar:

We were intercepted about 35 seconds before making our last turn. I think that the Americans reported our approach as we flew over many ships in the Mediterranean, and they might have had their [Grumman] E-2 Hawkeye airborne early warning aircraft up. It would have been hard for the Israelis to detect us as we were flying very low. When the Israeli Mirages appeared, my pair was about three kilometres behind Haider, and I was about one kilometre to the left of Moheb, but then lost sight to the front pair due to poor visibility. After the enemy appeared, I climbed slightly

An F-4E from No. 119 Squadron while escorting a giant C-5A Galaxy transport of the USAF, as the latter was approaching Israel, on 23 October 1973. (IDF via Albert Grandolini)

and jettisoned ordnance in preparation for an engagement. Then I saw Moheb and followed him. He did not respond to my radio calls. I saw at least six other Mirages, but could not distinguish friend from enemy. Thus, I focused on following Moheb's aircraft as he exited the battle towards Baltim. I noticed that he flew defensive manoeuvres in attempt to get rid of me, thinking I'm hostile. I then followed him from a distance. Upon landing, it turned out his radio malfunctioned.

Eventually, the chaotic dogfight in which both sides flew exactly the same aircraft and thus experienced extensive problems with visual identification, prevented the pilots from No. 69 Squadron from reaching their target. Two were killed while flying their aircraft into the sea, while one was shot down: Bassoumi ejected over Lake Bardavil and was rescued by one of the local farmers – who first beat him because of his fair hair and green eyes, but then handed him over to the military police. Concluding that el-Arish was heavily protected by the IDF/AF, the EAF subsequently abandoned any ideas for further plans vis-à-vis this airfield.[6]

AMAN'S FALSE ALERTS
During the night from 17 to 18 October, the Israeli military intelligence agency AMAN issued its next unsupported alert related to the Egyptian Scuds. Citing another re-deployment of the 65th Missile Brigade, it once again set the alarm bells ringing in Tel Aviv. This time, the 'Soviet-controlled' Scud missiles were not only re-deployed from one position to another, but meanwhile 'equipped with nuclear warheads', too. The reaction of the Israeli government and IDF's commanders is only partially known. It was around this point in time that Meir's cabinet – knowing that Nixon's National Security Adviser was on the way to Moscow – ordered Dinitz to forward the following message to Kissinger : 'If the Egyptians just think about firing their Scud missiles, Israel will know how to pay back twofold'.[7]

Although this was more than a 'serious threat', there would be no reply – neither from Cairo nor from Moscow – for the next four days. Then, on 21 October 1973, Antonov An-12B medium-sized transports and the giant An-22s of the Soviet Military Transport Aviation landed in Egypt to unload three additional MAZ-543 TELs and 15 Scud missiles. On the same day, the Soviet merchant ship *Maarnuli* delivered three MAZ-543s and another 15 missiles to Alexandria.[8]

When the AMAN then also misreported the activity of the 65th

Missile Brigade as 'preparations for a non-conventional attack' – the operation in question was actually little more than the continuation of routine training – the IDF/AF reacted by bombing Port Said with up to 140 aircraft on 22 October, this time killing up to 200 civilians. On the contrary, the Israeli sources stress that this attack had been run in preparation for an assault on Port Fuad, presented to Dayan on 19 October: the Israeli Minister of Defence presented this plan to the political leadership on 21-22 October, but the latter had turned it down 'because the IDF was not ready, not all the necessary troops were available, and they were keen to avoid civilian casualties'. Although Golda Meir then granted approval for the assault on Port Fuad, on the morning of 22 October, the operation was finally postponed due to the pending cease-fire.[9]

FINAL CRY OF THE 'LIBYAN' MIRAGES
The cease-fire in question was agreed during Kissinger's visit in Moscow, which resulted in Resolution 338 of the Security Council of the United Nations, and was announced for 1852hrs local time of 22 October. However, eager to avenge the shock of the surprise attack and their heavy casualties, now it was the Israelis that were not pleased with an 'imposed end of the war'. Supposedly, Golda Meir accepted the cease-fire only after Kissinger convinced her that a continuation of the conflict would lead to a radicalisation of the Arab world, irreparable damage to détente between the USA and the USSR, and 'extreme measures' by the Soviets in order to save their allies from a defeat. However, even then, once everything was agreed and Meir finally accepted the cease-fire – and exploiting the fact that the US public was preoccupied by the House of Representatives in Washington beginning the impeachment proceedings against president Nixon – Kissinger secretly gave Israel a green light to breach the cease-fire and continue the advance on Suez City, thus completing the encirclement of The Third Field Army: 'If the forces moved at night while I'm flying there would be no protests from Washington. Nothing can happen until tomorrow noon.' Meir replied, 'If they don't stop, we won't' – to which Kissinger replied, 'Even if they do…'[10]

Not to be outdone, Sadat was obviously keen to have his own, final word in the war: indeed, two of these. Firstly, No. 69 Squadron was ordered into its final action of the war, an attack on the Israeli-occupied Fayid AB, near the Great Bitter Lake. Magddin Rifaat recalled:

I took off as number four formation with Ahmed Hashim, Kamal Abdul Raouf, and Hussein Ezzat. Each aircraft was armed to the maximum: 10 250kg bombs, two drop tanks, and full load of internal cannon ammunition. The target was very close and we had enough fuel… we only needed the entire length of the runway to get airborne…

As we approached Fayid, we saw a big, long, white transport on finals, about to land there. My actual target was a specific corner of the air base where we suspected a concentration of enemy troops, but as a fighter pilot I could not resist this opportunity: a cargo plane is an easy yet precious target!

At first there were some doubts if it was one of ours, but Ahmed and Kamal passed by and identified it visually… I called Hussein to inform him about my new target, which was at his 4 o'clock, but he responded that he was in the final stage of his bombing run. I jettisoned my cargo instead; my Mirage lurched forward and accelerated. As I turned around, I saw two enemy Mirages behind the transport. They rapidly grew in size in my sight and then flashed by very close, one of them opening fire in the process. I fired with my cannon too, but missed. We all turned, and entered a high-speed yo-yo manoeuvre, after which I was behind one, but then I heard a loud beating at the rear of my aircraft: two other Mirages came in, took the advantage of my preoccupation with that enemy, and hit me with cannon. I was angry with myself because I had attacked alone, then took the bait while fighting that Mirage, and now ended up flying versus four. I forgot to warn my colleagues, and continued manoeuvring after the enemy in front of me… then I heard another series of hits on my aircraft. I looked back but saw only black smoke and then one fire warning after the other illuminated in my cockpit.

I realised my aircraft was badly damaged, but it still flew well so I decided to return to Abu Hammad. I did not want to eject. Hussein Ezzat joined me and made a visual inspection of my aircraft. He told me that thick black smoke was coming out directly behind the cockpit and it would be better if I ejected. That's when I gave up: I pulled the ejection handle, the cockpit hood flew away and then I was propelled upwards with acceleration of 18g. My helmet flew off and I blacked out for a few seconds: I only heard the crash of my plane… I landed in a rice field and heard a few shots fired in my direction. A group of peasants came towards me, I called out "Egyptian! Egyptian! Egyptian!" But they attacked me with axes and machetes and began beating me so I fell on the ground, until they saw my inflatable dinghy, which they thought was a bomb. This scared them and they fled… Then I heard several shots and an Army sergeant approached, telling me my safety was his responsibility and he would keep the farmers away from me. He gave me some water and helped me wash my face, which was full of blood. Finally, another group of soldiers arrived with a jeep to take me away: as we drove past the nearby village, there was still a big crowd there eager to kill me! 'I was treated by a doctor in the hospital of the Third Field Army, then brought to Zagazig, and then – finally – to Tanta. I slept badly that night due to nightmares and the next day was taken off flying and sent to our hospital, where I joined Samir Aziz [Mikhail] who was still suffering pains from compressed vertebrae during his ejection from a MiG-21. That was the end of the war for me.

Once again, the mission of the Mirages operated by No. 69 Squadron was spoiled by Israeli Mirages, and once again it ended with losses for no gain. If the IDF/AF ever had as serious concerns of 'Libyan Mirages' presence in Egypt as frequently claimed, such

must have disappeared at least on that afternoon.

SCUDS IN ACTION

Finally, at 1850hrs of 22 October 1973, only minutes before the cease-fire was to be enforced, the 65th Missile Brigade fired three 'Scud-As' from a position south of Cairo at the Israeli bridges spanning the Suez Canal north of the Great Bitter Lake. According to the inexplicably unsubstantiated yet widely published version in the West, all three missed by such a margin that the IDF would have failed to notice their impacts. Actually, at least one hit closely enough to kill at least seven Israeli troops.[11]

As could have been expected, this action kept the always hypersensitive Israelis on their toes – even more so because according to their intelligence reports Moscow delivered Scuds to Cairo under condition these would remain under 'full Soviet control' until the 65th Missile Brigade would become fully operational in 1974. Correspondingly, Sadat would have required Soviet permission for their combat deployment and, indeed, should have called the Soviet ambassador to Cairo, Vinogradov to obtain permission for their deployment. Supposedly explaining to the Soviet representative that the position of The Second and the Third Field Armies was approaching that of a catastrophe, he convinced Vinogradov to make a quick telephone call to Moscow. The Soviet ambassador attempted, but failed to reach Foreign Minister Andrei Gromyko. Instead, he reached the Defence Minister Andrei Grechko, who promptly granted permission for combat deployment of the Scuds. In turn, Vinogradov then made a telephone call to Sadat, forwarding him 'Moscow's agreement' to launch the missiles, and then another call to the Soviet advisors assigned to the 65th Missile Brigade. Grechko then returned to the meeting with the Soviet leader Leonid Brezhnev, informed him about the call from Cairo, and that he had granted permission to fire. Aroused, Brezhnev got very angry by the resulting situation and quickly issued the order for a cancellation. However, by the time this order was forwarded to Cairo and then to the Soviet advisors, it was too late: the three Scuds were already airborne.[12]

According to the available Egyptian documentation, the 65th Missile Brigade was already operational as of 6 October, and it was all the time under the control of the Ministry of War in Cairo, and its firing action was ordered by President Sadat. This is little surprising considering its personnel has previously operated incomplete rockets developed by German scientists and then Soviet-made FROG-7s, before undergoing conversion to Scuds in the USSR in early 1973 – which made it at least as experienced on ballistic missiles as the personnel of No. 150 Squadron of the IDF/AF was experienced on Jerichos.[13]

Indeed, none of the published Israeli explanations, and even less so any of those of the 'Israeli intelligence' can explain why Sadat would have let any Soviet advisors control a unit equipped with such an important weapon system once this was in Egypt? And even if: why the Egyptians would have been unable to remove the Soviets – if necessary at gun point? Traditional Israeli and Western prejudice about 'Arab' armed forces, and super-imposition of supposed Soviet involvement instead of serious studies of decision-making processes in Cairo do not offer answers to such questions. This is even more important considering the fact that, contrary to the Israeli expectations, the Egyptian armed forces did not collapse without the support of Soviet advisors after Sadat's kick-out order of 1972, and the Egyptians very much 'dared' initiating a new war with Israel. Indeed, the October 1973 Arab-Israeli War began with a joint Egyptian-Syrian attack on 6 October 1973, and not on 6 October

1977 or 1978. The conclusion is thus on hand that AMAN was, once again, plain wrong – which is something that can happen to anybody.

KISSINGER'S GAMES

To say that Kissinger's double game meanwhile precipitated a major crisis through angering the Soviets would be an understatement. When Washington turned down Sadat's call for a joint intervention by both superpowers (meant to force Israel into stopping its violations of a cease-fire), Moscow became even more alarmed. After the Israelis violated the second cease-fire, too, at 2200hrs on 24 October, Soviet Leader Leonid Brezhnev sent President Nixon a warning that if the US would not act, the USSR would do so unilaterally. Based on what is known about what would have happened afterwards, this was a big bluff: not only that Sadat never requested Moscow to deploy its armed forces in Egypt (he only demanded Soviet observers to monitor the implementation of the cease-fire), but there was no support in the Kremlin for sending troops to Egypt. Moreover, although US intelligence had indicated that 7 out of 12 Soviet airborne divisions stationed in East Germany and Poland – a total of about 42,000 troops – had been put on alert, and that the transport aircraft involved in hauling supplies and replacement armament to Egypt and Syria had been diverted to pick them up, while the Soviet warships in the Mediterranean Sea changed their course to move closer to Egypt, the USSR was actually not in a position to launch an outright military intervention. These moves had been ordered days before, and were an understandable result of the Israeli attacks on the Soviet Cultural Centre in Damascus on 9 October, and the sinking of the Soviet merchant ship *Ilya Mechnikov* in Syrian territorial waters, a few days later.[14]

Nevertheless, keen to 'prevent a Soviet military intervention in the Middle East', Kissinger then went a step further and, during the night of 24 to 25 October 1973, decided to raise the world-wide readiness state of the US armed forces to the Defence Condition (DEFCON) III, the highest state of nuclear readiness in peacetime. When the Soviet Ambassador in Washington inquired about reasons for this decision the following day, Kissinger advised him that it was prompted by 'domestic considerations' – i.e. the Watergate affair (which ultimately forced President Nixon to resign). Actually, Kissinger continued cheating the Egyptians and the Soviets and, amongst others, assured Dinitz that Washington had no intention of coercing Israel to withdraw to the 22 October lines in response to the Soviet threat.

Still, the Soviets backed down. At 1540hrs on 25 October, Nixon received a message from Brezhnev agreeing to cooperation with Washington. Unsurprisingly, the Israelis continued their advance, not only by firming the siege of The Third Field Army, but also by advancing past Suez City further south. Nevertheless, a day later, Brezhev went a step further and delivered a reconciliatory speech to the World Peace Congress in Moscow, emphasising the importance of detente, and stressing that all Soviet military actions were halted. It was only at that point that – assured that there would be no Soviet intervention – Kissinger began correcting his own mistake through warning the Israelis to spare the Third Field Army. In a telephone conversation with Dinitz on the same day, he openly stated, 'You will not be permitted to destroy this army'.[15]

WAS THERE A SOVIET NUCLEAR WEAPON IN EGYPT?[16]

The next result of Kissinger's machinations was the Security Council's Resolution 340 of 25 October, which demanded a third cease-fire. Unsurprisingly, this did not manage to stop further Israeli

This crater was left behind by one of three Scuds fired by the 65th Missile Brigade at the IDF's bridges spanning the Suez Canal, on 22 October 1973. Depending on the Israeli source in question, either 7 or 11 Israeli troops were killed by the Egyptian missile. (IDF)

advances south of Suez City, which sealed the siege of the Third Field Army: this was to last until 28 October, when Washington finally forced Israel into granting permission for a convoy with non-military supplies to reach the encircled Egyptian troops. There are strong indications that during this final drama of the October 1973 Arab-Israeli War, Kissinger was eventually forced to use a 'much stronger argument' to stop further Israeli violations of the cease-fire.

On 15 October 1973, a yacht operated by the US intelligence in the Bosporus and loaded with sensors for detecting traces of radiation left by nuclear weapons, had passed by the Soviet merchant *Mazhdorchinsky* as this was underway from the Black Sea to the Mediterranean. Because the sensors promptly sounded a 'red alert', the conclusion was that the ship 'absolutely contained nuclear weapons'. The involved intelligence operatives thus promptly reported their findings all the way to Washington. Although not entirely certain if the ship really carried nuclear warheads, the CIA analysed the options. Considering that *Mazhdorchinsky* reached Alexandria and dropped its anchor there on 25 October – on the same day as a 'brigade of Soviet officers of the Strategic Rocket Forces arrived at Cairo International' – the conclusion was that the ship was transporting Soviet nuclear warheads meant to be installed on the Egyptian Scuds. This theory further hardened when US satellite intelligence provided photographs showing Soviet transport aircraft unloading what appeared to be 'special warheads' for the Soviet ballistic missiles: in the light of Kissinger's order for DEFCON III, it was easy to conclude that the 'Soviet nuclear material' had reached Egypt and, at least from the US standpoint, the resulting situation began to resemble that during the Cuban Missile Crisis of 1962 – with the difference that this time it would have been Israel, and not the USA that was 'under a threat'.

Certainly enough, *Mazhdorchinsky* left Egyptian waters without ever unloading in Alexandria, two days later and returned home: a few months later the CIA 'discovered' that the ship actually carried no nuclear weapons, but that the sensors sounded alarm due to a mistake. Nevertheless, in the meantime, the Nixon administration used Israeli fears that the Egyptians had been given nuclear weapons to convince Meir to finally halt any further advance past Suez City.

If truth, this would have meant that Israel – a country that introduced nuclear weapons into the Middle East – was finally stopped by non-existing Soviet nuclear weapons in Egypt. The irony is even bigger considering that ever since it is 24 October 1973 that is considered the date on which this war finally came to an end.

CONCLUSIONS

On first appearances it might seem that there remain 'too many unknowns' to draw any useful conclusions about the entire affair involving the emergence of the Israeli nuclear weapons, Egyptian Scuds, Libyan Mirages, and the possible Soviet deployment of nuclear weapons in Egypt during the October 1973 Arab-Israeli War. Indeed, that there is no reason to describe all the related affairs as a 'nuclear war' even when these events are put within their context. Nevertheless, a few things are certain: conclusions such as that the full backgrounds and outcomes of diverse of military operations during this conflict are well-known and have been thoroughly researched; that air power played no important role in this war; that every known Israeli (or Egyptian) claim from diverse air combats has been completely cross-examined and can be considered as 'confirmed'; that the Israelis ran air strikes against places like Port Said or Tanta AB for reasons their

The first Mirage 5D manufactured for Libya, as seen during pre-delivery testing in France, while loaded with a total of 12 bombs – in a similar configuration to Mirage 5Ds of No. 69 Squadron during their attack on Israeli-occupied Fayid AB on 22 October 1973. (Albert Grandolini Collection)

One of the hardened aircraft shelters at Fayid, while this air base was under Israeli occupation, in late 1973. Notable is a Noratlas transport in the left foreground. The Israelis also used much bigger C-97s to deliver supplies there, which was the most likely type of aircraft sighted by Rifaat during his mission on 22 October. (David Nicolle Collection)

The second Mirage 5D manufactured for Libya, as seen during pre-delivery testing at Bordeaux. (Oscar Ruf Willson Collection)

available publications usually cite; that on 14 October 1973 Egypt and Israel fought the 'biggest tank battle since Kursk of 1943', that there was some kind of a super-big 'Air Battle of el-Mansourah'; that the MiG-21 possessed significant advantages in manoeuvrability in comparison to the F-4 Phantom II because it was such a joy to fly in peace-time, and many, many others – can all be only described as 'premature', even as 'futile'. Perhaps what is most important is the

fact that, as that designation clearly explains it, 'Israeli intelligence' is not the 'Egyptian leadership': just studying the former's reports and considering these as some sort of a dogma is not only futile because such agencies as the AMAN made a mass of mistakes prior to and during the October 1973 War, but is also unlikely to ever help find out exactly what was going on in Cairo – and even less so between Cairo and Moscow – or with the 65th Missile Brigade and its Scuds during that conflict. Moreover, there remain strong indications that much more was going on during this war than is usually reported, but that all the involved parties – Egypt, Israel, USA, and the USSR – had, and still have, plenty of good reasons to keep the details secret. This is little surprising considering the almost certain involvement of nuclear weapons – a topic no military, and very few political leaders are ready to discuss under the given circumstances.

Overall, all of these affairs are going to require much additional, and certainly much more objective research and cross-examination in the future. After all, the clandestine nuclear armament of any nation – not to mention Israel – is an affair exercising far too serious an impact upon our everyday lives to be swept aside with (usually oversimplifying) explanations published in diverse 'standard sources of reference' over the last 40 years.

An Egyptian Scud TEL loaded with a missile as shown on a military parade in Cairo in October 1974. (Albert Grandolini Collection)

BIBLIOGRAPHY

Adan, Avraham (Bren), *On the Banks of the Suez* (Novato: Presidio Press, 1991; ISBN 0-89141-043-0).

Aloni, S., 'Target Tanta', *International Air Power Review*, Volume 25.

Anderegg, C. R., *Sierra Hotel: Flying Air Force Fighters in the Decade after Vietnam* (Washington: Air Force History and Museums Program; ISBN 978-1782664345).

Artillery Department of the (Egyptian) Ministry of Defence, *War Diary of the 65th Missile Brigade* (Cairo: date of issue unknown; official document obtained from private sources by Dr. Abdallah Emran).

Asher, D., *The Egyptian Strategy for the Yom Kippur War, An Analysis* (Jefferson: McFarland & Co Inc., 2009; ISBN 978-0786442539).

Badri, H. el-, Magdoub, T. el-, Zohdy, M. D. el-Din, *The Ramadan War, 1973* (Dunn Loring: T. N. Dupuy Associates, 1978; ISBN 0-8824-460-8).

Bar-Joseph, U., 'Strategic Surprise or Fundamental Flaw? The Sources of Israel's Military Defeat at the Beginning of the 1973 War', *The Journal of Military History*, Volume 72, Number 2, April 2008 (pp. 509-530).

Bar-Noi, U., *Revelations From the Polish Archives*, Cold War International History Project at the Woodrow Wilson International Center for Scholars, e-Dossier No. 8 (based on 'On Soviet Policy Following the Israeli Aggression in the Middle East', by Comrade L. I. Brezhnev to the Plenum of the Central Committee of the CPSU, 20 June 1967, Archiwum Akt Nowych – a Polish document describing the speech given by Brezhnev to the Plenum of the Central Committee of the Communist Party of the Soviet Union on the actions undertaken by the Soviet leadership before and during the 1967 Arab-Israeli War).

Behiri, M. Al-, 'Secret Israeli Documents Reveal: Israel's Depth was in the Range of Egyptian Missiles at War' (in Arabic), *al-Masry al-Youm*, 2 October 2013.

Blum, H., *The Eve of Destruction: The Untold Story of the Yom Kippur War* (New York: HarperCollins Publishers, 2003; ISBN 0-06-001400-8).

Black, I. & Morris, B., *Israel's Secret Wars: A History of Israel's Intelligence Services*, (New York: Grove Press, 1991; ISBN: 0-8021-3286-3).

Carlier, C., & Berger, L., *Dassault, Volume 1: L'enterprise, 1945-1995, 50 ans d'aventure aeronautique* (Paris: Editions du Chene, 1996).

Carlier, C., & Berger, L., *Dassault, Volume 2: Les programes, 1945-1995, 50 ans d'aventure aeronautique* (Paris: Editions du Chene, 1996).

Carlowitz, D., *Egypt at War* (Publishamerica, 2007; ISBN: 978-1604411058).

Carter, J., *Sex and Rockets: The Occult World of Jack Parsons* (Port Townsend: Washington, Feral House; ISBN: 978-0-922915-97-2).

Chenel, B., Liebert, M., & Moreau, E., *Mirage III/5/50 en service a l'etranger* (Paris: Lela Presse, 2014).

Clausewitz, C. von, *Vom Kriege*, (Berlin: 1832).

Cohen, A., *Israel and the Bomb* (New York: Columbia University Press, 1999; ISBN: 978-0231104838).

Cohen, A., *The 1967 Six-Day War: New Israeli Perspective, 50 Years Later* (Wilson Center, Nuclear Proliferation International History Project, 3 June 2017).

Cooper, T. & Nicolle, D., *Arab MiGs Volume 2: Supersonic Fighters, 1958-1967* (Houston: Harpia Publishing, 2011; ISBN: 978-0-9825539-6-1).

Cooper, T & Nicolle, D., with Nordeen, L. & Salti, P, *Arab MiGs Volume 3: the June 1967 War* (Houston: Harpia Publishing, 2012; ISBN: 978-0-9825539-9-2).

Cooper, T., Nicolle, D., with Nordeen, L., Salti, P., and Smisek, M., *Arab MiGs, Volume 4: Attrition War, 1967-1973* (Houston: Harpia Publishing, 2013; ISBN: 978-09854554-1-5).

Cooper, T., Nicolle, D., with Müller, H., Nordeen, L., and Smisek, M., *Arab MiGs, Volume 5: October 1973 War, Part 1* (Houston: Harpia Publishing, 2014; ISBN: 978-0-9854554-4-6).

Cooper, T., Nicolle, D., with Grandolini, A., Nordeen, L., and Smisek, M., *Arab MiGs, Volume 6: October 1973 War, Part 2* (Houston: Harpia Publishing, 2015; ISBN: 978-0-9854554-6-0).

Cooper, T., *Hot Skies over Yemen, Volume 1: Aerial Warfare over the Southern Arabian Peninsula, 1961-1994* (Solihull: Helion & Co., 2017; ISBN: 978-1-912174-23-2).

Cooper, T., Grandolini, A., & Delallande, A., *Libyan Air Wars, Part 1* (Africa@War Series, No. 17), (Solihull: Helion & Co Ltd., 2014; ISBN: 978-1909982-39-0).

Crosbie, Sylvia, *A Tacit Alliance: France and Israel from Suez to the Six Day War* (Princeton: Princeton University Press, 1974).

Farr, W. D., *The Third Temple's Holy of Holies: Israel's Nuclear Weapons* (The Counterproliferation Papers, Future Wars Series No. 2), (Maxwell Air Force Base, USAF Counterproliferation Center, Air War College/Air University, 1999).

Fawzy, Maj Gen M., *The Three-Years War* (in Arabic), (Beirut: Dar Mustakbal al-Arabi, 1998).

Flaphan, S., 'Nuclear Power in the Middle East', *New Outlook*, July 1974.

Flintham, V., *Air Wars and Aircraft: A Detailed Record of Air Combat, 1945 to the Present* (London: Arms and Armour Press, 1989; ISBN: 0-85368-779-X).

Foreign Technologies Division (USAF), *Fishbed C/E Aerial Tactics* (tactical manual for MiG-21F-13, MiG-21PF, MiG-21FL and MiG-21PFM, obtained from Iraq in 1963 and translated to English by the Foreign Technologies Division USAF, in 1964).

Gamasy, FM M., A., G., el-, *The October War: Memoirs of Field Marshal el-Gamasy of Egypt* (Cairo: The American University of Cairo Press, 1993).

Gawrych, Dr. George W., *The 1973 Arab-Israeli War: The Albatross of Decisive Victory* (Fort Leavenworth: Combat Studies Institute, US Army Command and General Staff College, 1996).

Ginor, I. & Remez, G., *Foxbats over Dimona: The Soviet's Nuclear Gamble in the Six-Day War* (New Heaven & London: Yale University Press, 2008; ISBN: 978-0-300-12317-3).

Gordon, S., *Thirty Hours in October* (in Hebrew), (Tel Aviv: Ma'ariv Book Guild, 2008).

Green, S., *Living by the Sword: America and Israel in the Middle East* (Brattleboro: Amana Books, 1988; ISBN: 0-9155957-60-8).

Gunston, B. & Spick, M., Modern Air Combat: *The Aircraft, Tactics and Weapons Employed in Aerial Warfare Today* (London, Salamander Books Ltd., 1983; ISBN: 0-86101-1627).

Gurov, I. M., *Ground-based Air Defence Systems at Wars in Vietnam and the Middle East* (in Russian), (Moscow: Ministry of Defence of the USSR, 1980; published for internal use as a training tool).

Haloutz, D., *Straightforward* (in Hebrew), (Miskal: Yedioth Ahoronoth Books and Chemed Books, 2010; ISBN 978-965-482-870-3).

Hammad, G., *Military Battles on the Egyptian Front 1973* (in Arabic) (Cairo: Dar al-Shuruq, 2002; ISBN 0-8129-0567-9).

Golan, Lt. L. M. Dr. S., 'The Scud to Deter Israel' (in Hebrew), *Maarahot* (unknown volume), pp. 55-61.

Jaber, Fuad, *Israel and Nuclear Weapons* (London: Chatto and Windus for the International Institute of Strategic Studies, 1971).

Jauvert, V., 'Bombe Israelienne, quand de Gaulle a dit non a Ben-Gourion'; *Nouvel Observateur*, 17 November 2013.

Jawadi, Dr. M. al-, *In Between the Catastrophe: Memoirs of Egyptian Military Commanders from 1967 to 1972* (in Arabic), (Cairo: Dar al-Khiyal, 2001).

Karpin, M., *The Bomb in the Basement: How Israel Went Nuclear and What that means for the World* (London: Simon & Schuster, 2007; ISBN: 978-0743265959).

Klein, A., and Aloni, S., with Weiss, R., De Haven, L. R., and Myasnikov, A., *Israeli Phantoms: the Kurnass in IDF/AF Service, 1969-1988* (Erlangen: Double Ugly Books, 2010)

Kotlobovskiy, A. B., *MiG-21 in Local Wars* (in Russian) (Kiev: ArchivPress, 1997)

Langeron, J.-M., *F-4 Phantom II Flight Model Identification & Compared Air Combat Performances Analysis: MiG-21 versus F-4 Phantom II* (Parts 1, 2 and 3). These privately published assessments are based on the following documents:

- *Flight Manual F-4C,/D,E-1-S, T.O. 1F-4C-1*, 15th August 1973, Change 1
- *Performance Data Manual F-4C, D, E-1-1-S, T.O. 1F-4C-1-1*, 15 July 1969, Change 1
- *Flight Manual F-4E, T.O. 1F-4E*, 1 February 1979
- *NATOPS Flight Manual MiG-21M*
- *NATOPS Flight Manual MiG-21MF*
- *NATOPS Flight Manual F-4D blk37*
- *NATOPS Flight Manual F-4E blk31*
- *NATOPS Flight Manual F-4E blk41*
- *NATOPS Fight Manual F-4E blk46 To.556*
- *NATOPS Flight Manual F-4E blk50*
- Robert K Heffley & Wayne F Jewel, NASA CR-2144: *Aircraft Handling Qualities Data*, NASA, December 1972
- Joseph R Chambers & Ernie L Anglin, NASA TN D-5361: *Analysis of lateral-directional stability characteristics of a twin-jet airplane at high angles of attack*, NASA, August 1969.

Lake, J., & Donald, D. (editors), *McDonnell F-4 Phantom: Spirit in the Skies* (Updated and Expanded Edition), (Solihull: AIRtime Publishing, 2002; ISBN 1-880588-31-5).

Meir, G., *My Life*, (New York: G. P. Putnam, 1975).

Michel, Marshall L., *Clashes: Air Combat over North Vietnam, 1965-1972* (Annapolis: Naval Institute Press, 1997; ISBN 1-55-750-585-3)

Moneim el-, A. A., *Wolf in the Sun's Disc* (in Arabic), (Cairo: 1988).

Mustafa, Gen H., *The June War, 1967, Part II* (Lebanon: Establishment for Arab Studies and Publication, 1970).

Nordeen, L., *Fighters over Israel*, (London: Guild Publishing, 1991; ISBN 978-0517566039)

Nicolle, Dr. D., Cooper, T., & Gabr, Air Vice Marshal G. A., *Wings over Sinai: The Egyptian Air Force During the Sinai War, 1956* (Solihull: Helion & Co., 2016; ISBN: 978-1-911096-61-0).

O'Ballance, E., *No Victor, No Vanquished: The Yom Kippur War* (Novato: Presidio Press, 1996; ISBN 978-0-89141-615-9).

Okasha, Maj Gen Mohammed Abdel Moneim Zaki, *Conflict in the Sky: the Egyptian-Israeli Wars, 1948-1967* (Cairo: Ministry of Defence, 1976).

Okasha, Maj Gen Mohammed Abdel Moneim Zaki, *Soldiers in the Sky* (in Arabic), (Cairo: Ministry of Defence, 1976).

Okasha, Maj Gen Mohammed Abdel Moneim Zaki, *Operation Spark: I Wave* (in Arabic), (Cairo: Ministry of Defence, 2011).

Okasha, Maj Gen Mohammed Abdel Moneim Zaki, *69 Squadron at War* (in Arabic), (Cairo: Ministry of Defence, 2012).

Ovendale, R., *The Origins of the Arab-Israeli Wars* (Harlow: Longman Group UK Ltd, 1984; ISBN 0-582-49257-2).

Palit, Maj Gen D. K., *Return to The Sinai: The Arab Offensive, October 1973* (New Delhi: Lancer Publishers & Distributors, 1974, reprinted 2002; ISBN 81-7062-221-2).

Pean, P., *Les Deux Bombes* (Paris: Fayard, 1982).

Pedersen, D., *Top Gun: An American Story* (New York: Hachette Books, 2019; ISBN: 978-0-316-41627-6).

Peled, Gen. B., *Days of Reckoning* (Moshav Ben-Shemen: Modan Publishing House, 2004).

Pendle, G., *Strange Angel: The Otherworldly Life of Rocket Scientist John Whiteside Parsons* (London: Weidenfeld & Nicolson, 2005; ISBN: 978-0-7438-2065-0).

Pollack, K., *Arabs at War: Military Effectiveness, 1948-1991* (Lincoln: University of Nebraska Press, 2002; ISBN 0-8032-8783-6).

Price, Dr. A., *War in the Fourth Dimension: US Electronic Warfare, from the Vietnam War to the Present* (London: Greenhill Books, 2001; ISBN 1-85367-471-0).

Raspletin, Dr. A. A., *History PVO website* (historykpvo.narod2.ru), 2013.

Riad, M., *The Struggle for Peace in the Middle East* (Consett: Quartet Books, 1981; ISBN: 978-0704322974).

Rifaat, Major-General (ret.) M., *The Diary of a Mirage Pilot in the October War: Memoirs of Major-General Magd el-Din Rifaat, Former Head of the Armament Department*, Egyptian Air Force (private document in Arabic, translation kindly provided by Nour Bardai).

Shalom, D., *Like a Bolt out of the Blue: 'Moked' Operation in the Six-Day War, June 1967* (in Hebrew), (Rishon Le Zion: BAVIR Aviation Publications, 2002).

Sharmy, S., *The Eagles that Saved the October Victory* (unpublished manuscript).

Sharmy, S., & Nicolle, D., 'Battle of el-Mansourah', *Air Forces Monthly* magazine, January 1996.

Shazly, Sa'ad el-, *The Crossing of the Suez* (San Francisco: American Mideast Research, 2003; ISBN: 0-9604562-2-8).

Shevchuk, D., *The Soviet-Israeli War* (in Russian; unpublished manuscript).

Sokolov, A, 'PVO in Local Wars and Armed Conflicts: The Arab-Israeli Wars', *VKO*, No. 2 (2), 2001.

Sokolov, A., 'The Arab-Israeli Wars', *VKO*, No. 2 (5), 2002.

Tessler, M. A., *A History of the Israeli-Palestinian Conflict* (Bloomington and Indianapolis: Indiana University Press, 1994).

Transue, J. R. (project leader), *WSEG Report 249: Assessment of the Weapons and Tactics used in the October 1973 Middle East War*, (Arlington: Institute for Defense Analyses/Center for Naval Analyses, Weapons Systems Evaluation Group, October 1974, CIA/FOIA/ERR)

Vyhlidal, M., *Československá pomoc při výstavbě vojenského školství v arabském světě v letech 1948 – 1989* (in Czech), (Brno: Filozoficka fakulta Masarykovy University, 2010. 100 s. Magisterska diplomova prace, 2010).

WALKER, B., *Fighting Jets: The Epic of Flight* (New York: Time Life Books, 1983; ASIN: B003VTSU8G).

Zaloga, S., *Scud Ballistic Missile and Launch Systems, 1955-2005* (Oxford: Osprey Publishing Ltd, 2006; ISBN: 1-84176-947-9).

Zaloga, S., *Red SAM: The SA-2 Guideline Anti-Aircraft Missile* (Oxford: Osprey Publishing Ltd, 2007; ISBN 978-1-84603-062-8).

Zolotaryov, Maj Gen V. A., *Russia in Local Wars and Military Conflicts in the Second Half of the 20th Century* (in Russian), (Moscow: Institute of Military History, Ministry of Defence of the Russian Federation, 2000).

NOTES

Chapter 1

1 Tahsin Zaki, interview with Dr. David Nicolle, 02/1999.
2 Cohen, *The 1967 Six-Day War: New Israeli Perspective*. For an extensive study of the Egyptian military intelligence services in the 1950s and 1960s, see al-Jawadi, *In Between the Catastrophe*.
3 Pean, 'Les Deux Bombes'. Pean explained that the two nuclear programs – that of France and that of Israel – were closely intertwined. While the Israelis lacked the industrial infra-structure, it fell to the French to learn a lot about the technologies for developing and building nuclear weapons from the Israeli nuclear scientists – because many of these were US-born Jews that participated in the Manhattan Project (the original US project for development of nuclear weapons, run during the Second World War).
4 Jauvert, 'Bombe Israelienne…' & Farr. Until the publishing of Jauvert's article it was generally unknown whether the French had actually delivered a plutonium separation plant to Israel. Such a facility was necessary for reprocessing the reactor's spent fuel rods into weapons-grade plutonium. Instead, it was generally assessed that the Israelis made use of a much simpler and cheaper process of separating fissionable material from spent reactor fuel using a gas centrifuge, developed by West German scientists in 1960.
5 Crosbie, pp. 162.
6 NSC Briefing, *French Nuclear Test*, 29 December 1960, CIA/Freedom of Information Act/Electronic Reading Room (henceforth CIA/FOIA/ERR).
7 Flaphan, p. 50.

8 Jauvert, 'Bombe Israelienne…' Amongst others, the same article included extensive excerpts from negotiations between Ben-Gurion and de Gaule. Accordingly, after running out of arguments, Ben-Gurion concluded that 'Israel' understands such points of view and that 'Israel' does not want to develop nuclear weapons any more: 'I swear to you that we will not build a bomb, no other meetings will be needed to fulfil this agreement.'
9 CIA, *Memorandum to Holders of SNIE 30-2-63: the Advanced Weapons Programs of the UAR and Israel, Dated 8 May 1963*, 22 April 1964, CIA/FOIA/ERR.
10 Ibid; Chazly et al, pp. 39-42; Cohen, *The 1967 Six-Day War: New Israeli Perspective*; Green, *Taking Sides*, pp. 157-159; David Burnham, 'US Agencies Suspected Missing Uranium Went to Israel', *NYT*, 5 November 1977 & John J Flaika, 'CIA Found Israel Could Make Bomb', *Washington Post*, 6 November 1977.
11 Bar-Noi, *The Soviet Union and the Six-Day War*.
12 Cohen, *The 1967 Six-Day War: New Israeli Perspective*.
13 Ibid. Notably, Ginor et al (p. 124) state that the Israeli Military Censor prevented Danny Shalom from publishing the captured copy of Amer's 'Battle Order #4', which, 'apparently', related 'specifically' to an attack on the nuclear complex in his book *Like a Bolt out of the Blue*. For the full content of captured UARAF plans for air strikes on Israel captured during the June 1967 Arab-Israeli War, and released by the Israeli Military Censor, see Cooper et al, *Arab MiGs*, Volume 2, pp. 194-200. For Fawzy's statement, see Fawzy, Chapter 1, and for Soviet warnings to Egypt and Israel see Gluska, *The Israeli Military and the Origins of the 1967 War*, pp. 184-185.
14 Cohen, *The 1967 Six-Day War: New Israeli Perspective* & Fawzy, Chapter 1. For the full content of captured UARAF plans for air strikes on Israel captured during the June 1967 Arab-Israeli War, see Cooper et al, *Arab MiGs*, Volume 2, pp. 194-200.
15 Bar-Noi, *The Soviet Union and the Six-Day War* & Ginor et al, *Foxbats over Dimona*.
16 Abd el-Hamid, interview with Dr David Nicolle, 02/1999; this and all subsequent quotations from Abd el-Hamid are based on a transcription of the same interview.
17 *Fishbed C/E Aerial Tactics*, pp. 108-110. As explained not only in that manual, but also demonstrated by Abd el-Hamid and colleagues, these early variants of the MiG-21 could actually fly even higher than 18,000m – at so-called 'dynamic altitudes', though only if flown along a near-ballistic trajectory. Indeed, the same manual provided detailed instructions for operations at up to 24,000m (78,740ft) and speeds of up to Mach 2.4.
18 This map is based on one published in Shalom, *Like a Bolt out of the Blue*, and on interviews by Lon Nordeen with Egyptian pilots Qadri Abd el-Hamid and Fuad Kamal, 02/1999.
19 Cohen, *The 1967 Six-Day War: New Israeli Perspective*, based on the recollection of former Brigadier-General Yitzhak Ya'akov (in charge of weapons development, and the chief liaison officer between the IDF and all the civilian defence industries – including the nuclear project – as of 1967), and testimony by the former Chief of General Staff IDF, Zvi Tzur (chief aid to Moshe Dayan as of 1967).
20 For details on planning by the leaders of the Jewish Agency from 1948, according to which they intended to establish sovereignty over all of Palestine, then expand 'Erez Israel' into Transjordan, portions of Lebanon and Syria; and then establish 'Jewish military and economic hegemony over the entire Middle East', see Green, *Taking Sides*, pp. 20-21.
21 Carter, pp. 170-172, 286-287; Pendle, pp. 291-293, 296; Jauvert, 'Bombe Israelienne…' & Carlier et al, various chapters from Volumes 1 and 2.
22 Carlier et al, various chapters from Volumes 1 and 2 & Chazly et al, pp. 42-44.
23 Green p. 91.
24 Retired analyst of Defence Intelligence Agency (DIA), interview provided on condition of anonymity, 02/2001; Henry A Kissinger, *National Security Study Memorandum No. 40: Israeli Nuclear Weapons Program*, 11 April 1969 & Henry A Kissinger, *Memorandum for the President: Israeli Nuclear Program*, 1969 (precise date unclear), CIA/FOIA/ERR. On the contrary, platforms like the ArmsControlNetwork.com stress that the US intelligence community was wrong and Jerichos were not fully operational for a nuclear role even as of October 1973.
25 Green, p. 91.
26 Henry A Kissinger, 'Discussions with the Israelis on nuclear matters', *Memorandum for the President*, The White House, 7 October 1969 & Retired analyst of the DIA, interview, 02/2001. According to the latter source, the speed at which the Israelis were designing new nuclear weapons and at which they began turning them out amazed the US intelligence community. It was only following closer studies that it turned out this was possible thanks to clandestine, yet extensive help from multiple French, US, and British scientists, and numerous immigrants from these countries. Of equal importance would have been former US and British military personnel that included weapons-handlers trained in the use of nuclear weapons. The source further specified that the first Israeli nuclear test had already taken place on 22 May 1969, over a deep underwater abyss in the southern Indian Ocean. Undertaken by a heavily armed commercial vessel escorted by an Israeli submarine, this resulted in no fanfare: the Israelis lowered their test

weapon into the ocean, distanced and released it – all within only two days. For comparison, the CIA did officially acknowledge that Israel had 'already produced atomic weapons' as of September 1974, but assessed their number as 'at least 10' even as late as of 1976 (see David Burnham, 'CIA Said in 1974 Israel had A-Bombs', *NYT*, 27 January 1978.

27 Joe Mizrahi, 'The Designer of the B-1 Bomber's Airframe', *Wings*, Volume 36/Number 4 (August 2000); Carlier et al, *Dassault, Volume 1*; retired analyst of the DIA, interview, 02/2001 & Pedersen, p. 81. While the retired DIA analyst further specified that the Israeli Phantoms modified to carry nuclear weapons were known as 'F-4ENs' to the Americans, Jeffrey Lewis (in 'Israel, Nuclear Weapons and the 1973 Yom Kippur War', posted on ArmsControlNetwork.com on 21 October 2013), cited 'Mirages' as carriers of Israel's nuclear weapons. According to him, the idea was to avoid a conflict with the commitment Israel had given to Washington that its US-supplied aircraft would not be used for nuclear weapon missions. Accordingly, the IDF/AF had a small group of pilots pre-trained on flying nuclear missions on Mirages, and would need between 6 and 12 hours to prepare such missions.

28 For examples of US military intelligence assessments clearly pointing out the Israeli military superiority in comparison to all the neighbouring countries combined, see such as 'Israeli Arms Request', Document 23, Saunders Memos, National Security File, Lyndon Baines Johnson Library, and *SNIE 30-6-67*, from August 1967 (released by the DIA in response to FOIA enquiry).

29 Jauvert, 'Bombe Israelienne…'

30 Yair Evron, 'Israel and the Atom: The Uses and Misuses of Ambiguity, 1957-1967', *Orbis magazine*, Volume 17/Winter 1974, pp. 13-31.

31 Retired analyst of the DIA, interview, 02/2001. Notably, over recent years, the Qatari news channel al-Jazeera prepared a very detailed documentary titled 'Their Archive & Our History'. Based on extensive research in Western archives about the history of the Arab world, this included the episode titled 'Israel and the Nuclear threshold'. Planned for publication in 2013, this episode discussed findings from the archives of the CIA and the National Security Agency. For entirely unknown reasons, only the first episode of this documentary was ever aired: all the subsequent episodes were cancelled and the published part was deleted even from al-Janzeera's website.

Chapter 2

1 Clausewitz, *Vom Kriege* (for an English translation, see Michael Howard & Peter Paret [editors and translators], *On War* (Princeton: Princeton University Press; ISBN: 978-0-691-01854-6).

2 Chazly et al, p. 39.

3 Blum, p. 14; Shazly, pp. 13-14.

4 Asher, *Egyptian Strategy*, p. 103 & Shazly, pp. 24-28.

5 For classic examples of announcements that one or other Israeli soldier or military unit 'saved Israel' or 'the people of Israel' during the October 1973 War, see Asher et al, *Duel for the Golan* and Blum, *The Eve of Destruction*.

6 An alternative version for the motives behind Sadat's decision to initiate a limited war against Israel was offered by Israel Shamir in 'What Really Happened in the "Yom Kippur" War?', *counterpuch.org*, 22 February 2012. Correspondingly, the author – a veteran IDF paratrooper of the 1973 War – received a secret file written by the former Soviet ambassador to Cairo, Vladimir M. Vinogradov, according to which this conflict was, '…a collusive enterprise between the US, Egyptian and Israeli leaders, orchestrated by Henry Kissinger…', in which Sadat 'entered into a conspiracy with the Israelis, betrayed his ally Syria, condemned the Syrian army to destruction and Damascus to bombardment, allowed General Sharon's tanks to cross without hindrance to the western bank of the Suez Canal, and actually planned a defeat of the Egyptian troops in the October War…'. Similarly, Israeli Prime Minister Golda Meir had, '…knowingly sacrificed 2,000 of Israel's soldiers in order to give Sadat his moment of glory and to let the US secure its position in the Middle East'. Ending his dossier with a series of important questions, most of which still remain unanswered today, Vinogradov concluded that Sadat's behaviour allows for two explanations: '…an impossible one, of the Egyptian's total military ignorance, and an improbable one, of Sadat's intentions'. While frequently waved away as a 'conspiracy theory', Vinogradov's conclusions do offer an excellent explanation why Cairo would have had no concerns about a possible Israeli nuclear response to the surprise attack of 6 October, the successful crossing of the Suez Canal and then the limited advance into the Sinai.

7 Shazly, pp. 18-21.

8 M. Z. (former Tu-16 pilot), interview provided on condition of anonymity, 08/2001 & Ahmad Keraidy (son of Mohammad Abdel Wahab el-Keraidy, leading Egyptian Tu-16 pilot of the early 1970s), interviews, 09/2010 & 10/2010.

9 Ahmed Abbas Faraj (Su-17/20 pilot), interview, 02/2012 & Magdin Rifaat (MiG-21 and Mirage pilot), interviews, 04/2014 & 10/2017.

10 Mohammad Fathi Fat-hallah Rif'at (Mirage pilot, EAF), interview 10/2002;Mohammed Abdel Moneim Zaki Okasha (MiG-17 and Mirage pilot and leading Egyptian military aviation historian), interviews, 10/2008-05/2009 and 02/2011 & Medhat Zaki (MiG-21 pilot), interview, 11/2011.

11 CIA, *Intelligence Report: The Soviet Military Presence in Egypt*, February 1975, CIA/FOIA/ERR, p. 2.

12 Black et al, *Israel's Secret Wars*, pp. 193-200.

13 Shazly, pp. 79-80.

14 *War Diary of the 65th Missile Brigade*.

15 Ibid; DIA, Scud B Study, August 1974; Golan, 'The Scud'; Shazly, p. 72 & Zaloga, pp. 33-34. While Golan reports that Egypt originally received 10 old 8A61 launchers for R-11 missiles (ASCC-code 'SS-1b Scud-A'), supposedly because the 9K72 Elbrus was still a brand new weapon and rare even in Soviet service, Zaloga reports the delivery of 9 'TELs' and 18 R-17E missiles, the US intelligence reports cite 'Scud-Bs', and *The War Diary of the 65th Missile Brigade* cites 'Scud A' missiles. Theoretically, the strained nature of relations between Cairo and Moscow as of 1972-1973, and negative Egyptian experiences not only with Su-17MKs but diverse other Soviet weapons, make either version possible. Certainly enough, it is doubtful if Sadat's government would have accepted anything other than the 'latest' that the Soviets were able to deliver – which would be the Scud-B. However, considering the oppressive secrecy of the Soviets with regards to their weapons in general, and their 'tradition' of cheating their export customers, and also the Egyptian predilection for combining original Soviet with ASCC/NATO-codenames, other versions are perfectly possible too. One is that Moscow originally delivered the Scud-A, but then continued with deliveries of Scud-B; another is that it delivered some sort of a unique 'hybrid', including Scud-A missiles and Scud-B TELs; and yet another is that Moscow was all the time delivering Scud-B missiles and TELs, but the Egyptians designated them 'Scud-A' – in the same fashion that they designated the oldest variants of the SAM known as 'SA-2' in the West the 'SA-1'.

16 Golan, 'The Scud'; DIA, *Scud B Study*, August 1974 & Zaloga, pp. 33-34. Another notable detail is that while Golan stressed that the Israeli government was not concerned by Scuds, contemporary reports in the US media cited that during the summer 1973 – i.e. around the same time that the delivery of the Scuds to Egypt took place and then became known in public – the Israeli government allocated 250 million Israeli pounds in grants and loans for an intensified construction of 800 public shelters, each capable of housing up to 250 people, and announced its intention to extend the shelter program for years in advance. In comparison, in 1972 the government spent exactly 40 million for the same purpose.

17 CIA, *Intelligence Report: The Soviet Military Presence in Egypt*, February 1975, CIA/FOIA/ERR, p. 6.

18 Raspletin, *SAM Exports*.

19 Ayman Sayed Ahmad Hob el-Din (CO 418th Air Defence Battalion, ADC), interview, 11/2012.

20 Ibid & Gurov.

21 Unless stated otherwise, the following sub-chapter is based on Hob el-Din, interview, 11/2012 & Gurov (see Bibliography for details).

22 Okasha, interviews 10/2008-05/2009 and 02/2011. In comparison, Transue (in *WSEG Report 249*, CIA FOIA/ERR pp. 68-69, 72), cites the presence of 150 SAM-sites (including 10 SA-6s), while DIA (*Gaps in Egypt's Military Inventory and the Effects on its Wartime Capabilities*, 6 March 1975, CIA/FOIA/ERR) cites the presence of 140 SAM-sites in Egypt at the start of the war.

23 Transue, *WSEG Report 249*, CIA FOIA/ERR, p. 72 (henceforth 'Transue').

24 Raspletin, *SAM Exports*.

25 Ibid.

26 Based on cross-examination of data from Gurov, Raspletin, and interview with Hob el-Din, 11/2012.

27 For precise details on Egyptian acquisition of MiG-21s, and for sources on designations of units operating them, see Cooper et al, *Arab MiGs, Volumes 2-6*. The Indian nick-name for the MiG-21 is according to S. B. Shah (MiG-21 pilot of the IAF), interview, 04/2001.

28 Thanks to its Tumansky R-11F2S-300 engine, the MiG-21PFM was at least 'close' in performance to the Tumansky R-11F2SK-300-powered MiG-21M.

29 Shazly, pp. 24-28 & Bar-Joseph, 'Strategic Surprise or Fundamental Flaw'.

30 Transue, p. 3.

31 Lake et al, pp. 254-255; Mitchel, pp. 267-268.

32 Transue, p. 76 & Dr. Henry A. Kissinger, *Memorandum of Conversation: Military Briefing, The Guest House, Herzliyya*, 22 October 1973, p. 2, CIA/FOIA/ERR. According to the latter as of that date the IDF/AF was down to only '69-70 crews left' to fly '80-100 Phantoms'.

33 Transue, p. 22.

Chapter 3

1 Ibid, p. 21. For probably the 'best' (and certainly 'dominating') compilation of traditional Western conclusions about Arab militaries – including air forces – see Pollack, *Arabs at War*.

2 Although some Soviet instructors served in Egypt during the October 1973 War, even Israeli intelligence assessments with regards to the Egyptian military confirm that none became involved in combat against Israel (see Asher, p. 70).

3 For details, see Nicolle et al, *Wings over Sinai* and Cooper, *Hot Skies over Yemen, Volume 1*.

4 Conclusions based on research for the project *Arab MiGs*, run 2008-2014 (see Bibliography for details). Notably, contrary to the Egyptians, who regularly recall all four members of their formations, the Iraqis – who still

flew what the US Air Force called the 'Fluid Four' formation as of October 1973 – still recall only the Numbers 1 and 3 of their formations, who were the leaders of the two 'most important' elements in all of their flights.

5   Fawzy, *The Three Years War*, Chapters 14, 15 and 16; Okasha, *Soldiers in the Sky*, pp. 19-20 & Reda el-Iraqi (MiG-21 pilot), interviews, 10/2009 & 01/2010.

6   Transue, p. 21 & Moussa (MiG-21 pilot), interview, 04/2012. This and all following quotations from Moussa are based on the transcription of the same interview.

7   Rifaat, interview, 12/2014 & Rifaat, 'The Diary' (translation from Arabic provided by Nour Bardai, 12/2018). This and all subsequent quotations from Rifaat are based on the transcription of the same interview and the translation of the same narrative. Furthermore, Farouk el-Ghazzawy confirmed that he was the first CO of the first 'Libyan' Mirage squadron in an interview to Dr David Nicolle, in 02/1999.

8   Cooper et al, *Libyan Air Wars*, Part 1, pp. 15 & Rifaat, interview 12/2014.

9   Makarem (MiG-17 and Mirage pilot), interview with Nour Bardai, 12/2017; this and all following quotations from Makarem are based on the transcription of the same interview.

10   While the Israelis led the way by emphasising dissimilar air combat manoeuvring (DACM) training during the 1960s, the Egyptians introduced similar training methods in July 1967. In comparison, the US Navy started running similar exercises only in 1969 (see Pedersen for details), the USAF only in the early 1970s (see Anderegg, Mitchel, and Pedersen), and the Soviets only at a later point in time. Illustrative for the intensity of flying by Egyptian pilots during the period 1967-1973 are figures from others of interviewed officers. For example, Samir-Aziz Mikhail (MiG-21 pilot and brigade commander), Abd el-Moneim Zaki Okasha and Fikry el-Gindy (who served as a commanders of MiG-17 squadrons), Abd el-Moneim el-Shennawy (instructor on Sukhoi Su-7BMK fighter-bombers), and Salah Danish (instructor on Aero L-29 Delfins) were all regularly clocking 350-400, even more hours of flying time a year. Notable is that they flew short-ranged types, all 'renowned' – or notorious – for their short endurance: very few flights lasted longer than 30-40 minutes, which made long-range/navigational training flights a rarity, contrary to contemporary practice in the West. Instead, virtually 'every minute' of every single flight was spent on tactical training-related purposes.

11   Medhat Zaki, interviews, 01/2010 & 11/2011; this and all following quotations from Zaki are based on the transcription of the same interview.

12   el-Iraqi, interviews, 10/2009 & 01/2010; this and all following quotations from el-Iraqi are based on the transcription of the same interview.

13   Saqr (MiG-21 pilot), interview with Nour Bardai, 01/2019; this and all following quotations from Sakr are based on the transcription of the same interview.

14   For details, see Nicolle et al, *Wings over Sinai* and Cooper et al, *Arab MiGs*. As described in Volume 6 of the latter, especially Egyptian MiG-17F pilots claimed a number of hits with their 23mm and 37mm cannons on Israeli Mirages and Phantoms during the October 1973 War – though without scoring kills. While reviewing their gun-camera films, and to their astonishment, most were forced to conclude that although frequently receiving multiple hits, Israeli aircraft rarely went down. On the contrary, just a few hits by Israeli cannons, not to mention US and Israeli-made air-to-air missiles, frequently caused catastrophic damage to the MiG-17Fs. Although proving more survivable than the older design, the MiG-21 would frequently run out of fuel due to combat damage.

15   Data based on computations by Jean-Marie Langeron (see bibliography for details).

16   Ibid.

17   Gunston et al, pp. 122-123.

18   Transue, p. 22.

19   For details on Israeli tapping operations, see Cooper et al, *Arab MiGs Volume 3*, pp. 74-76, partially based on such reports as Offer Drori, 'Operation Kachal' (in Hebrew), www.global-report.com, September 2009. The most recent known case of an Israeli tap on a telephone cable being discovered reportedly took place in Iraq in the mid-1990s (Sadik, interview, 03/2005).

20   While the debate about how much ECM can degrade the function of radar is unlikely to ever end, there is no doubt that even the performance of the most modern, tremendously sophisticated, computer-supported detection systems of the present day would be significantly degraded by advanced ECM-systems almost certain to be deployed in any major war.

21   Transue, p. 72 & Iftach Spector (Mirage- and F-4E-pilot), interview, 02/2019.

22   Conclusions based on computations by Jean-Marie Langeron.

23   *Fishbed C/E Aerial Tactics*, p. 56-60, 69-70, 115, 120, 131-132, 153.

24   Abraham Rabinovich, 'The Air Force's Lost Chances to Turn around the Yom Kippur War', *Jerusalem Post*, 30 September 2017.

25   Transue, p. 20. The report cited post-war tests against aircraft shelters captured at Fayid AB, near the Great Bitter Lake, all of which confirmed their relative invulnerability to attack with available conventional ammunition.

26   Transue, p. 16.

27   Years later, the rate of failure of much more sophisticated submunitions for such systems like the US-made MLRS or M4831 artillery shells was still ranging from 5%, via 14% up to 23% (see Office of the Undersecretary of Defense for Acquisition, Technology and Logistics, 'Unexploded Ordnance Report', Table 2-3, p. 5, *US Congress*, 29 February 2000; *Operation Desert Storm: Casualties Caused by Improper Handling of Unexploded US Submunitions*, US General Accounting Office, August 1993 and similar).

28   Data based on computations by Jean-Marie Langeron.

Chapter 4

1   Mitch Ginsburg, 'Golda Meir: "My heart was drawn to a preemptive strike, but I was scared"', *The Times of Israel,* 12 September 2013.

2   Unless stated otherwise, this sub-chapter is based on the *War Diary of the 65th Missile Brigade*.

3   *War Diary of the 65th Missile Brigade*.

4   Around the same time, an EAF Tu-16K-11-16 bomber hit the Israeli radar site at Umm Qashiba using two KSR-11 anti-radar missiles.

5   Sadik, interview, 03/2006. Some recently released Israeli accounts are confirm such conclusions. For example, Ariel Sharon's testimony to the Agranat Commission (Sharon testified on 29 July 1974) revealed that for most of the time between the moment he reached Refidim AB on the afternoon of the first day of the war and at least a week later, he was unsuccessfully trying to find out what the Egyptians were doing. Left without useful intelligence, the Israeli division commander ended up doing the same as most of other military commanders have done for centuries when attempting to figure out developments: monitoring the battlefield with his binoculars.

6   For further details, see Cooper et al, *Arab MiGs, Vol.5*, pp. 117-118.

7   Unless stated otherwise, the following sub-chapter is based on Rifaat, *The Diary*.

8   Klein et al, pp. 65-69; Weiss, pp. 38-47; Abraham Rabinovich, 'The Air Force's Lost Chances to Turn around the Yom Kippur War', *Jerusalem Post*, 30 September 2017.

9   Saqr (MiG-21 pilot that shot down Giora Rom, on 11 September 1969), interview with Nour Bardai, 01/2019.

10   With Israeli narratives about this and the following operations being widely published, the narrative in this book concentrates on Egyptian recollections, which are forwarded 'as provided', with bare minimum of editing during translation. The reason is that the aim of this book is to record and inform about what both sides have reported, without 'revising' anybody or anything, without a confirmation or denial – either of which the authors feel is impossible without full approach to the official records of *both* sides.

11   Mikhail, interview with Lon Nordeen, 03/1989 & with Abdallah Emran, 11/2009. This and all subsequent quotations from Mikhail are based on transcriptions of the same interview.

12   Moussa, interview, 04/2012 & Sharmy, *The Eagles that Saved the October Victory*, pp. 3.

13   Klein et al, p. 67.

14   O'Balance, p. 107 & Behiri, 'Secret Israeli Documents'.

15   Weiss, pp. 58.

16   Unless stated otherwise, this sub-chapter is based on Meir, pp. 428-430; Green, pp. 89-92; Burr, W., *The October War and the U.S. Policy*, The National Security Archive, 7 October 2003, Document 21B. The other usual primary source for reports on the activation of the Israeli nuclear arsenal during the October 1973 War is Seymour Hersh's book *The Samson Option* (New York: Random House, 1991), pp. 225-230. Hersh's source appears to have been Eli Mizrachi, one of Golda Meir's office aides, who left Israel in the late 1970s – supposedly under the cloud of a security investigation (he was suspected of leaking information to the USA) – and immigrated to the United States. Further sources with similar thesis are such as Avner Cohen, 'The Last Nuclear Moment', *NYT*, 6 October 2003; Erol Araf, 'Incalculable Consequences', *National Post*, 7 October 2003 and others. So far, no positive confirmation has been provided for these allegations and at least two prominent Israelis attempted to openly and firmly deny such claims. Especially Freier sought vigorously and publicly to discredit Hersh's narrative in any possible platform, although he refused to provide his own account or any kind of specific reservations. More recently, Dr Dima Adamsky and Professor Uri Bar-Joseph (see Behiri, 'Secret Israeli Documents') stated that they did not find any document confirming reports about an Israeli nuclear alert, or the IDF preparing to launch Jericho missiles. However, they did conclude that, 'Israel was worried about Scud missiles in the hands of the Egyptians because there were no practical solutions to deal with these and that during a meeting held on the morning of 6 October, Dayan ordered the IDF/AF to be ready for the possibility of a Scud-attack on Tel Aviv. The thesis about 'nuclear demonstration' (instead of 'arming and targeting the nuclear arsenal') was published by Jeffrey Lewis 'Israel, Nuclear Weapons and the 1973 Yom Kippur War' (posted on ArmsControlNetwork.com on 21 October 2013), in which the author attempted to reconstruct the flow of related events foremost on the basis of an interview with Azarayahu 'Sini' Arnan, a former senior advisor in the Israeli government. Lewis concluded that Sini's testimony showed that the Israeli government recognized the danger of the nuclear brink and, 'recognizing its own commitment to the nuclear taboo' – 'refused to approach it'.

17   Behiri, 'Secret Israeli Documents'.

18 Memcon between Dinitz and Kissinger, 9 October 1973, 6:10-6:35 p.m. National Security Archives & Green, pp. 94-95. Of course, while it is widely accepted that Meir – via Dinitz – thus exercised the threat of a nuclear war to blackmail Washington into sending massive quantities of ammunition and new armament, definite evidence for this was never released to the public, whether by the USA or Israel. Israel has never confirmed possession of nuclear weapons, and the official US standpoint with regards to Israeli nuclear weapons is, 'no comment'.

19 Green, p. 94-95.

20 Retired analyst of the DIA, interview, 02/2001. Ironically, while the number of operational aircraft thus increased, the number of Israeli crews qualified to fly F-4Es continued to decline. As a post-war Israeli report to Kissinger explained (see Chapter 7), the IDF/AF was short by at least 10 qualified crews for available Phantoms. Due to the delivery of replacement aircraft from the USA, this gap further increased as by the end of the war the IDF/AF had up to 100 F-4Es on hand but only 70 crews to fly them. This detail is of particular importance because the usual legends about every one of the Arab-Israeli Wars – and so also the October 1973 War – is that it was the Egyptian and Syrian air forces that were short on pilots for their aircraft.

Chapter 5

1 Hob el-Din, interview, 11/2012; Nabil Shuwakry (MiG-21 pilot, 104th Air Brigade), interview with Lon Nordeen, 02/1999 & retired analyst of the DIA, interview, 02/2001. Independently from each other, all these sources stressed the importance of the Port Said area as the 'only one from which the Egyptians could deploy R-17Es against Israel from the western side of the Suez Canal'. As we are about to see, both the 418th Air Defence Battalion and 104th Fighter Brigade were to receive explicit orders to, 'protect the 65th Missile Brigade' and/or 'protect sites selected for Scud-attacks on Israel', too.

2 Golan, 'The Scud' & Behiri, 'Secret Israeli Documents'. Notably, Behiri based his article on research by Israeli historians Dr Dima Adamsky and Professor Uri Bar-Joseph, 'about strategic implications of the confrontation between USA and USSR in October 1973 War'.

3 Spector, interview, 05/2019; Golan, 'The Scud' & Aloni, 'Target Tanta'.

4 Badri et al, The Ramadan War, p. 149.

5 Klein et al, pp. 73.

6 Badri et al, The Ramadan War, p. 150.

7 Moussa, interview, 04/2012 & Sharmy, The Eagles that Saved the October Victory, pp. 3.

8 Mikhail, interviews, 03/1989 & 11/2009; Moneim, Wolf in the Sun's Disc; Weiss, pp. 54-55.

9 Hob el-Din, interview, 11/2012 & Weiss, pp. 49, 62.

10 Klein et al, pp. 76-77; Bourdos (MiG-21 pilot, SyAAF), interview, 03/2007; Duha (retired air defence officer), interview, 08/2004 & 03/2007 & Jabbar (retired officer of the Syrian Military Intelligence), interviews, 06/2003 & 03/2006. For a discussion of all available reports about the status of the Lebanese radar station at Jebel Barouk, see Cooper et al, Arab MiGs, Vol.6, p. 39.

11 Rifaat, The Diary. Okasha (interview, 10/2008) confirmed the sortie by four Mirages of No. 69 Squadron by citing from that unit's War Diary.

12 Hob el-Din, interview, 11/2012.

13 Moneim, Wolf in the Sun's Disc & Weiss, p. 73.

14 Sharmy, The Eagles that Saved the October Victory, pp. 2.

15 Moussa, interview, 04/2012. Notable is that in the manuscript of The Eagles that Saved the October Victory, Adoub's claim for a Phantom-kill was related to the 'Battle of el-Mansoura', fought on 14 October, although Moussa did not put it in relation.

16 Ibid & Weiss, p. 81.

17 Behiri, 'Secret Israeli Documents'.

18 Hob el-Din, interview, 11/2012 & Weiss, p. 85. Notable is that Hob el-Din did not recall any attacks by AGM-45 Shrike anti-radar missiles on his battalion. In comparison, Transue (pp. 22 & 73) described, 'extensive use of chaff bombs and AGM-45 Shrike missiles' by the IDF/AF during this war. Correspondingly, the IDF/AF's inventory of 145 such missiles as of early October 1973 was bolstered through deliveries of 150 additional Shrikes before the cease-fires of 22, 24 and 25 October: still, no less than 197 out of these 295 missile were fired in combat scoring between 10 and 14 hits. Furthermore, Transue précised that they proved 'useful for countering SA-2s and SA-3s' only, and 'ineffective against SA-6s and ZSU-23-4s'.

19 Spector, interview, 05/2019.

20 Conclusions based on cross-examination of all the interviewed Egyptian and Israeli participants, and secondary Israeli sources.

Chapter 6

1 For 'classic' narratives in this regards see Pollack, Arabs at War; O'Ballance, No Victor no Vanquished; diverse works by Dupuy and Dunstan, Abrahamovich, Herzog (The War of Atonement), all works by Aloni and Weiss covering 14 October 1973, and others. Ironically, the instigator of this operation, Egyptian President Anwar el-Sadat, neither mentioned the 14 October offensive nor the 'Air Battle of el-Mansourah' with a single word in his memoirs (In Search for Identity). Another irony is the usual comparison of the battle from 14 October with the tank battle of Kursk between Germans

and Soviets in 1943: contrary to usual claims, this was not the largest ever armour battle, but was declared as 'the one' precisely because it was the first major armour battle from which the Soviets came out as victorious. As such it stood in strong contrast to several bigger armour battles from summer 1941, all of which ended with disastrous Soviet defeats.

2 Shazly, pp. 243-251; the events of 14 October probably proved too much for Ma'amon: he died of a heart attack and had to be replaced by Gen Abdel al-Moneim Wassel.

3 Specifically, in the sector of the Second Field Army: 15th Independent Armoured Brigade (equipped with Soviet-made T-62 MBTs) advanced for about four kilometres before it was stopped short of the so-called Artillery Road; 24th Armoured Brigade (23rd Mechanized Division, but detached to the 2nd Infantry Division) made a wide sweep in the Firdan sector, but was blocked every time it attempted to break out of the bridgehead; 1st Armoured and 14th Armoured Brigades (21st Mechanized Division) deployed the largest number of tanks during this operation but launched only a few uncoordinated piecemeal approaches of Israeli positions. Similarly, in the sector of the Third Field Army: 24th Independent Armoured Brigade (attached to 7th Infantry Division) made a half-hearted attempt to advance on the Artillery Road, which was easily stopped; 3rd Armoured Brigade (from 4th Armoured Division, but attached to the 19th Infantry Division) made the deepest advance of this operation against Israeli infantry supported by armour and the IDF/AF before being stopped at Wadi Mabuk, while the 22nd Armoured Brigade (6th Mechanized Division, but attached to the 19th Infantry Division) made a parallel flanking move further south that was easily impeded. Transue (p. 4) reported de-facto the same at a much earlier date.

4 For an in-depth study of the true nature of this Egyptian operation and subsequent reactions by top Egyptian military commanders, see Asher, pp. 147-151. Citing Israeli intelligence assessments, captured Egyptian documents, and a number of Israeli military publications based on the latter, Asher concluded that instead of fighting 'the biggest armour battle since Kursk' and losing 250 tanks in the process, Egyptians lost around 100 out of a mere 300 tanks involved in this operation, perhaps '150 if damaged tanks would be included'. Ironically, while the US intelligence was very fast in gathering quite precise information about Egyptian losses (for example, see 'Situation Report #32, titled 'Situation in the Middle East, as of 1200 EDT, Oct 15, 1973', issued by the Department of State, Operations Center, Middle East Task Force, National Security Archives, which cited Egyptian sources claiming to have 'captured two forward Israeli airstrips while losing 76 tanks in the process'), this fact remains entirely ignored by most Israeli and Western historians.

5 Hob el-Din, interview, 11/2012; Shuwakry, interview to Lon Nordeen, 02/1999; Aloni, 'Target Tanta'; Retired DIA analyst, interview, 02/2001 & Roi Kais, '40 Years after Yom Kippur War: The Egyptian Perspective', Ynetnews. com, 13 September 2013. The most fantastic Egyptian claims for the 'Air Battle of el-Mansourah' cite the involvement of up to 300 Israeli aircraft, of which 44 were shot down – 'all of these over the Mediterranean Sea' – and that just one Egyptian unit deployed at el-Mansourah was targeted by no less than 48 bombs (not one of which hit). On the more serious side, independently from each other, Hob el-Din and Shuwakry both stressed that Port Said was the only site west of the Suez Canal from which the 65th Missile Brigade's Scuds could reach Israel. As mentioned above, Hob el-Din stressed that the order for him to re-deploy the 418th Air Defence Battalion included the explicit statement to, 'replace battalions protecting… sites selected for Scud-attacks on Israel'.

6 Notable is that not only Spector but diverse other Israeli sources erroneously cite the presence of 'two Libyan Mirage squadrons' in Egypt during the October 1973 War. For example, Weiss (p. 148) cites a second unit with 14 aircraft joining No. 69 Squadron at Tanta during the second week of the war. For comparison, all available Egyptian sources are unmistakable in this regard: No. 69 Squadron was the only Mirage-equipped unit around. The Libyans deployed their first operation unit equipped with Mirage 5Ds to Egypt only on 24 October. Indeed, considering the Israeli sources stress the sufficient importance of these aircraft for the IDF/AF to repeatedly bomb Tanta AB, it is rather amazing how poor other Israeli intelligence about the activity of No. 69 Squadron was. The best-known detail mentioned in all related Israeli publications – including those supposedly based on official documentation (like Weiss) – cite that the 'Libyan Mirages' flew '400 combat sorties' during the October 1973 War. However, this figure was published in the Libyan newspaper al-Fatah, on 19 May 1974, in a quote from Muamar el-Qaddaffi's speech, in which the Libyan leader actually stated, '…the Libyan Arab Air Force made some 400 sorties against the Israelis'. Even then, this figure is flatly denied by Rifaat's Diary of a Mirage Pilot, which is indicative of No. 69 Squadron flying less than 50 combat sorties during the entire war, and the later-coming Libyan unit none at all. Ironically, because the Israeli figure was never seriously cross-examined, all related Western publications have repeated the same, wrong claim about '400 combat sorties' flown by 'Libyan Mirages'.

7 Retired DIA analyst, interview, 10/2005.

8   Sharmy, *The Eagles that Saved the October Victory*, pp. 2. This three-page write-up in the English language came into being in 1995, through a combination of several interviews with involved EAF commanders and an older write-up, apparently created as early as 1974. Considering Sharmy's relations to Mubarak and top ranks of the EAF, it can be considered as an 'official' Egyptian version of this air battle.

9   Pedersen, p. 82.

10 Wakeel (MiG-21 pilot), interview, 03/2010 & Klein et al, pp. 86.

11 Ibid, pp. 90 & Sharmy, pp. 2.

12 Sharmy, pp. 3.

13 Aloni, 'Target Tanta'.

14 Spector, interview, 03/2019.

15 Conclusions based on cross-examination of recollections by involved Egyptian pilots, and Aloni, 'Target Tanta'.

16 Sharmy, *The Eagles that Saved the October Victory*, pp. 3; Sherif Sharmy and David Nicolle, 'Battle of el-Mansourah', *Air Forces Monthly*, January 1996.

17 A. G., interview provided on condition of anonymity, 06/2018.

18 Conclusions based on all available sources of reference. Detail on several Israeli Phantoms being damaged during the air battles over the Nile Delta on the afternoon of 14 October 1973, is from a retired DIA analyst, interview, 10/2005.

19 For related explanations by Okasha, see Cooper et al, *Arab MiGs, Volume 5*, pp. 139.

Chapter 7

1   Rifaat, interview, 12/2014; el-Iraqi, interview, 01/2010; Mamdouh Heshmat (MiG-21-pilot), interview 07/2008.

2   Spector, interview, 03/2019. According to Spector, reports according to which the F-4 crews demanded top cover by Mirages, but the IDF/AF turned them down, are not true.

3   Peled, p. 366; Spector, interview, 05/2019 & Nassr Moussa, interview, 04/2012; curiously, in his earlier book *Israeli F-4 Phantom Aces* (pp. 69), Aloni cited the reason for the damaged Phantom as, '...an AA-2...'.

4   Weiss, p. 111. Notably, Klein et al (p. 159) listed the Livneh's and Sofer's F-4E as shot down 'over Tanta/Syria', on '16 October 1973'.

5   Behiri, 'Secret Israeli Documents' & Anwar el-Sadat, 'Excerpts of a Speech Calling for an Arab-Israeli Peace Conference', 16 October 1973 (sadat.umd.edu).

6   For comparison, the IDF/AF credited its pilots with three confirmed kills (see Weiss, p. 129).

7   Behiri, 'Secret Israeli Documents'.

8   'Soviet Delivery of Arms to Egypt During October 1973', Department of State Telegram N00497/E.O. 11652: XGDS-1, CIA/FOIA/ERR. According to Shazly (pp. 197-198) the missiles in question belonged to the second Egyptian order, placed in February 1973.

9   Golan, 'The Scud' & Behiri, 'Secret Israeli Documents' & Hob el-Din, interview, 11/2012.

10 Memcon between Meir and Kissinger, 22 October 1973, 1:35-2:15 p.m. National Security Archives. Kissinger subsequently admitted this flow of events.

11 Zaloga, p. 34; Golan, 'The Scud'; Behiri, 'Secret Israeli Documents' & *War Diary of the 65th Missile Brigade*.

12 Golan, 'The Scud' & Behiri, 'Secret Israeli Documents'.

13 *War Diary of the 65th Missile Brigade*

14 Ibid. One is left to wonder about possible Israeli or US reactions if their cultural centres and merchant ships had been bombed by any kind of foreign powers.

15 O'Ballance, pp. 262-265 & Golan, 'The Scud'.

16 Unless stated otherwise, this sub-chapter is based on CIA, 'Is there a Soviet Nuclear Weapon in Egypt', 30 October 1973, CIA FOIA Electronic Reading Room; John W Finney, 'Officials Suspect Russians Sent Atom Arms to Egypt', NYT, 21 November 1973; 'Egypt got Soviet A-arms in '73, ex-aide says', Baltimore Sun, 21 May 1983; Behiri, .'Secret Israeli Documents', Golan, 'The Scud'.

ABOUT THE AUTHORS

TOM COOPER

Tom Cooper is an Austrian aerial warfare analyst and historian. Following a career in the worldwide transportation business – during which he established a network of contacts in the Middle East and Africa – he moved into narrow-focus analysis and writing on small, little-known air forces and conflicts, about which he has collected extensive archives. That resulted in specialisation in such Middle Eastern air forces as those of Egypt, Iran, Iraq and Syria, plus various African and Asian air forces. As well as authoring and co-authoring 30 other books and over 500 articles, he has co-authored an in-depth analysis of major Arab air forces at war with Israel in the period 1955–1973, resulting in the six-volume book series *Arab MiGs*.

ABDALLAH EMRAN

Abdallah Emran is an Egyptian historian researching and documenting 20th Century Egyptian military history with the help of participant's accounts, official documentation, film, photography and videos. Co-founder and former member of the Group 73 Historians, he has conducted hundreds of interviews with participants and eyewitnesses of the Arab-Israeli wars, from all branches of the Egyptian military. He has participated in the production of dozens of acknowledged documentaries, including such TV programmes as *Wings of Fury*, *Ababil*, and *Battalion 418*, and books including *Golden Eagles*, published in Arabic, in Egypt. This is his first work for Helion.